BECOMING A GLOBALLY COMPETENT TEACHER

Ariel **Tichnor-Wagner**
Hillary **Parkhouse**
Jocelyn **Glazier**
J. Montana **Cain**

BECOMING A GLOBALLY COMPETENT TEACHER

Arlington, Virginia USA

2800 Shirlington Road, Suite 1001 • Arlington, VA 22206 USA
Phone: 800-933-2723 or 703-578-9600 • Fax: 703-575-5400
Website: www.ascd.org • E-mail: member@ascd.org
Author guidelines: www.ascd.org/write

Ronn Nozoe, *Interim CEO and Executive Director;* Stefani Roth, *Publisher;* Genny Ostertag, *Director, Content Acquisitions;* Allison Scott, *Acquisitions Editor;* Julie Houtz, *Director, Book Editing & Production;* Jamie Greene, *Associate Editor;* Judi Connelly, *Senior Art Director;* Valerie Younkin, *Senior Production Designer;* Donald Ely, *Senior Graphic Designer;* Kelly Marshall, *Interim Manager, Production Services;* Shajuan Martin, *E-Publishing Specialist*

All web links in this book are correct as of the publication date below but may have become inactive or otherwise modified since that time. If you notice a deactivated or changed link, please e-mail books@ascd.org with the words "Link Update" in the subject line. In your message, please specify the web link, the book title, and the page number on which the link appears.

PAPERBACK ISBN: 978-1-4166-2751-7   ASCD product #119012   n07/19
PDF E-BOOK ISBN: 978-1-4166-2753-1; see Books in Print for other formats.

Quantity discounts: 10–49, 10%; 50+, 15%; 1,000+, special discounts (e-mail programteam@ascd.org or call 800-933-2723, ext. 5773, or 703-575-5773). For desk copies, go to www.ascd.org/deskcopy.

Library of Congress Cataloging-in-Publication Data
LCCN: 2019942004

BECOMING A GLOBALLY COMPETENT TEACHER

Acknowledgments

The origins of what would eventually become this book began in 2012 in Jocelyn's doctoral-level course *Teacher Education in the United States* in the School of Education at the University of North Carolina at Chapel Hill. Jocelyn was part of a teacher education working group within NAFSA: Association of International Educators that had drafted standards for globally competent teaching. The group was seeking assistance in refining these standards and developing a corresponding rubric. Jocelyn included this as one of three options for the final projects in the class. Ariel, Hillary, and Montana, who were students in the class that semester, selected the option to help articulate a vision of globally competent teaching. From this class project, the first iteration of the Globally Competent Learning Continuum was created. We thank the NAFSA working group for issuing the call to operationalize what it means to teach for global competence.

Our work may have ended there if not for the generous support from the Longview Foundation, who awarded the four of us an Internationalizing Teacher Preparation grant to transform the rubric we had created into a validated interactive, self-guided professional development tool for teachers. This funding allowed us to test and refine our conceptualization of globally competent teaching and what it looks like at different developmental and grade levels, to document best practices for globally competent teaching from exemplary educators, and to disseminate this work at conferences and through free online courses. We wish to thank the global education experts and over 100 educators who provided feedback on these earlier drafts, which shaped the final version we refer to throughout this book.

We are particularly indebted to the 10 exceptional globally minded educators from across North Carolina who opened their classroom doors to us to further our understanding of global competence. They graciously allowed us to video and document their teaching practices, interview them about their global education experiences, and make these materials available to guide other teachers' development. They also willingly shared lesson plans, websites, and other instructional resources that helped them teach with a global lens. Many of the examples found throughout the book come from these observations and interviews. We want to express our deepest gratitude to these extraordinary educators: Yolanda Barnham, Matt Cramer, Marget Garner, Nicholas Gattis, Chadd McGlone, Courtney Money, Alexis Gines, Krista Pool, Mariette van der Sluijs, and Andi Webb.

We also thank the staff of World View, a not-for-profit organization based at the University of North Carolina at Chapel Hill that provides global professional development and other resources for K–12 and community college educators. World View partnered with us on the Longview Foundation grant to connect us with globally minded educators in North Carolina and to disseminate the resources we created. We also express our gratitude to ASCD for recognizing and elevating global competence as a crucial component of educating the whole child and for giving the Globally Competent Learning Continuum a new digital home at globallearning.ascd.org (and this companion book to go with it).

Finally, we wish to thank the many educators who, over the past six years, have shared with us their experiences with globally competent teaching as they self-reflect using the Globally Competent Learning Continuum. This book would not have been possible without the insights provided by globally minded educators who added nuance, complexity, and comprehensiveness to our understanding of the elements that constitute globally competent teaching. We give special thanks to the teachers who contributed to this book: Kelisa Wing for contributing to various sections of Chapters 1 and 8; Steve Goldberg for writing the vignette, helping to edit, and providing resources for Chapter 3; and Maddy Krautwurst for writing the vignette and sharing resources for Chapter 5. We hope this book serves as a vehicle for bringing the wisdom of these inspiring and passionate educators to a wide audience and, in doing so, transforms classrooms around the world.

Introduction

All Teachers Are Global Educators

The responsibilities of the teacher have dramatically shifted over the past decade to include preparing students for a complex, interconnected world. On the one hand, teaching in an isolated classroom can feel like an especially local endeavor. Other than the occasional field trip or guest speaker, students may not be interacting with people and cultures beyond their classroom walls. On the other hand, teachers are facing increasing pressures to prepare students for today's global, knowledge-based economy. They also must effectively teach an increasingly diverse student population affected by real-world issues that have an impact on their physical and mental health and social-emotional well-being. The pushes and pulls teachers face as they seek to provide an equitable education to every student are multifaceted, and the responsibility to prepare students for a global world is rarely well defined.

State and federal education policies are increasingly pushing for high-quality standards aimed at effectively preparing students for college and careers in today's rapidly shifting, global economy. An early goal of the Common Core State Standards (CCSS)—originally adopted by 46 states—was to equip students "with the necessary knowledge and skills to be globally competitive" (National Governors Association Center for Best Practices and Council of Chief State School Officers, 2008, p. 6). Indeed, the mission statement of the U.S. Department of Education reads, "Our mission is to promote students' achievement and preparation for global competitiveness by fostering educational excellence and ensuring equal access" (U.S. Department of Education, 2017).

At the same time, teachers' classrooms are becoming more global with growing numbers of students born outside the United States, and school demographics are becoming increasingly diverse, requiring teachers to adapt new strategies to effectively reach students whose racial, cultural, and linguistic backgrounds may differ from their own. Approximately one in four students in the United States are first- or second-generation immigrants, 4.5 million are English language learners who speak one or more of 350 languages, and—as of 2016—a majority of children under the age of 5 are ethnoracial minorities, signaling that the diversity in our schools is a long-term trend that is here to stay. At the same time, the U.S. teaching force does not reflect these demographic changes. In the 2015–2016 school year, 80 percent of teachers identified as white (Taie & Goldring, 2018).

Students are also living in what military and business leaders have dubbed a VUCA world—one that is volatile, uncertain, complex, and ambiguous. At the macro level, this includes unpredictable government elections, the rise of new political movements, shifts in international alliances, the advent of new technologies, and more. At the micro level, students are grasping with volatility and uncertainty in immediate, personal ways: public health crises, such as the opioid epidemic and lead-contaminated water; a surge in hate crimes that target individuals' religion, race, or sexual identity; a constant barrage of school shootings; fears that parents or loved ones will get incarcerated or deported at any time.

Students cannot simply check the baggage they carry with them at the door. Research on the science of learning and development has repeatedly shown that physical and mental stress and trauma affect students' cognitive development (Cantor, Osher, Berg, Steyer, & Rose, 2018). Unless society addresses the underlying causes that adversely affect students' physical and mental health, these undue impediments to learning will remain.

In this current landscape, what does a true vision of equitable teaching and learning look like? We argue that it is a comprehensive approach that addresses students' cognitive, social-emotional, and behavioral development. It is teaching that arms students with the knowledge and skillset to not merely survive but thrive in an ever-changing, interconnected world—one that both paves a pathway for students to pursue their passions and dreams and opens windows to opportunities students might not have known existed. It is teaching that addresses the unique background each student brings and the institutional barriers students face on account of the racial, ethnic, cultural, or linguistic group with which they identify. It is teaching that provides students with the foundation to be the change they want to see in their own communities and the wider world.

This is not a utopic vision of teaching. Imagine a 1st grade classroom where English language learners in a semirural North Carolina community discuss the causes and effects of deforestation in the Amazon and articulate concrete actions they will take to protect the rainforest. Imagine 8th grade students in a town with a military base debate the pros and cons of the Vietnam War from the perspectives of both the Americans and the Vietnamese. Imagine 10th graders in Washington, DC and Ghana who collaborate across continents to discuss a lack of access to potable drinking water and devise STEM solutions to the problem. These are all realities. Teaching for global competence is one way that educators are already working toward this holistic vision of education.

What Is Global Competence?

Global competence is the set of knowledge, skills, mindsets, and values needed to thrive in a diverse, globalized society. In essence, global competence is the toolbox that equips students to reach their career aspirations in a globally connected economy (Asia Society & Longview Foundation, 2016) and take individual and collective responsibility as global citizens who make their local communities, their countries, and the world a more just, sustainable place for all of humankind (Banks, 2014; Zhao, 2010).

Global competence, global awareness, global citizenship, global literacy, intercultural competence, international education, and *global education* are often used interchangeably. We recognize that there are distinctions among these terms and even ambiguity within them (Kirkwood, 2001a; Oxley & Morris, 2013). However, for the purposes of this book, we are less concerned about getting hung up on terminology than we are about supporting teachers as they cultivate the underlying attributes that allow students to thrive in a world that is complex, interconnected, and filled with a diversity of landscapes, people, and perspectives. Throughout this book, we use the term *global competence* to describe these attributes, though we recognize that some schools, districts, or policy guidelines may use others.

Global competence is multidimensional in nature (Organisation for Economic Cooperation and Development [OECD], 2018a; Reimers, 2009; UNESCO, 2015), addressing social-emotional, behavioral, and cognitive domains of learning. The cognitive domain covers "knowledge and thinking skills necessary to better understand the world and its complexities," the social-emotional domain emphasizes "values, attitudes, and social skills... that enable learners to live together with others respectfully and peacefully," and the behavioral domain relates to "conduct, performance, practical application, and engagement" (UNESCO, 2015, p. 22).

Nongovernmental, governmental, and supranational organizations—such as the Asia Society, World Savvy, the U.S. Department of Education, the OECD, and UNESCO—have created frameworks that delineate specific attributes that collectively comprise global competence. Figure 0.1 provides an overview of these different frameworks. Despite differences in wording, these frameworks coalesce around the following cognitive, social-emotional, and behavioral domains:

- Knowledge of global issues, trends, and globalization processes using analytic and critical thinking (cognitive domain).
- Dispositions of empathy, valuing multiple perspectives, appreciation for diversity, and a sense of responsibility toward a common humanity (social-emotional domain).

- Skills related to effective intercultural communication and collaboration, including speaking more than one language and acting on issues of global importance (behavioral domain).

Importantly, global competence is not about the world "out there." It is rooted in understanding ourselves and our place in the world as a foundation for understanding those around us. Developing global competence also does not mean trading in one's cultural or national identity for global citizenship or "one-world government." Rather, it embraces how "cultural, national, regional, and global identifications are interrelated, complex, and evolving" (Banks, 2008, p. 134). Indeed, one can develop global citizenship while maintaining strong cultural, national, and local affiliations.

In addition, global competence is also not a content area unto itself. It is instead rooted in disciplinary and interdisciplinary knowledge that cuts across all disciplines (Mansilla & Jackson, 2011). Therefore, it should not be treated as an "add-on"—limited to an elective course in which a handful of students enroll, a one-time international day, or a multicultural fair—but integrated into existing courses and curricula to which all students are exposed throughout the school year (Tichnor-Wagner, Parkhouse, Glazier, & Cain, 2016).

Because global competence is a multifaceted construct, it can help prepare students to thrive in a variety of ways. From a career-readiness perspective, business and industry leaders argue that global competence is desired and required of employees and will give students a leg up in a competitive, global marketplace. From a civic perspective, global competence helps students learn to live together in communities marked by increasing diversity, and it illuminates the root causes of inequities that exist in our world and how students can combat such injustices (Tichnor-Wagner, 2016). This all points back to equity, whether it is providing students with equitable access to opportunities that will help them succeed in postsecondary education (and beyond) or giving students the tools to disrupt global injustices that play out in their local communities. Therefore, global competence is not a "nice-to-have"; it is a "must have" for all students, for both their individual betterment and the betterment of the world in which they live.

Figure 0.1 | Global Competence Frameworks

Organization	Global Competence Framework
Mansila & Jackson (2011): *Four Domains of Global Competence*	• Investigate the world. • Recognize perspectives. • Communicate ideas. • Take action.
OECD (2018a): *The OECD PISA Global Competence Framework*	Dimensions of Global Competence • Examine local, global, and intercultural issues. • Understand and appreciate the perspectives and world views of others. • Engage in open, appropriate, and effective interactions across cultures. • Take collective action for well-being and sustainable development. Knowledge, Attitudes, Skills, and Values • Recognize global and intercultural issues. • Value human dignity and diversity. • Evaluate information, formulate arguments, and explain complex situations or problems. • Identify and analyze multiple perspectives. • Understand differences in communication. • Evaluate actions and consequences.
UNESCO (2015): *Global Citizenship Education Key Learner Outcomes*	• Learners acquire knowledge and understanding of local, national, and global issues and interconnectedness and interdependency of different countries and populations. • Learners develop skills for critical thinking and analysis. • Learners experience a sense of belonging to a common humanity, sharing values and responsibilities, based on human rights. • Learners develop attitudes of empathy, solidarity, and respect for differences and diversity. • Learners act effectively and responsibly at local, national, and global levels for a more peaceful and sustainable world. • Learners develop motivation and willingness to take necessary actions.

Organization	Global Competence Framework
U.S. Department of Education (2017): *Framework for Developing Global and Cultural Competencies to Advance Equity, Excellence and Economic Competitiveness*	<u>Domains</u> • Collaboration and communication • World and heritage languages • Diverse perspectives • Civic and global engagement <u>Outcomes</u> • Critical and creative thinkers who can apply understanding of diverse cultures, beliefs, economies, technology, and forms of government in order to work effectively in cross-cultural settings to address societal, environmental, or entrepreneurial challenges. • Aware of differences that exist between cultures, open to diverse perspectives, and appreciative of insight gained through open cultural exchange. • Proficient in at least two languages. • Able to operate at a professional level in intercultural and international contexts and to continue to develop new skills and harness technology to support continued growth.
World Savvy (2018): *Global Competence Matrix*	• *Core Concepts*: World events and global issues are complex and interdependent; one's own culture and history is key to understanding one's relationship to others; multiple conditions fundamentally affect diverse global forces, events, conditions, and issues. • *Values and Attitudes*: Openness to new opportunities, ideas, and ways of thinking; desire to engage with others; self-awareness about identity and culture; sensitivity and respect for differences; valuing multiple perspectives; comfort with ambiguity and unfamiliar situations; reflection on context and meaning of our lives in relation to something bigger; question prevailing assumptions; adaptability and the ability to be cognitively nimble; empathy; humility. • *Skills*: Investigates the world; recognizes, articulates, and applies an understanding of different perspectives; selects and applies appropriate tools and strategies to communicate and collaborate effectively; listens actively and engages in inclusive dialogue; is fluent in 21st century digital technology; demonstrates resiliency in new situations; applies critical, comparative, and creative thinking and problem solving.

(continued)

Figure 0.1 | Global Competence Frameworks (continued)

Organization	Global Competence Framework
World Savvy (2018): *Global Competence Matrix—(continued)*	• *Behaviors*: Seeks out and applies an understanding of different perspectives to problem solving and decision making; forms opinions based on exploration and evidence; commits to the process of continuous learning and reflection; adopts shared responsibility and takes cooperative action; shares knowledge and encourages discourse; translates ideas, concerns, and findings into individual or collaborative actions to improve conditions; approaches thinking and problem solving collaboratively.

Globally Competent Teaching

More states, districts, and schools are inserting terms such as *global awareness*, *global citizen*, *global competence*, and *international* into school names, mission and vision statements, teacher evaluations, and more (Parker, 2008; Tichnor-Wagner, 2016). School, district, and state global scholar certificate programs are on the rise, with the purpose of recognizing global competence in both students and teachers (Singmaster, Norman, & Manise, 2018), as are Seals of Biliteracy, which acknowledge students' bilingualism achievement on high school diplomas (Heineke, Davin, & Bedford, 2018). This has left educators asking, "Becoming more global sounds great, but how do we actually do it?"

When we first embarked on this work in 2013, definitions for what global competence meant for students abounded. Missing, though, was a clear delineation of the knowledge, skills, and dispositions teachers need to instill global competence in their students. This interrelated set of dispositions, knowledge, and skills is what we refer to as *globally competent teaching* (Figure 0.2).

Globally competent teaching is composed of 12 distinct yet interrelated elements. We identified these elements through a systematic review of scholarly literature that addressed how K–12 teachers develop global competence. We also conducted a systematic literature review of publications and frameworks produced by leading education organizations that address K–12 teachers' global competence development (including the Asia Society, Global Teacher Education, the Longview Foundation, NAFSA: Association of International Educators, and World Savvy). Following state-adopted professional standards for teachers—which require educators to demonstrate professional knowledge, skills, and dispositions for licensure (e.g., National Council for the Accreditation of Teacher Education [NCATE])—we delineated the 12 elements by dispositions, knowledge, and skills because globally competent teaching is part and parcel of what effective teachers are already doing.

Figure 0.2 | Elements of Globally Competent Teaching

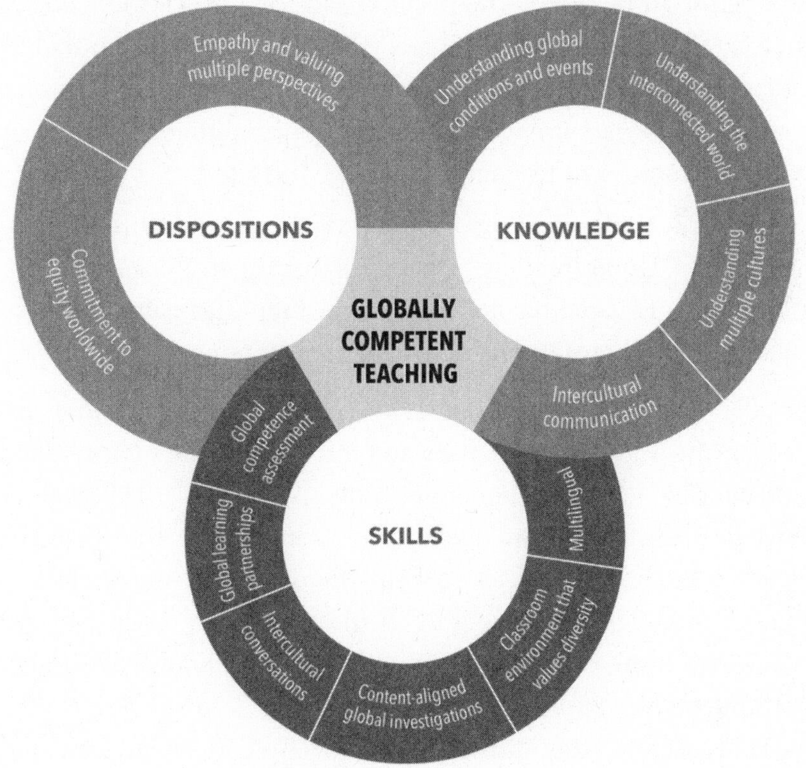

Teaching dispositions encompass the "professional attitudes, values, and beliefs demonstrated through both verbal and nonverbal behaviors as educators interact with students, families, colleagues, and communities" (NCATE, 2008). Globally competent teaching dispositions specifically emphasize the attitudes, values, and beliefs needed to work effectively with students and families from all backgrounds and instill a global mindset in students. Such a mindset embraces an appreciation of diversity, universal rights and commonalities across humanity, and a responsibility for the planet we inhabit and the diversity of people who live on it. They include

- Element 1: Empathy and valuing multiple perspectives.
- Element 2: Commitment to promoting equity worldwide.

Because global competence is not in itself a discipline but a way of teaching that cuts across all disciplines (Mansilla & Jackson, 2011), the "subject-matter" knowledge of global competence reflects a disciplinary and interdisciplinary understanding of the cultures, systems, structures, and events around the world and how they are interconnected with one another and with our own lives. Globally competent teaching knowledge includes

- Element 3: Understanding of global conditions and current events.
- Element 4: Understanding of the ways that the world is interconnected.
- Element 5: Experiential understanding of multiple cultures.
- Element 6: Understanding of intercultural communication.

Globally competent teaching skills emphasize pedagogical content knowledge: "the ways of representing and formulating the subject that makes it comprehensible to others" (Shulman, 1986, p. 9). As NCATE (2008) defines it, pedagogical content knowledge is "the interaction of the subject matter and effective teaching strategies to help students learn the subject matter. It requires a thorough understanding of the content to teach it in multiple ways, drawing on the cultural backgrounds and prior knowledge and experiences of students" (p. 89).

The skills section truly differentiates globally competent teaching from other models of global competence (see Figure 0.1), as it integrates global dispositions and knowledge into how teachers manage their classroom environment, plan for and implement instruction, and assess student learning. The six globally competent teaching skills cover the core components of instructional practice delineated in the InTASC Model Core Teaching Standards (2013), developed by the Interstate Teacher Assessment and Support Consortium convened by the Council for Chief State School Officers, and outline what teachers across all content areas and grade levels should know and be able to do. This includes "planning for instruction by drawing upon knowledge of content areas, curriculum, cross-disciplinary skills, and pedagogy, as well as knowledge of learners and the community context" (Standard 7); using a variety of instructional strategies to understand content, make connections, and meaningfully apply knowledge (Standard 8); and using a range of formative and summative assessments to "engage learners in their own growth, to monitor learner progress, and to guide the teacher's and learner's decision making" (Standard 6).

Globally competent teaching skills include the ability to

- Element 7: Communicate in multiple languages.
- Element 8: Create a classroom environment that values diversity and global engagement.
- Element 9: Integrate learning experiences for students that promote content-aligned explorations of the world.
- Element 10: Facilitate intercultural and international conversations that promote active listening, critical thinking, and perspective recognition.
- Element 11: Develop local, national, and international partnerships that provide real-world contexts for global learning opportunities.
- Element 12: Develop and use appropriate methods of inquiry to assess students' global competence development.

These 12 elements of globally competent teaching incorporate best teaching practices that emphasize providing real-world contexts for learning in order to develop higher-order thinking skills and validate students' unique backgrounds. As written in the InTASC standards (2013):

Effective teachers have high expectations for each and every learner and implement developmentally appropriate, challenging learning experiences within a variety of learning environments that help all learners meet high standards and reach their full potential. Teachers do this by combining a base of professional knowledge, including an understanding of how cognitive, linguistic, social, emotional, and physical development occurs, with the recognition that learners are individuals who bring differing personal and family backgrounds, skills, abilities, perspectives, talents, and interests. (p. 8)

Integrating learning experiences that promote content-aligned investigations of the world and assessing global competence development promote the teaching of challenging standards using authentic and inquiry-based instruction and assessment. Together, empathy and valuing multiple perspectives, understanding multiple cultures, understanding intercultural communication, and communicating in multiple languages incorporate and validate students' diverse perspectives and experiences, reflective of culturally relevant and sustaining pedagogies that best reach culturally and linguistically diverse learners (Ladson-Billings, 1995; Paris, 2012). Both facilitating intercultural conversations and developing partnerships for global learning teach students to communicate and collaborate with people from diverse backgrounds, an emphasized skill for college and career readiness. In this regard, as with the "meat" or "content" of the concept of global competence, globally competent teaching is not an add-on but a compilation of dispositions, knowledge, and skills proven to help all learners succeed academically, socially, and emotionally.

Developing Globally Competent Teaching Practices

Once we identified the 12 elements of globally competent teaching, a second question immediately emerged. How do teachers operationalize this in their daily practice? Some tools exist that measure global or cultural competence. For example the Intercultural Development Inventory—commonly used as pre-post measures in studies on the effect of cross-cultural experiences such as study abroad—measures orientation toward cultural differences through a 50-item Likert scale questionnaire (Hammer, Bennett, & Wiseman, 2003). However, such tools do not provide insight into steps teachers should take to become more globally aware, nor do they directly translate to practical classroom applications.

Therefore, we developed the Globally Competent Learning Continuum (GCLC) as a self-reflection tool to drive professional growth by breaking down the broad—and sometimes daunting—construct of globally competent teaching into manageable steps for implementation and steady improvement. The GCLC delineates the 12 elements of globally competent teaching and breaks each down into five developmental levels: nascent, beginning, progressing, proficient, and advanced. Unlike Likert-scale assessments that place teachers at a particular level of global or cultural competence based on their responses to a cluster of questions, rubrics allow users to rate themselves based on descriptors for each level, identify clear benchmarks for success, and document progress over time (McGury, Shallenberg, & Tolliver, 2008).

As teachers progress from nascent to advanced, the continuum moves from the personal to the interpersonal, with teachers taking the work upon themselves in the early stages and gradually releasing responsibility to students in the advanced stages. At the later stages, students initiate their own intercultural and international conversations and partnerships and evaluate their own global learning. Likewise, under a commitment to equity worldwide, teachers come to recognize inequities that exist locally (and globally) before encouraging students and the school community to take action on those inequities.

The continuum also moves from the local to the global. In the early levels, teachers recognize their own perspective, culture, language, and context before extending outward to recognize the perspectives, cultures, languages, and contexts of others. This embraces a "glocal" mindset that recognizes the intersecting cultural, regional, national, and global identities and affiliations we hold (Banks, 2008). It also reinforces a recognition that our personal, local actions are interconnected with the actions of others around the world (Robertson, 1995). Finally, as teachers move through the levels, they also move from basic awareness and exposure to the world to critically analyzing global inequities and taking actions to address them (Merryfield, 1998; O'Connor & Zeichner, 2011).

The GCLC uses self-reflection as a key driver for teacher learning. For each element, teachers first read through each developmental level and select the level that best describes them, reflecting on the professional and personal experiences that justify their choice. Second, teachers identify an element (or elements) they would like to improve and then read the description for the next highest level to understand what is required for growth. Third, teachers take actions that help them reach the next developmental level—for example, reading a series of articles and books, participating in a professional learning opportunity abroad, teaching a new unit that infuses global perspectives, or researching organizations that provide service-learning opportunities around issues of global concern. Finally, teachers reflect to see if their actions have led them to reach the next developmental level. They can continue the process for the next level or move on to a different element. Because developing global competence is a lifelong journey—and the world we live in is ever-changing—even when the advanced level is reached, there is always room for continued growth.

Research, Development, and Validation

We developed the GCLC through a two-year iterative research process consisting of four stages that developed the construct of globally competent teaching and tested the content validity, internal consistency reliability, and internal structure of the self-reflection tool. Stage 1 identified the 12 elements of globally competent teaching through a systematic literature review (described earlier). Stage 2 broke down each globally competent teaching element into developmental levels. This initial rubric underwent extensive review by 57 practicing K–12 teachers, 7 teacher educators, and 8 global education field experts to determine the representative and relevance of the elements and their developmental levels. Based on the data, modifications to the continuum were made. Stage 3 evaluated internal consistency and overall stability of the 12 elements and their 5 developmental levels through a pilot test with 111 practicing K–12 teachers and a focus group of educators. During Stage 4, final revisions were made. We assessed participant interpretation and use along with overall content validity by conducting cognitive interviews with nine in-service teachers, representing elementary, middle, and high school, and asked a second round of global education experts to provide an expert review.

Teachers and administrators across the United States who have used the GCLC in online courses, district-based professional development, and national global learning cohorts have overwhelmingly stated in evaluations that it is a valuable resource for exploring global issues, gaining global and cultural knowledge, and self-reflecting. Comments that educators have made about the GCLC include "This has changed a lot of views I had and made me reflect about issues that I usually did not pay attention to," "It has helped me to understand my students better," "It will enable me to design more activities that incorporate global awareness," and "It has helped us see where the gaps are and provide those resources for teachers and students in curriculum and strategic plans."

Using This Book

Trends in globalization highlight that all of us are part of a wider world. Historic increases in migration have reshaped our local communities. Technology can connect us in nanoseconds to people and ideas around the globe. The clothing we wear, the food we buy, and the devices on which we rely often get into our wardrobes, refrigerators, and hands through complex global supply chains. Regardless of where you live or the student population you teach, the purpose of this book is to bring out the global educator in you.

This book is written for teachers of all experience levels and grade levels from PreK through 12, teaching any and all subject areas. Preservice and inservice teachers can use this book as a tool to evolve their teaching practice to incorporate globally competent teaching elements. Through this book, teachers can develop a deeper understanding of what global competence means for themselves and their students, reflect on their strengths and areas for improvement across the 12 elements of globally competent teaching, and explore professional learning resources to aid their professional growth.

This book is also valuable for school administrators interested in supporting their staff's and students' global competence development. It gives insights into what you should look for in a classroom that regularly integrates global competence, along with resources you can provide to teachers as they embark on the journey of developing global competence. Since it provides a nuanced conceptualization of what global teaching and learning entails, school administrators can also use this book as a guidepost for designing professional development, instructional coaching, and curriculum that is focused on global competence.

Similarly, teacher educators who want to weave global competence into coursework and programs can use this book as a framework for planning and running both teacher preparation programs for preservice teachers and continuing education programs for inservice teachers. Teacher educators can use the chapters in this book as guideposts to assess whether the courses or additional learning experiences their programs provide are helping preservice and inservice teachers' global competence growth for specific elements. They can also be a tool for personal introspection as teacher educators incorporate global competence into their courses.

This book is divided into three sections—Dispositions, Knowledge, and Skills—and each chapter is devoted to an element of globally competent teaching. Chapters include a description of each element, tips for implementation delineated by developmental levels on the GCLC, and links to additional resources for continuing the journey. Each chapter also invites you to rate yourself on that particular globally competent teaching element. We encourage you to use the Globally Competent Learning Continuum Self-Reflection Tool (see Appendix) as a place to document the level you rate yourself (nascent, beginning, progressing, proficient, advanced) and note the evidence from your personal and professional experiences that justify your rating.

Examples of how these elements have been operationalized by real teachers in real schools are also prominent throughout the chapters and highlighted in real-life vignettes. These examples come from interviews, observations, and surveys of practicing K–12 teachers from a cross-section of grade levels (elementary, middle, and high school), subject areas (math, science, language arts, social studies, world language, and the arts), and locales (urban, suburban, and rural). Note that all teacher names are pseudonyms to protect confidentiality. We also infuse our own personal experiences as teacher educators and elementary, middle, and high school teachers working with diverse student populations.

There is no prescribed order for developing these 12 elements of globally competent teaching—or for reading these chapters. Just as teacher beliefs (dispositions) shape practice (skills), practices can also reshape teachers' beliefs (McLaughlin, 1990). The globally competent teaching elements themselves are interconnected and can be conceived as developing simultaneously and iteratively—as opposed to consecutively and linearly. For example, research suggests that learning to communicate in another language can increase empathy (Goetz, 2003). In gaining an experiential understanding of multiple cultures, a teacher may simultaneously come to value the perspectives of others and learn intercultural communication skills that facilitate international conversations. In developing international partnerships, a teacher may learn about a global inequity that sparks a desire to take action. Because of the interconnectedness of these elements, you will find that some of the same resources will cut across them, such as the Sustainable Development Goals (SDGs), Skype in the Classroom, the Global Read Aloud, and virtual exchange tools, to name a few.

At the same time, we encourage teachers to start with dispositions because those are the foundational lenses through which we engage with our world, our students, and our content. As will be made clear throughout the following chapters, a mindset that values multiple perspectives is requisite to understanding global conditions and current events, understanding intercultural communication, creating a classroom environment that values diversity, and facilitating intercultural conversations. A commitment to equity is likewise foundational to critically analyzing how global interconnectedness contributes to inequities within and across nations, understanding power dynamics that relate to language and intercultural communication, and developing partnerships that allow students to learn with and through the world.

No matter where you fall on the Globally Competent Learning Continuum—and whether you're just thinking about this work for the first time, have recently dabbled, or have 20 years of global teaching experience—the information in this book will help you further develop as a global educator in preparing all students for academic success, social-emotional well-being, and the ability to thrive in an ever-changing world.

DISPOSITIONS

Dispositions are the attitudes, values, and commitments teachers hold and espouse that inevitably influence how they teach. All teaching follows from your dispositions: your classroom setup, classroom curriculum, pedagogy, and assessment practices. Dispositions are essentially the driver of your overall practice, whether you are conscious of it or not. In the next two chapters, we aim to make explicit the dispositions we believe are critical for globally competent teachers:

- Empathy and valuing multiple perspectives.
- Commitment to promoting equity worldwide.

As described in Chapter 1, empathy is a critical element in being a globally competent teacher. Empathy, or the ability to understand others, requires a teacher to be open to listening to others. Empathetic teachers seek out and invite multiple perspectives. Further, they are aware of the limits of their own perspectives and thus value opportunities to see the world through others' eyes. Empathetic teachers engage in regular reflection to better understand their biases and preconceptions. They seek to reframe their understandings in ways that enable them to hold and value multiple perspectives simultaneously.

Chapter 2 details how globally competent teachers reflect a commitment to promoting equity worldwide. These teachers are committed to addressing larger systemic issues in and through their teaching. For example, they are committed to promoting peace, addressing world hunger and poverty, and tackling illiteracy and gender inequity around the globe. This commitment is as much local as it is global, and it is at the heart of both *teaching about* inequity and social justice and *acting for* equity and human rights beyond the classroom.

These two dispositions are truly foundational to the personal and professional actions globally competent teachers take to gain an understanding of the world and our place in it. They also help teachers foster those same understandings among students so they are primed to succeed in a global marketplace, live peacefully with those from backgrounds different from their own, and strive to make their own communities and the wider global village more just and sustainable for their own and future generations.

1

Empathy and Valuing Multiple Perspectives

Open-mindedness, empathy, and perspective consciousness are the foundations for global competence. All three are also at the heart of good teaching. Part of what moves a teacher from good to great is the ability to model empathy and an appreciation for the variety of perspectives (and the many influences on those perspectives) that exist on any given topic. In modeling these dispositions, a teacher can cultivate empathy and perspective consciousness in students. This fosters not only global competence but also trusting relationships among students and between the teacher and students. Consequently, students are more willing to take risks and consider perspectives they never thought of before.

Examining multiple perspectives also means examining biases. It is important to acknowledge that we all hold biases, and we must face our own head-on. Once we have done so, we can begin to understand the limitations of our own and others' perspectives. If we approach one another with empathy, however, we can open ourselves up to challenging our perspectives. As George Bernard Shaw said, "Progress is impossible without change, and those who cannot change their minds cannot change anything."

It is not easy to admit that our prior viewpoints may have been faulty—or that a viewpoint that contradicts our own may have merit. However, being willing to do so is necessary for truly considering the perspectives of others.

This, in turn, is crucial for understanding those who seem different from ourselves at first blush. By valuing multiple perspectives, having empathy for others, and identifying our own biases, we can set the stage for deepening students' global awareness and empathy.

What Does It Mean to Express Empathy and Value Multiple Perspectives?

Empathy is the ability to step into another person's shoes and understand that person's thoughts and feelings from his or her point of view, rather than your own. If we are in someone else's shoes, then we are standing where they are standing, seeing what they are seeing, and feeling what they are feeling. Thus, to truly empathize with another person or group, we need to be able to understand their perspective, which is difficult to do because our minds, personalities, and life experiences are all so unique. That is why the closest we may get to seeing from another's eyes is to learn everything we can about *their* experiences and understand how those experiences shape their worldviews. This takes commitment, since a considerable amount of work and time is required for such introspection.

Perspective consciousness is "the recognition or awareness on the part of the individual that he or she has a view of the world that is not universally shared, that this view of the world has been and continues to be shaped by influences that often escape conscious detection, and that others have views of the world that are profoundly different from one's own" (Hanvey, 1982, p. 162). The first step to being able to understand someone else's perspective is to understand your own. This requires identifying your personal beliefs and experiences and recognizing how they shape your view of the world. It requires recognizing that we each hold certain stereotypes and that our biases limit our ability to understand an issue from all angles. Once we recognize that our perspectives are inherently incomplete, we can understand the importance of seeking out alternative perspectives and even trying them on, so to speak. Genuinely valuing multiple perspectives means being willing to consider viewpoints that directly challenge our own and being open to change our minds. When we can honor someone else's perspective to that degree, then we come much closer to knowing what it's like to stand in that person's shoes.

As educators, we also must be able to reflect on how our own worldviews and subconscious biases shape our decisions in the classroom and the effect those decisions have on students. For example, when Ariel gave her 5th grade students math assignments, she required students to show their work. That was how she was taught math in school, and it was how she was taught to teach math. By having students show their work on a long division problem, for example, she could identify areas where their understanding of the process broke down. However, her students' parents—who went to school in Mexico—considered that process messy, and when their children turned in homework assignments, they only submitted their final answers. Ariel would constantly reiterate to those students the need to show their work. However, in doing so, Ariel unintentionally put her students in an uncomfortable situation, one where they didn't know whether to listen to their teacher or their parents.

The stereotypes we may consciously or subconsciously hold about specific racial, ethnic, gender, socioeconomic, or cultural groups also have negative ramifications for students' scholastic achievement. Stereotype threat, a phenomenon widely studied in social psychology, puts students at risk of underperforming when the group with which they identify is negatively stereotyped to be inferior intellectually or academically (Steele & Aronson, 1995). For example, researchers found that African American students perform worse than white students on the Graduate Record Exam (GRE) when placed in a stereotype-threat condition, but they perform equally well when in a nonthreatening setting (Steele & Aronson, 1995). Likewise, female students perform worse than men when told that a test shows gender differences (Spencer, Steele, & Quinn, 1999).

We also need to consider how our students may have views that differ from our own. For instance, we need to attend to moments where we may be intentionally or unintentionally advocating for particular positions with which not all students agree. These might include positions about tax cuts, gender roles, religion, free speech, welfare programs, environmental protection, and universal health care, just to name a few. We may unconsciously express a rejection of the view that is counter to our own, which could leave some students feeling alienated or defensive. We do not mean to suggest that teachers should never share their positions. Pretending to be neutral denies students the opportunity to learn the important democratic citizenship skills of deliberation and rational debate (Journell, 2016). However, teachers need to take care that they foster a classroom in which multiple, potentially opposing, perspectives are encouraged. If teachers share their opinions, they should invite others to share counterpoints so democratic deliberation can be practiced and students' diverse perspectives are validated.

Self-Reflection and Implementation Tips for Developing Empathy and Multiple Perspectives

Look at Figure 1.1 and rate yourself along the GCLC for the element "Empathy and valuing multiple perspectives."

1. Where do you rate yourself and why?
2. What steps do you need to take to move along the continuum?

The following implementation tips will help you think through the next steps you can take to develop empathy and value multiple perspectives, regardless of what grade levels and subject areas you teach.

Stepping outside our own minds to examine our beliefs and where they come from does not come naturally or easily to most people. Psychology researchers have used the term *motivated reasoning* to describe how humans tend to seek out evidence that aligns with their prior views and dismiss evidence that contradicts those views (Kunda, 1990). In other words, we are psychologically predisposed to confirm, rather than question or revise, our beliefs. As a result, moving along the continuum from nascent to advanced may be quite challenging because it requires us to seek viewpoints that challenge our own. It may be helpful to pause frequently and ask ourselves, "Is motivated

Figure 1.1 | Empathy and Valuing Multiple Perspectives

Element	Nascent	Beginning	Progressing	Proficient	Advanced
Empathy and Valuing Multiple Perspectives	I have not yet explored how my personal beliefs have shaped my worldview.	• I can identify my personal beliefs and experiences and recognize how they shape my view of the world. • I recognize that I might hold stereotypes.	• I understand that my beliefs and experiences are not universally shared. • I can identify the influences that shape how others and I view the world. • I am willing to explore the experiences and perspectives of people who challenge my beliefs.	• I recognize biases and limitations of my own perspective and those of others' perspectives. • I recognize how my personal beliefs influence my decisions as a teacher. • I empathize by seeking to understand the perspectives of others.	• I challenge my personal assumptions to understand viewpoints that differ from my own. • I value diverse perspectives, including those that challenge my own.

reasoning shaping my opinion on this issue?" More to the point, we should ask, "*How* is motivated reasoning shaping my opinion on this issue?"

The following are implementation tips on empathy and valuing multiple perspectives specific to your developmental level along the GCLC.

Nascent

A first step you can take to develop empathy and seek multiple perspectives is to list your personal beliefs and values and try to identify the experiences throughout your life that have shaped these beliefs. For example, you may believe that more farming should be organic or that more state funding should go to public schools. What led you to these beliefs? Were they formed through messages transmitted by your parents, interactions with others, scientific articles you read, documentaries you watched, newsfeeds you clicked on, or other experiences?

Try to list some of the stereotypes you hold. We don't generally like to think of ourselves as having biases, but we all do. Stereotyping is part of being human; it results from our brain's propensity to notice patterns and make generalizations (Payne, Niemi, & Doris, 2018). Since stereotypes and biases are often unconscious, it can be hard to identify them in ourselves. Try to pay attention to any assumptions you make when you meet new people. For example, when you meet someone who has a different political ideology than you, do you assume he or she will have certain personality characteristics or background experiences? When you meet someone from your hometown, do you assume anything about that person? How about people from certain religious, racial, ethnic, or sexuality groups? By paying attention to your internal thoughts when you meet new people, you may get a small window into your unconscious.

Think back upon previous interactions you have had with individuals from various backgrounds. Howard (2003) suggests the following reflection questions to uncover and unpack the prejudices you may harbor:

1. How frequently and what types of interactions did I have with individuals different from my own growing up?

2. Who were the primary persons that helped to shape my perspectives of individuals from different groups? How were their opinions formed?
3. Do I currently, or have I ever harbored prejudiced thoughts toward people from different backgrounds?
4. If I do harbor prejudiced thoughts, what effects do such thoughts have on students who come from those backgrounds?
5. Do I create negative profiles of individuals who come from different racial backgrounds? (p. 198)

You may feel some guilt or shame when you realize assumptions you've been making, but remember that we *all* have biases, and in recognizing your own, you are taking steps toward dismantling them. Try not to let any feelings of guilt discourage you from continuing to uncover additional stereotypes and develop greater empathy and perspective recognition.

Beginning/Progressing

Once you have identified your beliefs and listed your biases, you are now ready to trace the origins of your biases. Asking yourself questions such as "Why do I feel this way about this particular situation?" is a great way to recognize what influenced your biases and help you break them down. For example, Lisa declared at the age of 10 that she would never get married. As she grew older, she held on to this declaration, believing that all marriages ended in divorce. But what exactly led her to that assumption? She had to reflect on her youth and identify that watching the dissolution of her parents' marriage made her develop a bias against marriage in general. By tracing back to that time in her life, she was able to examine her deeply held beliefs, and, at the same time, recall other successful marriages to which she was exposed and recognize that her assumption that all marriages ended in divorce was not true. Rather, the trauma of her personal experience caused her to believe every marriage was bad.

As a second example, Hillary noticed that, while teaching high school social studies, she paid more attention to her outspoken and gregarious students than to her quieter students. When funny students would call out, she would often unintentionally reward the behavior by laughing or smiling. Hillary actually could relate better to her quiet students—having been a shy, rule-following student herself. However, as she reflected on her preference for the outgoing students, she realized that it was *because* she was introverted that she was more intrigued by extroverted students. Perhaps she even admired them to some extent for having the ability to entertain the group and provide a lively atmosphere. Nevertheless, she realized this was problematic not only because it unevenly distributed her attention among the students but also because it usually meant she attended more to male students. Once she identified the source of her bias, she found greater motivation for constantly reflecting on whether she was paying sufficient attention to shy students like her former self.

As the examples of Lisa and Hillary show, an important part of facing our biases is getting to the root cause analysis of why we feel or believe the way we do. Once we have identified our biases and traced their origins, the next step is to reduce those biases for a clearer view of reality.

Proficient/Advanced

Expand the number of viewpoints you can see at one time. Notice when you are using motivated reasoning when you are trusting sources that confirm your prior opinions and dismissing sources that contradict your views. Try to step into the shoes of someone with the opposite view. If you support organic farming, for example, ask yourself what the arguments might be against the expansion of organic farming (e.g., issues of scale in feeding a growing global population). Can you imagine how these positions could be justified? Perhaps you might seek out readings that reflect these alternative perspectives to better understand them. Even if you are not convinced by these arguments, can you empathize with someone who is?

Another way to recognize multiple perspectives on a particular topic—be it gun control, immigration, or teacher salaries—is to seek out alternative perspectives. For example, if you come across an opinion article with which you disagree, see if you can "try on" the author's perspective. This may help you more deeply consider the author's points, rather than dismiss them without weighing the arguments and evidence he or she provides. Try to notice how your own perspective impedes you from being able to see through someone else's eyes, thus preventing you from truly empathizing with that person. What biases cause you to have knee-jerk reactions to certain viewpoints, and how can you work to overcome those? By seeking to truly understand—and not just tolerate—perspectives that oppose your own, you are demonstrating a foundational element of living and working in a diverse, interconnected world.

Taking on opposing perspectives can be quite difficult, especially in the current polarized world. By self-selecting the news channels we watch, the radio shows and podcasts we listen to, and the people and organizations we follow on social media, we can literally tune out any viewpoint that doesn't jive with our own and live in an echo chamber of agreement. Understanding human psychology can help us trace the confluence of biological and social influences on our beliefs about morally correct behavior. In his book *The Righteous Mind: Why Good People Are Divided by Politics and Religion,* psychologist Jonathan Haidt (2012) describes how people on different ends of the political spectrum tend to prioritize different values within their morality frameworks.

Whereas people on the political right tend to prioritize fairness, authority, loyalty, and sanctity, people on the political left tend to prioritize care. Both groups believe their framework is the most righteous one and have a hard time seeing the other group as having an equally valid morality framework. Haidt also points out that most societies consist of both groups, suggesting that a balance of the two may contribute to a society's stability. Perhaps we can better empathize with and understand one another if we register that it could be beneficial to society to have some variety of moral foundations.

It's also important to understand how your personal beliefs influence your professional actions and decisions as a teacher. Pay careful attention to how you respond to different students depending on how similar they are to you in terms of personality, background, ideology, or other characteristics. Film a lesson, and then watch it with an eye open for any biases you show toward your students—whom you call on, how you respond to their questions, and how they are seated.

In addition, examine how your beliefs shape the content you include, exclude, emphasize, or fail to even consider in your curriculum. For instance, high school social studies teacher Tina realized that the traditional curriculum made almost no mention of LGBTQ individuals throughout history, which could leave many of her LGBTQ students feeling invisible. Therefore, she intentionally supplemented her U.S. history textbook with content such as the Lavender Scare (which resulted when President Eisenhower banned federal employment of gay and lesbian individuals).

Go as far as to challenge, critique, reconsider, and even change your own beliefs. American culture tends to value "sticking to your guns" and not being "wishy-washy," but this can lead people to cling to misconceptions or prejudices about the world, other people, or places and not take others' perspectives into account when making decisions. Understanding other people's viewpoints can help us confront our own deeply held beliefs that may be problematic and oppressive.

Another way to demonstrate valuing multiple perspectives is to overcome your desire to pick a side. We often feel uneasy when we have not made up our minds about which side is "right" in a conflict, but quickly choosing a side may not always be the most productive decision. Some conflicts, particularly on the global scale, are so deep, complicated, and fraught that the best option might be to maintain an ability to see all opposing positions as legitimate, even if you tend to favor one position over another. For instance, when teaching the history of the Israeli-Palestinian conflict, the Cold War, or the Syrian Civil War, present students with the diverse perspectives of individuals on different sides of the conflict and model that well-informed adults do not always have to choose one side. In fact, the best chance of peace in war-torn regions depends on diplomats and leaders who can understand and truly empathize with all sides of a conflict in order to reach consensus on a solution.

Special Considerations for Elementary School Teachers (PK–5)

- Connect students with other classrooms from different geographical locations to learn about other students who have different life and cultural experiences than they might. (See Chapter 11 for a list of tools and programs that can help students forge these connections.) Learning about others in this interactive way allows students to learn more about themselves in the process—and you to learn along with them. Young students are especially impressionable, so starting early in the building of empathy promotes a strong foundation that students can carry into their lives as they get older.

- Learn about new perspectives and worldviews from your own classroom community. For example, Adrian begins each school year with a heritage project for his elementary students. Rather than have students present an "All About Me" project, he pairs students together to learn about each other's backgrounds, which they then present to the class. Adrian finds that students get excited to learn about and present their peers' backgrounds (e.g., the languages they speak, the holidays they celebrate, their favorite foods, their hobbies), and the project builds a strong sense of community and models how to embrace differences while also showing similarities across students.

- Become cognizant of "teachable" moments that show students to be more aware and tolerant of differences. For example, when 1st grade teacher Shauna shared a slide show of foods around the world, a number of students responded to unfamiliar foods and instinctively said, "Ew!" Instead of ignoring the comments, Shauna paused the lesson and explained that just because a food is different from what you are used to, it doesn't make it gross. She then asked students to think about their favorite foods and what another kid might think about that food if they had never seen it before.

Special Considerations for Secondary School Teachers (6–12)

- Even if you can't set aside time for explicit lessons on empathy and multiple perspectives within the confines of content-area standards and curriculum, you can still intentionally address these dispositions by infusing them into your everyday lessons. For example, before starting a collaborative learning activity, spend 5–10 minutes discussing how to engage in perspective-taking and how to communicate this with one's peers. Post several sentence starters or frames, such as "What I hear you saying is _____"; "You have a perspective on this that I hadn't thought of before"; and "I like how when you said _____, you were raising a new viewpoint." Use these sentence frames as a reminder for you to model this language as well!

- Instead of reactively addressing respect and empathy after students fight, be proactive by beginning the school year with ample opportunities for students to learn and practice expressing empathy, inviting opposing perspectives, and considering changing their own minds on a topic. This could include lessons on being a bystander versus an upstander (i.e., witnessing versus taking action to defend someone), using respectful language to disagree or question, and practicing active listening and rephrasing another student's views in their own words. Such lessons can establish an atmosphere of trust, open-mindedness, and respectful disagreement that will reduce the likelihood of conflict and hurt feelings throughout the year. (See Chapter 8 for additional ideas on creating a classroom environment that values multiple perspectives and global engagement.)

Element 1 in Action: Teaching War from Multiple Perspectives

Simone Jackson teaches 8th grade social studies in a public middle school in rural North Carolina with a population that is about 73 percent white, 20 percent black, and 6 percent Latinx. One of Simone's primary goals is to develop students' empathy and ability to view an issue from multiple perspectives, maybe even challenging or changing their own opinions in the process. She works toward these goals in her unit on the Vietnam War.

Simone explains that her students tend to be familiar with the pro- and anti-war stances within the United States, but they are less familiar with the opposing stances within Vietnam. She wants her students to realize that the people living in these two countries had quite different understandings of the war. Prior to teaching this unit, Simone, like her students, had little familiarity with what the Vietnamese population thought of the war, and she used the unit as an opportunity to seek to understand the perspectives of others.

She tells her 8th graders that the Vietnamese called the conflict "the American War," and the class views a video showing how, in Vietnamese schools today, children are taught that the conflict was not a civil war between the North and South but a revolution to expel the American colonial power from the region.

To help students understand the war from the perspective of the North and South Vietnamese, Simone created an activity in which groups analyze four sets of primary source documents and fill out a chart in which they describe "what the documents said" and "how this will make people feel." The sets of documents include

- North Vietnamese sources: Declaration of Independence, Ho Chi Minh appeal
- South Vietnamese sources: protest songs
- Pro-war U.S. sources: U.S. Department of State letter, pro-war song lyrics
- Anti-war U.S. sources: John Kerry's speech, protest song lyrics

Students discuss how both the North and South Vietnamese might have felt about the French colonization and American intervention in the region. Throughout the conversation, Simone encourages students to put themselves in the shoes of the Vietnamese. She says, "I know you all are taught basically to hate communism, but if you're in this situation, you can see where that might sound appealing." Students' comments in class reflect an understanding of the motive to support communism as a means of obtaining national independence.

For homework, students answer the questions "Would you have been pro- or anti-war if you lived in the United States at that time? Do you think something could have caused you to change sides? If so, what?" Simone tells students that the pivotal moment need not be realistic. For example, it could be meeting a member of the North Vietnamese army. By asking students to consider how their minds could be changed, Simone encourages students to think of a perspective as something that is open to revision rather than as a stance that must be adhered to no matter what evidence one encounters. She models this by giving each student the opportunity to develop and share his or her own perspective on the Vietnam War without imposing her own view. By doing so, some of her students' perspectives challenge Simone to think differently about her own stance.

Further Developing This Disposition

- Begin with a "personal inward journey" by self-reflecting on the following questions:
  - Who am I?
  - What do I value?
  - What stereotypes do I hold?
  - Why?

- These are difficult to detect in ourselves, so ask someone close to you to help you on this journey of discovery. It should be someone who will be forthright with you and whose feedback you will be able to accept without pushback, defensiveness, or hurt feelings.
- Then move to an "outward journey" and seek perspectives that differ from your own. Don't start with issues you feel most passionately about; you're less likely to change your mind or understand the counterpoints on those issues. Instead, start with an issue on which you have an opinion but are willing to explore further. Consider choosing

an issue that a loved one disagrees with you about. That might provide some motivation for really trying to understand the counterview. Deeply examine all of the evidence for the other side and consider the possibility that your view could use some modification. Finally, consider how you might transmit to your students this openness to reassessing one's opinion.

Continuing the Journey

Explore these additional resources as starting points for moving forward in your own development of empathy and valuing multiple perspectives and how you can apply it to your classroom practice.

❯ **Ashoka: Start Empathy Resources**
(https://startempathy.org/resources): This resource library provides books, articles, PDFs, videos, and weblinks to resources that show what empathy looks like in education and why it matters.

❯ **TED Talk: The Danger of a Single Story**
(www.ted.com/talks/chimamanda_adichie_the_danger_of_a_single_story): Nigerian author Chimamanda Adichie describes why it is important not to tell a "single story" about a place or a people.

❯ **TED Talk: A Radical Experiment in Empathy**
(www.ted.com/talks/sam_richards_a_radical_experiment_in_empathy): Sociologist Sam Richards leads the audience, step-by-step, through stepping into the shoes of an Iraqi insurgent in order to understand the motivations and experiences that shape anti-American sentiments.

❯ **RSA Short Video: Empathy Versus Sympathy**
(www.thersa.org/discover/videos/rsa-shorts/2013/12/Brene-Brown-on-Empathy): This short animated video defines *empathy* and contrasts it with *sympathy*. In it, Dr. Brene Brown explains how empathy requires connection, whereas sympathy—or feeling sorry for someone—distances us from the other person.

❯ *The Righteous Mind: Why Good People Are Divided by Politics and Religion*
This book by Jonathan Haidt draws on research from psychology to show how humans have developed different moral frameworks that shape our sometimes conflicting understandings of justice.

Commitment to Equity

Let's start with a visual activity. Imagine a baseball field while a game is in session. There is a group of fans trying to watch the game over a fence. The people in this group are of varying heights, so not everyone is able to see the game over the fence. To help them reach their goal, in the name of equality, you have to treat everyone fairly. In other words, you give them all the same supports—the same-height chair, for example. This solution is effective for some and allows them to see the game. However, it does not take into account that there are some who were already able to see the game and are now at an even greater advantage. Similarly, there are some who, even with the added support, are still unable to see the game.

Equality, though well intentioned, assumes that everyone starts off on an even playing field with the same needs, thereby justifying the same support. *Equity*, on the other hand, considers individuals' varying needs and, therefore, provides varying supports so that each person is able to see the game. This means that those who were already able to see will not receive additional support. Instead, the fans who were unable to see will receive the supports that meet their needs and allow them to see the game. With this solution, some will receive more support than others. The result is that every fan will be able to see the game—even if that means the supports are not distributed evenly.

The image in Figure 2.1 is how Angus Maguire, commissioned by the Interaction Institute for Social Change, visually distinguishes between equity and equality. The goal of equity is justice, which questions why the fence is there in the first place and what we can do to dismantle it. Justice seeks to provide a world where everyone has the opportunity to thrive, and a commitment to equity is a foundational building block toward a just world.

Figure 2.1 | Illustrating Equality Versus Equity

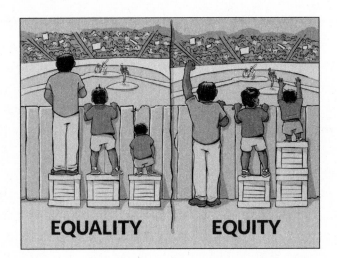

EQUALITY   EQUITY

Source: From Interaction Institute for Social Change (https://interactioninstitute.org), artist: Angus Maguire (https://madewithangus.com).

To cultivate global citizens who seek to shape a more just and sustainable world, it is important for teachers and students to acknowledge and appreciate the diversity of people and perspectives in their local communities and around the world. It is equally important to understand and address the inequities that people around the world experience because of their sociodemographic characteristics. We live in a world that is riddled with inequities. For example, the United States has wide disparities in incarceration rates, with black Americans being 4.6 times as likely to be incarcerated than their white counterparts (National Research Council, 2014). Globally, children from the poorest 20 percent of households are almost four times as likely to be out of school as compared to their more affluent peers, with out-of-school rates being highest for children in rural areas (United Nations, 2016). Addressing these inequities and countless others is a fundamental part of understanding and acting as a responsible citizen of the world.

Let's reconsider the opening example and replace baseball with the opportunity to thrive in society. A globally competent teacher who is committed to equity *is aware* of the fences that block people's access to an opportunity to thrive and *acts* to find the supports needed for people to jump over those fences on the journey toward justice. In this chapter, we will explore what it means and looks like to be committed to equity worldwide and how you can work toward that within yourself, your classroom, and your school.

What Does It Mean to Have a Commitment to Equity?

Educators who espouse a commitment to equity are critically conscious. That is, they are aware "that our ideas come from a particular set of life experiences, an ability to trace our ideas to their sources in our experience, and acknowledgement that others will have equally valid, if different, life experiences and ideas" (Hinchey, 2004, p. 25). Around the world people are socialized to hold beliefs about what or who is "right" and what is "wrong," and human differences (e.g., race, gender, sexual orientation, level of educational attainment, language, and socioeconomic status) are used to justify inequities. Take, for example, the labels *expatriates*, *immigrant*, or *alien* and the connotations they conjure. In his article "Why Are White People Expats When the Rest of Us Are Immigrants?" Koutonin (2015) points out that the use of these labels depends on social class, country of origin, and economic status.

In hand with critical consciousness is a recognition of the privilege and oppression that comes with human differences. Dominant groups, which vary across communities, experience privilege demonstrated by better life outcomes, such as greater access to high-quality education, healthcare, and wealth. By contrast, marginalized groups, which also vary across communities, experience poorer life outcomes. According to the Organisation for

Economic Co-operation and Development (OECD, 2018b), the following hold true on a global scale:

- The average income of the richest 10 percent of the population is about nine times that of the poorest 10 percent.
- On average, women earn 16 percent less than men, and even the top-earning females are paid 21 percent less than their male counterparts.
- Poorer students struggle to compete with their wealthier classmates and experience lower levels of educational attainment.

The United Nations has likewise acknowledged vast global disparities that presently exist around opportunity, wealth, and power. To address these inequities and their systemic causes, the United Nations adopted 17 Sustainable Development Goals (SDGs) for the world to achieve by 2030. These ambitious goals include, among others, ending poverty in all forms everywhere, ending hunger, ensuring healthy lives, ensuring inclusive and equitable high-quality education, achieving gender equality and empowerment of all women and girls, ensuring availability and sustainable management of water and sanitation, ensuring affordable and clean energy, ensuring decent work and economic growth, and reducing inequality within and among countries (United Nations, 2015).

Given the current state of our world, we agree with global education scholar Kenneth Tye (1990) that "the ultimate goal of education is to cause people to transcend more limited levels of interest and to take personal and collective action on behalf of all humankind" (p. 6). The ability to recite statistics is not enough to take action. This awareness must be paired with an ethic of care, which postulates that the carer acts responsively to the needs of the cared-for, based on what the actual needs of the cared-for are—not what the carer perceives the needs to be (Noddings, 1984). This requires a sense of engrossment, or empathy, whereby the carer can see the cared-for's reality as a possibility for his or her own reality and make a commitment to addressing those realities. Ladson-Billings (2011) considered an ethic of care to be a prerequisite to equity-focused pedagogy. She described *care* as informed empathy, which goes beyond "feeling with" to "feeling for." Feeling with does not require a sense of accountability, whereas feeling for does.

Moving from a place of feeling with toward feeling for can depend on your personal experience. Merryfield (2000) conducted a study that identified the experiences that influenced teacher educators committed to multicultural and global education. Her participants of color had an experiential understanding of discrimination. For example, Deborah Wei described her experiences growing up Chinese American as painful. Many of her peers held negative stereotypes about countries and cultures in Asia. As a child, trying to make sense of the ridicule, she "[laid] the blame on the accident of [her] identity" (p. 433). As she got older, she recognized that that was not the case and became committed to ensuring that her English language learner students did not have the same experience. By contrast, due to the nature of white privilege and racism, the white middle-class teacher educators in Merryfield's study were largely influenced by experiences outside their own country. For example, Vic Martuza described himself as politically conservative and assimilationist prior to his travel to Central America and Mexico. His experiences there changed his perspective and "sensitized [him] to the demographic changes in the U.S. and elsewhere as well as the global systems and their impact on the quality of our daily lives" (p. 438).

Following the recognition that inequities exist both locally and globally, educators who are committed to equity can identify the barriers to equity. However, in order to identify the strategies that will ameliorate inequity and disparities on a local and global scale, educators must examine their ideologies around these issues. Your ideological position determines how you define and pursue a problem. To that point, Gorski (2016) argues that teachers must avoid a deficit ideology that blames people as the sole agents of their social conditions. Instead, he suggests a structural ideology that understands disparities from an institutional and not an individualistic perspective. In other words, policies and practices in place play a large role in the inequities that people around the world experience. He uses poverty as an example.

In the United States, there is an individualistic narrative of meritocracy that says success is the result of hard work. Thus, those who are economically disadvantaged did not work hard and are to blame for the situations they are in. A solution that follows an individualistic perspective would solely involve fixing people and ignore institutionalized structures that influence poverty, such as food insecurity, inequitable access to high-quality schools, and housing instability. Solutions that reflect a structural ideology would include providing resources that those who are economically disadvantaged lack, such as healthcare, affordable housing, and accessible job training programs.

As this example shows, solutions are driven by how the problem is defined. Moving toward justice requires challenging structures in place that exacerbate inequities—for example, by challenging the ways in which schools are funded that deny access to high-quality education for all. By engaging in conversations with our students and colleagues that identify institutionalized inequities and devise solutions for how to overcome them, "schools become the incubators of social change" (Gaudelli & Hewitt, 2010, p. 93).

Self-Reflection and Implementation Tips for Solidifying a Commitment to Equity

Look at Figure 2.2 and rate yourself along the GCLC for the element "Commitment to promoting equity worldwide."

1. Where do you rate yourself and why?
2. What steps do you need to take to move along the continuum?

The following implementation tips will help you think through the next steps you can take to strengthen your commitment to promoting equity worldwide.

Find your why. What experiences have you had that drive your commitment to equity? If you don't have any, what authentic experiences can you design to help you understand the differences among the lived experiences of others? An oft-mentioned quote by Lilla Watson cautions, "If you have come here to help me, you are wasting your time, but if you have come because

Figure 2.2 | Commitment to Promoting Equity Worldwide

Element	Nascent	Beginning	Progressing	Proficient	Advanced
Commitment to Promoting Equity Worldwide	I have not yet considered local and global inequities.	• I care about the well-being of others. • I recognize that inequities exist locally and globally (e.g., poverty and discrimination).	• I understand that there are barriers to equity locally and globally. • I seek opportunities to contribute to efforts to address inequities.	• I engage in opportunities that address particular issues of local and/or global inequity (e.g., poverty and discrimination). • I take responsibility for helping my students and others in my school to recognize inequities.	• I actively seek to understand why inequities exist and challenge those underlying causes. • I lead students and others in my school to act on issues of equity locally and globally.

your liberation is bound up with mine, then let us work together" (Watson, 1985). What is it that will help you find your place in the fight for justice worldwide?

Engage in critical reflection. Experiences alone don't lead to a commitment to equity. It is crucial to pair these experiences with an understanding of the interrelationships among power, identity, and experiences in order to lead to a shift in perspective (Merryfield, 2000). To aid in this process, engage in the practice of critical reflection. This goes beyond reading autobiographies to critically reflecting on personal beliefs to uncover biases, a point raised in Chapter 1. Albeit difficult, Howard (2003) considered this skill to be essential for teachers. It requires honest self-reflection and a critique of thoughts and behaviors.

Think globally; act locally. It can be easier to focus on inequities in an international context and avoid the uncomfortable reality of inequities that hit closer to home—and may directly affect your students. Take, for example, Sustainable Development Goal 6: the achievement of universal and equitable access to safe and affordable drinking water for all. Although we in the United States may immediately think of the lack of water access in poor rural villages in sub-Sahara Africa, the reality is that millions of Americans also lack access to potable drinking water. The Flint, Michigan, water crisis exposed the unsafe tap water that municipal leaders allowed to flow into homes of predominantly lower-income African American residents. But African Americans in the rural South, Latinos in the rural Southwest, Native Americans, Alaskan Natives, residents of deep Appalachia, and migrant farmworkers are also likely to experience water poverty (McGraw, 2018). By realizing common inequities that people around the world face, we allow ourselves and our students to develop empathy and the capacity to truly care for fellow human beings. This is key because the interdependence of nations and people requires "multinational solutions to be negotiated and carried out by individuals who can and do simultaneously participate in local, national, and global civic life" (Colvin & Edwards, 2018, p. 5).

Address inequities across the content areas. Shape your classroom practice to engage students and help your school community recognize and tackle inequities. Design learning activities that show a commitment to equity within content areas. Figure 2.3 provides examples of how you can address inequities within math, science, language arts, social studies, music, art, and physical education. For a deeper exploration of a local or global inequity from a variety of perspectives, create interdisciplinary lessons and units around a particular issue. You can also engage students in service learning projects, which serve the dual purpose of addressing curricular learning goals and real community needs.

The following are implementation tips on a commitment to equity specific to your developmental level along the GCLC.

Nascent/Beginning

First, become familiar with disparities at a local and global level. You can do so by following current events that address inequities and diving into deeper research on the global conditions that fuel these events (further explored in Chapter 3). For example, at the time this book was written in 2018, teachers in West Virginia, Oklahoma, Arizona, and Colorado went on strike demanding higher salaries and an increase in state education budgets. These events brought to light labor inequities since these teachers were in non-unionized states, and disparities in youth's access to high-quality education were revealed due to a lack of funding for vital school resources. As you increase your awareness of conditions and events both locally and around the world that disadvantage certain groups, ask *why* this is happening and utilize a structural ideology to help you unmask the root causes.

Second, find your personal entry point. The inequities in our local communities and around the world are vast and can be overwhelming to tackle all at once. As you develop an ethic of care, identify the issues you are the most passionate about. It is also important to explore how your identity in the context of power might influence your perception of why certain inequities exist and how to best combat them. For someone who has never experienced

Figure 2.3 | Solidifying a Commitment to Equity Across the Content Areas

Content Area	Examples of Solidifying a Commitment to Equity
Math	• Create math problems that explore inequities, such as mass incarceration (www.prisonpolicy.org/global/2018.html and www.naacp.org/criminal-justice-fact-sheet) and educational disparities (www.education-inequalities.org). • Discuss wealth inequality and create simulations to model how tax progressivity can be a tool to combat inequality.
Science	Introduce access to clean water on a local, national, and global scale. Create lessons in which students explore filtration and the qualities of potable drinking water, and have them test local water sources. Questions to have students reflect on include: Who has water? Who does not? What are the challenges to clean water in different contexts? What sorts of waterborne illnesses are prevalent in different contexts?
Language Arts	Have students read the UN Convention on the Rights of the Child and consider situations in which children are not able to access certain rights. Have students consider position statements.
Social Studies	• Examine how governments in different countries respond to illegal activity. Discuss the disproportionate representation among those incarcerated and what activities are considered illegal. • Compare the historical context of national anthems and discuss whose voice is present and whose voice is absent in these anthems.
Music	• Explore ways in which music has been used to document struggles and communicate among marginalized groups (e.g., African American spirituals in the United States, Palestinian hip-hop.) • Examine differences in literacy rates around the world and how music can be a tool to improve literacy.
Art	Introduce artivism (Sandoval & Latorre, 2008), the pairing of art and activism, and have students create art around an issue they care about that can be displayed around the school and/or community.
Physical Education	Share the ways in which dance has been used as a form of social protest for marginalized groups around the world (e.g., gumboot dancing in South Africa to protest apartheid, indigenous tribes dancing at the Standing Rock Sioux Reservation to protest the Dakota Access Pipeline).

poverty, it may be difficult to truly understand the barriers people face in reaching financial stability. This would be a good opportunity to seek authentic conversations with those who have relevant experiences. This should not be done in a way to "other" them but to create a personal connection and truly understand their perspectives. This helps avoid an approach to global citizenship where those in positions of privilege feel a responsibility to instill their own worldviews and solutions onto others. Instead, it promotes one in which global citizens seek to change inequitable conditions by critically reflecting on power relations and communicating with those who experience inequities. In this way, all parties have an equal footing and can take responsibility for their actions in moving forward a more equitable vision of society (Andreotti & Pashby, 2013).

The Privilege Walk is one activity you can do in your classroom to help students come to understand their own position(s) of power within society. A facilitator reads a series of statements and asks participants to take either a step forward or a step back, based on their response.

Forward steps that denote positions of privilege may include statements such as

- Your ethnic identity is "American."
- Your parents were "white-collar" professionals.
- You studied the culture of your ancestors in school.
- You attended private school or summer camp.
- You are legally able to marry the person you love.
- Your parents attended college.
- You are able to take steps forward and backward.

Backward steps may include statements such as

- Your ancestors were forced to come the United States, not by choice.
- You were a victim of bullying or violence based on your race, class, ethnicity, gender, or sexual orientation.
- You were made to feel ashamed about your clothes, house, car, or other material possessions.

- You entered school speaking a language other than English.
- You had to skip meals because you didn't have enough money.
- Your parents did not grow up in the United States.

You can also personally reflect on these statements to understand areas where you hold power and areas where you are disadvantaged. For example, you might find yourself in a privileged position regarding your level of education and sexual orientation but disadvantaged regarding your gender, economic standing, and ethnicity. Reflecting on your own power status can help you think about the areas you want to address and who and how you should be partnering with to achieve your goals.

Progressing/Proficient

At these levels, you are moving into action to address the root causes of inequities that you've identified and explored with your students. As you make the leap toward action, Gorski (2016) suggests the following questions to ensure that efforts address the problem and do not focus on fixing the people who are marginalized:

- Am I helping students develop a language that problematizes deficit framings?
- Am I in any way suggesting that disparities can be eradicated by fixing marginalized people rather than by fixing the conditions that marginalize people?

Introduce community service or service learning as an opportunity to take action and bridge the gap between classroom and community. For example, if eradicating poverty is what you are passionate about, there are various ways to address this goal within your classroom. Students might donate needed resources, such as clothing, food, or school supplies, to a sister school with whom they've been communicating, or, as part of a unit on microfinancing, they can fundraise money to lend to a low-income entrepreneur.

Remember, everyone's context, community, and comfort level are different. It may be easier for you to start taking action as a global citizen outside your work hours (e.g., volunteering at a local food bank, making calls to your elected officials about policy actions) and then progress into embedding equity-oriented action in your role as an educator. Alternatively, you may feel more comfortable jumping into this work through school-based projects.

Advanced

Returning to the metaphor that opened this chapter, at this level, you are working to dismantle the fence. If educational equality is the issue you are committed to, you are not only working toward providing resources that help level the playing field between economically disadvantaged students and their counterparts but also questioning the structural conditions that allow these conditions to exist, such as school funding, wealth attainment, and food security.

At this level, you are also expanding awareness of inequitable conditions among your students and colleagues and leading them to take action. As you, your students, and your colleagues devise plans to address inequities—whether it's through curriculum-embedded service learning, a capstone project, or an extracurricular community service project—constantly ask yourself the following questions (adapted from Hinchey, 2004, p. 14):

- Who made this decision or devised this plan—and based on what criteria?
- Who will gain what from it? Who will lose what?

These questions allow for a deep dive into the inequities we see around us and reflect a structural understanding of the roots of inequity and the underlying power dynamics that could impede real progress if we don't consider all voices—especially those who are experiencing inequity.

Special Considerations for Elementary School Teachers (PK–5)

- Use visuals to model what inequities look like. For example, a kindergarten teacher shared pictures of communities with varying levels of trash on the ground. From looking at the pictures, students were able to articulate problems that kids might face who live in highly polluted areas. Early elementary school students can understand concepts such as "more" and "less." You can model food inequities by distributing large handfuls of a healthy snack (e.g., raisins, crackers) to some students, one or two pieces to other students, and nothing to other students. Kids will quickly pick up on why that isn't fair.

- Remember that students are never too young to recognize inequities and act on them. When observing a 2nd grade class in Washington, DC, reading a picture book about the devasting 2010 earthquake in Haiti, Ariel was struck by comments students made about how the main character had no food, house, or water, and because they had those things, it was their responsibility to help. As one student simply stated, "We should care about other people." Examples abound of young kids who have started organizations, fundraising initiatives, and awareness campaigns to address hunger, poverty, and more (Tavangar & Mladic-Morales, 2014).

Special Considerations for Secondary School Teachers (6–12)

- Engage students in a design challenge to create a solution for a global inequity that a population is facing. The design thinking process consists of five steps: (1) empathy, which focuses on understanding the true needs and issues of the population (your "user" of the solution) through interviewing and observations; (2) define, which focuses on developing the point of view of the user; (3) ideate, in which you generate as many potential solutions as possible; (4) prototype, which involves building representations of your solution; and (5) test, which involves getting feedback on the prototype from the people who would be using it (Hasso Plattner, Institute of Design at Stanford, n.d.). The empathy and testing steps allow for students to probe deeply into why inequities exist from the perspective of those who are experiencing them and to take action in ways that will dismantle the true root causes.

Element 2 in Action: Using Music to Explore Global Educational Inequities

Nelson is a middle school band teacher at an urban school located in the southeast United States. The community where he teaches has a large number of Spanish-speaking and Latinx students. Nelson challenges the traditional curriculum by ensuring that his students and their culture are represented in his lessons. One way he does this is by using Latin American folk music as a vehicle to discuss literacy in Latin America and help his students understand the effect of limited access to education that millions of youth around the world experience.

During one class, Nelson and his students examined adult literacy rates from 1985 to 2011 in Latin America. In small groups, students hypothesized why some countries had higher literacy rates than others and shared their thoughts in a whole-class discussion. He realized that for many of his students, the concept of illiteracy and a lack of access to education were difficult to grasp because of their own experiences in the United States. Therefore, throughout the discussion, Nelson asked probing questions to help students consider the lack of access to education and technology that some communities face and why those conditions exist in some countries but not others. To tie the discussion back to the content area, he discussed ways in which music has been a vehicle for teaching literacy. At the end of the lesson, students completed an exit ticket answering the essential question that Nelson hoped students grasped from incorporating global inequities into his music lesson: "How can we use the folk tunes we have learned to become greater world citizens?"

Further Developing This Disposition

- Seek a historical perspective on current power structures. Though this task might seem daunting, it's important to understand how the inequities we see today are the products of past events, policies, and practices. It can seem like a scavenger hunt, but it starts with a series of *why*s and an exploration of the issue from multiple perspectives. Take, for instance, the issue of mass incarceration. Michelle Alexander (2012) traces it back to the Jim Crow laws instituted to enforce racial segregation.

- Review the 17 Sustainable Development Goals. Which goals resonate the most with you? Why? Of the goals you've identified, come up with examples of how these goals are—or are not—being achieved in your local community, region, or country.

- Identify local concerns via community exploration and review local statistics to understand the inequities that your students, families, and surrounding school community are grappling with. These explorations should move beyond voyeurism and include opportunities to engage with community members in genuine ways.

Continuing the Journey

Explore these additional resources as you continue to strengthen your commitment to equity.

❯ Edutopia: What the Heck Is Service Learning?
(www.edutopia.org/blog/what-heck-service-learning-heather-wolpert-gaw-ron): This is a good place to start for those who are new to service learning. The website provides a definition of service learning, along with guidelines, project ideas, and assessment strategies.

❯ Asia Society: Service Learning
(https://asiasociety.org/education/service-learning): This website is a resource for service learning specific to global education. Reflection questions, examples, resources, and a list of potential organizations are shared.

❯ United Nations Sustainable Development Goals
(www.un.org/sustainabledevelopment/sustainable-development-goals): Declared by the United Nations in 2015 to target areas of critical importance for humanity and the planet by 2030, the Sustainable Development Goals (SDGs) outline 17 goals and associated indicators that focus on people, the

planet, prosperity, peace, and partnership, and they provide data points on the extent to which these goals are being achieved. This website houses all 17 goals but also includes relevant facts, targets, and additional resources.

❍ TeachSDGs

(www.teachsdgs.org): This website includes resources for teaching and learning about the SDGs.

❍ The Global Goals YouTube Channel

(www.youtube.com/channel/UCRfuAYy7MesZmgOi1Ezy0ng): This channel includes short films that focus on each of the SDGs.

❍ World Inequality Database on Education

(www.education-inequalities.org): This database highlights global education inequity, which is related to wealth, gender, ethnicity, and location. Data can be sorted by country and/or indicator (e.g., literacy, achievement, years of education).

❍ Organisation for Economic Co-operation and Development

(www.oecd.org/social/inequality.htm): The OECD is a platform that promotes and conducts policy-oriented research on the trends, causes, and consequences of inequalities in society and the economy, and it includes a forum to discuss how policies can best address such inequalities.

❍ Stanford d.school

(https://dschool.stanford.edu/): The Stanford d.school provides tools, guides, and other resources for educators to facilitate design challenges that can help them take action by creating solutions that address local and global inequities.

KNOWLEDGE

A teacher's knowledge is commonly defined as a mixture of understanding, demonstrating through synthesis and critical analysis, and applying content knowledge of the subjects they teach (InTASC, 2013; NCATE, 2008). Because knowledge of the world is vast and constantly changing, the knowledge that globally competent teachers possess can be parsed into two broad concepts: (1) an understanding of events, conditions, systems, and structures that connect the world, and (2) an understanding of the people who live in it.

The first two knowledge elements discussed in this section touch upon the former:

- Understanding of global conditions and current events (Chapter 3)
- Understanding of the ways that the world is interconnected (Chapter 4)

The following two knowledge elements examine the latter:

- Experiential understanding of multiple cultures (Chapter 5)
- Understanding of intercultural communication (Chapter 6)

These knowledge elements do not ask teachers to recall information about populations in different countries or practices of specific cultures. Instead, they focus on reflection, synthesis, and critical analysis of resources, events, and experiences. These knowledge elements are also not meant to supplant content-area knowledge. As the four chapters in this section illustrate, globally competent teachers infuse cultural and global knowledge across the content areas, thus necessitating that teachers have a solid disciplinary foundation to make global content-area connections (Mansilla & Jackson, 2011).

Foundational to these four knowledge elements are the dispositions described in Section I. Understanding global conditions and current events requires an openness toward seeking multiple perspectives on different issues. An experiential understanding of multiple cultures follows a similar progression—understanding one's self before understanding others and being open-minded to unfamiliar ideas and experiences. Understanding how the world is interconnected emphasizes addressing inequities spurred by globalization, whereas understanding intercultural communication specifically examines inequitable power dynamics that linguistic minority students face.

In addition, this knowledge base becomes important for the pedagogical practices described in the skills section. For example, an understanding of intercultural communication can help teachers communicate in multiple languages and facilitate intercultural conversations and partnerships with their students. An experiential understanding of multiple cultures can help teachers create a classroom environment that values student diversity. An understanding of global conditions and current events can help teachers create an environment that values global engagement and can serve as the basis for content-aligned explorations of the world. As you actively acquire knowledge of global systems and structures and the diversity of cultures, languages, and contexts that people across the planet experience, we encourage you to make local connections to your teaching practice, your students, and yourself.

3

Global Conditions and Current Events

How do current local, national, and world events affect what and how we teach? Schools are part of a larger society. They, along with the teachers and students within them, are not immune to the twists and turns of the world. Everyday events—from local weather conditions and their consequences to political upheaval and ethnic conflicts—affect our students, their families, and us as teachers.

Becoming knowledgeable of the current issues that influence our students' lives is a critical part of what globally competent teachers do. Furthermore, these teachers look beyond their own classroom population to consider the ways local and global issues influence the world at large to help their students become informed and able to better influence their world. Topics of exploration with students might include anything from economic development, gender equality, global warming, global health, human rights, immigration, peace and conflict, racism, religion, and world hunger (Armstrong, 2008; Kirkwood, 2001b; Roberts, 2007; Selby & Pike, 2000). The list seems endless, so how do teachers come to understand global conditions and current events and be able to teach them to their students? What do teachers need to know in order to guide their students toward a greater awareness of the world around them?

What Does It Mean to Understand Global Conditions and Current Events?

There is not a defined set of facts and figures that teachers must memorize to gain an understanding of global conditions and current events. Rather, much of the knowledge that teachers need depends on a commitment to becoming lifelong learners. Indeed, the world around us is constantly changing. Globally competent teachers recognize the need to have a "state of the planet" awareness (Hanvey, 1982), which allows them both to understand the interconnectedness between local issues and the wider global community and to help students make those connections.

Further, globally competent teachers recognize the ways the past intersects with the present. In other words, globally competent teachers understand the historical foundation or antecedents on which present issues arise. Current events do not happen in a vacuum and are far more complicated than something that could be assessed on a simple multiple-choice test. As such, globally competent teachers seek to comprehend the complexity of today's events in light of the historical past, and they consider implications of today's current events on the future—be it local, national, or global.

In addition to a growing knowledge of current events, globally competent teachers must also be able to contextualize these events in ways that make them real to students. This includes having a basic knowledge of world geography to situate events not only in time but also in place so students can truly visualize and understand where events are happening in relation to themselves and others. Teachers can develop a more complex understanding of world geography through resources such as Mapfight (https://mapfight. appspot.com), a size comparison tool that enables students to understand geography at a deeper level. The tool helps students compare the actual size of a potentially unfamiliar place with the size of someplace else they may be more familiar with. It helps students understand, for example, that the Pacific Ocean is more than 1.5 times as large as the Atlantic Ocean, Africa is twice the size of Russia, and Texas is six times bigger than North Korea.

Finally, globally competent teachers consider local and global current events through multiple lenses. To understand contrasting perspectives on a single event, globally competent teachers seek out multiple resources. For example, teachers read across sources rather than rely on single sources of information. They may read about an event in a local or national newspaper that prompts them to recognize how the event is described in news reports from around the world. Doing so enables teachers to better understand the historical, social, cultural, political, and geographic influences on a particular event. Further, teachers then recognize the effects of current events on different people (Armstrong, 2008; Roberts, 2007; Tate, 2011). They are then better able to help their students see diverse perspectives, thus moving beyond a single articulation of an event.

Self-Reflection and Implementation Tips for Understanding Global Conditions and Current Events

Look at Figure 3.1 and rate yourself along the GCLC for the element "Understanding of global conditions and current events."

1. Where do you rank yourself and why?
2. What steps do you need to take to move along the continuum?

The following implementation tips will help you think through the next steps you can take to better understand global conditions and current events.

Learn the local geography. In coming to understand global conditions and current events, begin at home. Come to understand the issues that most affect your students and local community. One way to begin is to start with a map of the local school community to get a sense of the geography. This enables a better understanding of where your students come from and where they live. Using Google Maps for this exercise, for instance, will also help you get a sense of the various resources within the community. For example, you can determine where the local libraries are, where the supermarkets are, where houses of worship are, and so on. Coming to understand the layout of the school community also helps teachers better understand their students'

Figure 3.1 | Understanding of Global Conditions and Current Events

Element	Nascent	Beginning	Progressing	Proficient	Advanced
Understanding of Global Conditions and Current Events	I do not yet have knowledge of world conditions and current events.	• I have a basic understanding of world geography. • I have a basic understanding of current local and/or global events.	• I can articulate geographical, historical, political, economic, social, and/or cultural influences on current events. • I can access multiple resources that portray current events.	• I seek out multiple sources to understand contrasting perspectives on an issue. • I stay informed on current local and global issues.	• I regularly seek resources from varied perspectives and opportunities to stay informed on local and global issues. • I think critically about the potential impact of current events on future conditions, both locally and globally.

commute to school or how far they must go to visit a local library. Involve students in this activity. For example, a middle school social studies teacher had students create a local map and highlight a different community service, such as schools, libraries, supermarkets, and public transit. When each group presented its map to the class, the conversation cascaded into a deeper discussion about food and education deserts and the implications for local residents.

Come to know the community: read, ask, and listen. When Paul, a middle school science teacher, began his first year of teaching at a new school, he was interested in doing a project with his students that engaged them in addressing an environmental issue affecting the community. He set out to learn about the environmental history of his school community. He sent e-mails to a local environmental organization and spoke with one of the group's founders to get a sense of the issues prevalent in the community. He also read the town's newspapers and conducted internet searches on relevant issues in the local community. This process helped him recognize the significant effort the town was making to reduce carbon emissions. Thus, carbon emissions—and their reduction—became a focal area of study in his earth science class.

In order to become knowledgeable about local events, immerse yourself in getting to know the past and present of where you teach. Like Paul, reach out to local organizations, read local newspapers, and conduct online research to learn about the community. Furthermore, ask students and their families about their experiences in the town, city, or region where they live. For example, Louise, a 4th grade teacher, begins each year asking her students to complete a quick survey that includes the following question: *What about your community do you care deeply about?* She then follows up with students to learn more about the issues they identified so she can incorporate those topics into her lessons throughout the year.

Pay attention to world events. Sometimes, the easiest way to learn about global events is to simply pay attention to them. We often assume that what happens in the world does not affect us, but world events generally have some influence on our own lives, be it economically, socially, or otherwise.

Furthermore, these global events directly—or indirectly—affect some of our students. (See Chapter 4 for detailed examples of global interconnectedness.) So how do we learn about these events? Listen to or watch various international news programs. There are many radio news programs or podcasts you can access through the internet (e.g., http://bbcworldservice.radio.net or www.aljazeera.com/topics/categories/audio.html). Also, it's important to read a variety of news outlets and seek out multiple perspectives. Don't rely on a single representation of an event. As you read and listen to different versions of current events, ask critical questions such as, Who is the author? From whose perspective is the story told? What or whose perspectives are missing here? In what ways do the different versions of the event differ? Which details are missing from each version? Why might that be the case?

Dig in. Don't begin and end with the news story itself. Instead, read widely around the story. For example, veteran secondary history teacher Steve often locates places where events take place on a map as his starting point. If an event happened in Syria, for example, Steve will look up the city on Google Maps to situate the event in its geographic context. He then reads about the present event, examining it through a few different sources that reflect different perspectives (e.g., *The New York Times, Al Jazeera, The Guardian*). Finally, he sets out to contextualize the event even more fully by learning about the history of the city in question. In other words, he peels back the layers to determine how the current event fits into the larger historical timeline. For this, he relies on internet searches, using key words about the topic. As illustrated in Figure 3.2, digging in is particularly salient in providing real-world relevance across content areas.

The following are implementation tips on global conditions and current events specific to your developmental level along the GCLC.

Nascent

If you feel overwhelmed by the prospect of learning about current events and global conditions, start small. For example, Catherine, a 9th grade Spanish teacher, was interested in bringing global issues into her classroom.

Figure 3.2 | Understanding Global Conditions and Current Events Across the Content Areas

Content Area	Significance of Understanding Global Conditions and Current Events
Math	• Enables math teachers to connect math to the "real world." Having this knowledge enables teachers to use real-world data related to current issues (e.g., wealth and poverty, illness). • Understanding global conditions and current events through different perspectives enables math teachers to help students understand such things as the purpose of statistics in discussions of current events.
Science	Provides science teachers with authentic and directly applicable ways to teach a number of science topics (e.g., water use and conservation, energy sources, global warming, the relationship between the environment and the economy).
Language Arts	• Informational texts are required reading in schools. By being familiar with local and global issues, teachers can provide timely informational texts for students. • Becoming familiar with multiple perspectives and stories on the same current event, teachers are better prepared to help students seek out the same and learn to compare/contrast perspectives.
Social Studies	• Teachers' own understanding of current local and global conditions enables them to better teach these concepts to students in a social studies classroom. • Seeking out multiple primary sources to understand an event most fully supports teachers' ability to share these resources with students. • Understanding world geography and the ways in which maps differently project that geography empowers teachers to support students in understanding inherent biases in mapping based on cartographers' perspectives.
Foreign Language	• Providing opportunities for students to read about current global events that directly influence countries in which the focal language is spoken makes language teaching more authentic.

However, she lacked confidence in her own knowledge of current events around the world to incorporate them into her lessons. She felt like she had to know everything there was to know about a topic before she brought it to her students. Her mentor teacher, though, suggested she start with a fairly simple topic rather than one that was more complex. Her mentor also convinced her that she could learn alongside her students; she did not have to know everything about the topic prior to teaching it. She simply had to be prepared with materials and ready to learn alongside her students. Armed with newfound confidence, Catherine introduced her students to two news articles about the running of the bulls event in Pamplona, Spain, since a recent event had resulted in more than one fatality. There were opinions as to whether the event should continue as it had for centuries. She had students read different opinion pieces from Spanish newspapers and then develop their own positions. Although this particular event may seem far from momentous, it provided an initial gateway for Catherine.

Beginning/Progressing

To develop a basic understanding of world geography and of current local and global events, let your curiosity take hold as you expose yourself to new resources. One of the things middle school social studies teacher Simone had done while traveling was collect maps of various cities and countries she visited. She became fascinated by what was included in some maps and excluded on others. She began to use these maps in her world history class to help students develop an understanding of geography, the limits of maps to explain the world in simple ways, and the effect that maps have on our perceptions of the world.

As part of this exercise, she shared with her students a short clip from the television series *The West Wing*, which highlights the differences between the Mercator and the Peters Projection maps. The Mercator projection is the one we commonly see. However, in this version, sizes of objects on the map are distorted, leading people to develop misunderstandings of the relative size of certain countries and continents to others (e.g., a common misconception based on the viewing of the Mercator projection map is that Greenland is the same size as the continent of Africa. In reality, Africa is nearly 15 times as large as Greenland). By contrast, the Peters Projection map reflects more area accuracy. This clip from *The West Wing* further illustrated for Simone's students the ways that maps can influence our perception of power, depending on where a country is located on a map and how large or small that country is depicted. Because Earth is a sphere, any flat map necessarily distorts some aspect of the world, even the Peters Projection. This is a good point to make with students: maps are documents and have biases just like any other source.

Just as Simone did with maps, try to seek out and consume a wide range of sources to learn about global conditions and events and the historical, political, social, economic, and cultural aspects of that event or world condition. This not only includes newspaper and magazine articles and websites but also resources such as memoirs, documentaries, and maps. The wider the range of source materials, the larger the potential range of perspectives.

Proficient/Advanced

At this level, consider current events and conditions along with how those events and conditions may affect the future. Matt, a high school math teacher, had recently sought a loan to purchase his first house. Matt was surprised at how challenging the experience was for him. The experience prompted him to consider the history of the loan market and the ways that different people in the United States, across time, had experienced the loan market. Of particular interest to him, as a black male, was the way his experience differed from or was similar to his own parents' and grandparents' experiences of home loans. Matt's research revealed patterns of discrimination in mortgage lending, so he introduced the concepts of loans and mortgages to his statistics students.

Together, Matt and his students examined past trends of home loans, particularly for people of color in the United States. They then set out to predict future patterns based on past trends. Matt's own experience with the lending process and his own research into the past trends prompted him to work with his students to examine the ways past and current conditions might play out in the future.

Anticipating future consequences of today's events is certainly not an easy process. However, like Matt did in this example, look to past patterns and trends to begin to predict future effects. Ask yourself, "What in the past does this current event or condition remind me of? How did this event or condition affect the local, national, and/or global community at the time? What were the long-term impacts?" For better or worse, history repeats itself; thus, the globally competent teacher should consider the past when working to link the present to the future.

Special Considerations for Elementary School Teachers (PK–5)

- Keep a globe handy or a world map hanging on your wall. Anytime you talk about a city, state, or country, pull out the globe or map and point to where it is you are talking about in relation to where you live. This reinforces geography skills while also engaging students. (One 1st grade teacher shared that every time she picked up her classroom globe, her students got so excited!)
- Focus on your local community and what conditions look like where students live so they can see real-life examples of what environmental, government, economic, and social issues affecting communities look like before they explore those issues in different communities and parts of the world.
- Get a class subscription to a news magazine such as *Time for Kids* or *Scholastic News Magazine*. Incorporate these weekly issues into nonfiction reading lessons so your students (and you) stay on top of the news and get in the habit of regularly reading about current events.

Special Considerations for Secondary School Teachers (6–12)

- Most students at this age have their own mobile devices. Encourage them to download news apps and incentivize them to share current events they read from around the world.
- When introducing a global issue to students, examine that single issue from a variety of vantage points (e.g., what the issue looks like

in different countries or what it looks like from the perspective of people of different genders, races, ethnicities, and sexual orientations). For example, when a high school English teacher introduced a unit on civic engagement, she compared the civil rights movement in the United States to the anti-apartheid movement in South Africa.

Element 3 in Action: Using Google Earth to Learn about Global Events and Empathize with Other People in the World

What does it look like for a teacher to gain an understanding of global conditions and current events? Here, Steve Goldberg, a veteran secondary history teacher, describes his own process of coming to these understandings and provides a glimpse into how he helped his students develop the same sorts of understandings.

"The first years of teaching are so difficult and all-encompassing that it is often hard to make time to keep up with world events and think about how it might influence your students' learning. But in my experience, it is crucial that teachers make the effort and do so in a thoughtful way. Here are a few stories that might be useful as you consider your own journey of developing an understanding of global conditions.

"I have taught high school students world and U.S. history for more than two decades. When I got my Master of Arts in Teaching degree in May 1995, the Rwandan genocide was still a current event, but we never once talked about it in my courses. Indeed, I was largely unaware of this genocide that killed roughly 800,000 people in 100 days until much later in my teaching career, after I saw the 2004 movie *Hotel Rwanda*. At that point in my career and my life, I would say that I was at the nascent to beginning stage of understanding global conditions and current events. My MAT program missed an opportunity to discuss a hugely important international event.

"The cost of not paying attention to the world around you is that some of your students *will* pay attention, and you can be perceived as insensitive if you don't know what's happening. In my first year of teaching (1995–1996), I had a student from Israel in my U.S. history class who usually participated in class discussions. When our class met on Monday, November 7, 1995, she spent the whole class silently glaring at me. I did not know what was wrong. At the end of class, she gave me a note she had written. I asked students to write me suggestions any time they had them, and she gave me her suggestion at the end of class. I wish I kept her note, but it essentially said, 'You are such a hypocrite. You tell us to pay attention to current events and you connect world events today to events we are learning about in early U.S. history. Well, my president was killed over the weekend, and we did not even mention it in class.'

"I knew about Yitzhak Rabin's assassination on Saturday, but I was so consumed with preparing lessons for my classes and just surviving as a first-year teacher that I did not think to make a connection between Rabin's assassination and our class. I corrected my mistake the next day, but it was not the same, and the student never forgave me. That episode made me commit to being more globally aware and to bringing world events into my classroom.

"As I would learn, there are emotional considerations when you *do* talk about current events that you don't often have to contend with when you teach about historical figures such as George Washington or Martin Luther King Jr. A few years later, in 1999, as a 'seasoned' fourth-year teacher committed to bringing current events into my classroom, I mentioned Matthew Shepard, a college student at the University of Wyoming who had been beaten and murdered in October 1998. I do not recall the exact point I was making in mentioning Shepard, but as I was making my point, it became clear that most of my students did not know about him, so I started to tell them about him. As I did so, one of my students teared up and ran out of the room—I had no idea why.

"It turned out that she had attended high school in Saudi Arabia with Matthew Shepard, and she knew him—so I was bringing up a very raw memory for her. I talked with her later that day, and she understood what I was trying to do. I mean, how could I have known that she had a connection to a student from Wyoming? But the lesson I learned from that episode is that whenever you talk about current events, it is respectful and thoughtful (and necessary) to first ask whether anyone has any personal connection to the event in question. Sadly, in today's climate of school shootings, I have to ask my students whether anyone knows any of the students or teachers killed in X shooting or Y shooting before we have a moment of silence in class and take time to talk about school shootings since Columbine.

"Over the years, I have been mindful and intentional about bringing current events into my classroom. I often use Google Earth as a tool to help students contextualize and understand these events. Here's one example of how to use Google Earth to help enhance a current events discussion in class. One of the issues that surfaced during the 2016 U.S. presidential election was the topic of how many Syrian refugees the United States should accept each year. An article from about a month before the election framed the difference between the candidates nicely:

'Democrat Hillary Clinton has said she would expand President Barack Obama's refugee program to accept about 65,000 Syrian refugees, while Republican Donald Trump has called for an all-out moratorium' (Associated Press, 2016, para. 1).

"A teacher who started to discuss the issue of Syrian refugees would probably raise the question 'Why are there Syrian refugees in the first place?' That question necessarily brings us to the civil war in Syria, which started in 2011 when people within Syria opposed President Bashar al-Assad. In my research about the conflict, I learned about the Za'atari refugee camp. As of 2018, it was home to 80,000 people. Back in 2013, it housed nearly twice that number. The camp is located in Jordan, about eight miles from the border Jordan shares with Syria.

"An image from Google Earth in 2018 shows that the camp is about 1.75 miles long by a little more than 1 mile wide. However, an image from mid-2012 shows that this camp did not exist. Google Earth images such as these usually lead to some great questions from students. If there are 80,000 people living there, where are the schools in the camp? What happens when people are born in the camp? Are there hospitals? What jobs do people do? Where does the food come from? Looking at the camp using Google Earth helps bring the abstract idea of Syrian refugees to life and begin to help students empathize with the event.

"The trick when you are teaching is to find time to discuss something like Syrian refugees with students when that topic is not the sort of thing that will naturally be part of the curriculum you are asked to cover. It's a constant challenge to keep up with world events—particularly in a culture that seems easily distracted by celebrity gossip and domestic concerns. The benefit to doing so is that it not only allows you to make more connections to what students are learning but also makes you a more informed global citizen, and students benefit from being around adults who take the world and its issues seriously."

Further Developing This Knowledge

- Begin to follow the news from a variety of sources (e.g., national, international, different political leanings and scopes).
- Reflect on how the same event is portrayed from different news sources and why that might be the case.
- Identify an event currently making international headlines. Consider the impact of that global current event on you, your family and friends, your students, and your community immediately and into the future.

Continuing the Journey

Explore these additional resources as you move forward in your and your students' understanding of global conditions and current events.

Global Conditions

⊙ The World Factbook
(www.cia.gov/library/publications/the-world-factbook): This website, hosted by the Central Intelligence Agency, provides a detailed profile for every country in the world and includes information on the history, people, government,

economy, geography, communications, transportation, military, and transnational issues for each.

❷ World Atlas

(www.worldatlas.com): This website provides facts and maps on the continents, countries, cities, and landforms of the world.

❷ Google Earth

(https://google.com/earth): Google Earth allows students to virtually tour the globe and users to add annotations, text, and images.

❷ Worldmapper

(https://worldmapper.org): Worldmapper is a collection of world maps, where territories are resized on each map according to the subject of interest.

❷ EyeWitness to History

(www.eyewitnesstohistory.com/index.html): This website provides primary sources and accounts of historical events from multiple perspectives. Students can use these accounts for making connections to present-day conditions and events.

Current Events

❷ Time for Kids

(www.timeforkids.com): This eight-page magazine and companion website provides current events for K–6 students in a way that helps them build information reading skills, understand the complex world in which we live, and become informed and active citizens.

❷ BBC Newsround

(www.bbc.co.uk/newsround): This site provides a daily five-minute clip of news around the world that is appropriate for kids and is an easy way to start conversations about global events with students.

❷ CNN 10

(www.cnn.com/CNN10): This student-based daily news program covers current events on an accessible level for secondary students.

⊃ Newsela

(https://newsela.com): This news outlet provides nonfiction and news articles for students from lower elementary school through high school and is organized by different reading levels.

Global Interconnectedness

Many mornings on the way to work, I stop at a local coffee shop to fuel up. On the surface, this simple act is as personal as it gets. I need caffeine to wake up, and I go to the closest coffee shop because it's the most convenient. Though my actions are local, my purchase supports coffee bean farms around the world. Likewise, what happens at coffee farms in Nicaragua, Colombia, and Kenya—from economic downturns and upswings, climate change, and plant diseases—affects the bean selection on offer and the price I pay at my local shop. *Think globally, act locally* is at the heart of what it means for educators to understand how our world is interconnected and interdependent—and the implications that has for our students, schools, and local communities.

What Does It Mean to Understand Global Interconnectedness?

Globalization—the spread of people, products, and ideas across borders—has connected our world economically, politically, socially, culturally, politically, and ecologically. Today, the goods we consume (i.e., the food we buy in supermarkets, the phones we use, the clothes we wear) are often produced and distributed via complex global supply chains. Governments have long worked with other nations through treaties, alliances, and supranational organizations to address issues that transcend national borders: from climate change (e.g., the Paris Climate Agreement) to security (e.g., the North Atlantic Treaty

Organization) to trade (e.g., the North American Free Trade Agreement) to human rights (the United Nations).

The movement of people, products, and ideas across physical and perceived borders has spread cultural practices and ignited new hybrid cultural forms. Technological advances and innovations have spawned the virtual spread of people and ideas at nanosecond speed as we upload, download, stream, and share content via constantly evolving digital platforms. Entirely new social movements born out of viral hashtags and videos have spread around the globe: the Arab Spring, the #MeToo movement, and #BlackLivesMatter being just a few examples. Our planet, filled with diverse species, climates, and biomes, is but one delicate interconnected ecological system. To illustrate this point: the burning of fossil fuels from Lexington, Kentucky, to Shanghai, China, and the deforestation of large swathes of the Amazon in South America are melting the icecaps over the North and South Poles, which in turn causes flooding in coastal towns and cities from Miami, Florida, to small fishing villages in Bangladesh.

Though NAFTA, #MeToo, Facebook, and climate change make the headlines, globalization is not a 21st century phenomenon. In fact, it goes back centuries. The 1492 journey of Christopher Columbus to the "new" world ignited over four centuries of European colonization of most of the known world, and with it came the cross-continental spread of people, food, animals, diseases, natural resources, and religious doctrines. In the 19th and 20th centuries, multinational companies replaced colonizing countries as the main drivers of shrinking the world, as the falling costs of transportation and telecommunication allowed for the creation of global markets for goods and services (Friedman, 2007).

There is a dark side to this long history of globalization. The genocide and displacement of indigenous communities, the loss of language and culture, ecological destruction, job outsourcing, and nativism and xenophobia are emerging as a backlash to globalization. The shrinking of the world is not a steady, inevitable march toward progress. Larry Summers, Harvard professor and former U.S. Secretary of the Treasury, warned, "Global integration won't work if it means local disintegration" (Gerber, 2018, para. 22). Therefore, it is important to think critically about the pros and cons of globalization—both past and present—whom it benefits, and who pays the steepest price.

When we come to understand how the world is interconnected, we see ourselves as a part of this web of interdependence and understand that the actions we take affect and are affected by people and places around the globe: past, present, and future (Pike & Selby, 2000). As social justice educators Bigelow and Peterson noted (2002), "The more we taught about issues of globalization, the more we found ourselves telling our students: 'Everything is connected. You can't really understand what's going on in one part of the world without looking at how it's related to everything else'" (para. 4).

In essence, the global and local are so interconnected that sociologist Roland Robertson (1995) used the term *glocal* to describe how the two influence each other in a cyclical, reciprocal manner. This element encourages teachers to adopt a glocal perspective in their understanding of the world and how they impart that global awareness to students.

Self-Reflection and Implementation Tips for Understanding Global Interconnectedness

Look at Figure 4.1 and rate yourself along the GCLC for the element "Understanding of the ways the world is interconnected."

1. Where do you rate yourself and why?
2. What steps do you need to take to move along the continuum?

The following implementation tips will help you develop an understanding of global interconnectedness and how you can apply that understanding to your teaching.

Start locally. To see how the world is interconnected, you don't have to look far. Globalization is locally rooted. In each community, global interconnectedness plays out as a melding of international connections with local traditions (Peacock, 2007). Placing your feet on the ground of your own neighborhood and school can help you "ground" the global. Survey the businesses,

Figure 4.1 | Understanding of the Ways the World Is Interconnected

Element	Nascent	Beginning	Progressing	Proficient	Advanced
Understanding of the Ways the World Is Interconnected	I have not yet considered the ways the world is interconnected.	• I recognize that our world is interconnected and interdependent (e.g., economically, socially, culturally, and environmentally). • I recognize that the ways in which the world is interconnected are constantly changing.	• I understand ways that a global issue affects my local context (including myself, my students, and my local community). • I understand ways that a global issue affects cultures or nations aside from my own.	• I can explain ways that global issues affect my local context and individuals in other nations. • I can explain global influences on local issues and local influences on global issues.	• I can critically analyze ways that global interconnectedness contributes to inequities within and between nations. • I can explain how actions I take at the local, national, or international level address inequities related to our interconnected world.

population, and student body to map out global connections in your own community. Questions you might ask include, "Which ethnic groups are represented in your classroom and community? What languages are spoken by the families in your classroom and community? How many companies and businesses in your community are foreign owned or owned and operated by immigrants?"

You may be surprised to learn how connected your community is. For example, as of 2016, 458 foreign-owned companies in Columbus, Ohio, employed 57,762 residents; 22 local companies operated facilities in 71 countries outside the United States, 7 percent of the population was born outside the United States (the top five countries of origin being India, Mexico, Somalia, China, and Ghana); and public school students spoke 74 different languages at home, including Spanish, Somali, and Arabic (Columbus World Affairs Council, 2017). Don't be afraid to examine the negative ramifications of globalization in your community, too. Have plants been outsourced, leaving a dearth of employment opportunities for students' parents? Has your community seen an increase in hate crimes? What is the status of local indigenous languages and cultures?

Getting to know the stories of your own students can be a fertile ground for seeing how global events affect your classroom and school community. In *The Newcomers: Finding Refuge, Friendship, and Hope in America,* journalist Helen Thorpe (2018) shadowed 21 students in a newcomer class from places as far-reaching as Iraq, Burma, El Salvador, Tajikistan, and the Democratic Republic of Congo. Her book illuminates how complex and harrowing global affairs that these students survived—from genocide to civil war—in every corner of the globe led them to the same Denver classroom and ultimately changed the identity of the school itself. Though teachers may not have the same time and resources as a journalist to conduct extensive research on the various regions students come from and ongoing in-depth interviews with students' parents, you can take time to read news articles and books about regions where your students have immigrated from to better understand the push-and-pull factors that led them to your classroom. Doing so provides an understanding of how events around the world affect your school population, while also giving you a deeper understanding of the experiences these students may have lived through and the social-emotional and cognitive supports they may need as a result.

You can also create opportunities to learn from your students. For example, an upper elementary school teacher from a southern U.S. town with a large influx of students from Central America designed a research project where students traced their families' origins. This provided a safe space for immigrant students to share their stories with their nonimmigrant peers and for nonimmigrant students to realize that they have global connections through their own ancestry.

Weave yourself, your students, and your subject area into the web of global interconnectedness. Embrace a systems approach mindset as you look at the relationships between and among people, places, events, and ideas. Regardless of the subject area you teach, topics you cover are bound to have connections between students, their communities, and the world, along with connections to other content areas. In Alyssa's high school English language arts class—where students are learning strategies for writing argumentative essays—students often watch CNN 10 as a warm-up activity. As they watch, Alyssa asks students to explain why different news stories around the world are relevant to them and to explain how local news stories might have a global impact.

A middle school science teacher in rural North Carolina keeps the following sentence frames on her door: "Why does _____ matter to me? Why does _____ matter to my country? Why does _____ matter to the world?" At the end of lessons, she has students complete the sentences with the topic under study and answer all three questions in a notebook. Asking students to contemplate these types of questions not only illuminates how global issues can affect one's local context but also makes learning personally relevant by answering the question "How does this relate to me?"

Consider everyday consumer products that you and your students use as inspiration to map out the global supply chains that got them to you. Dissect where the raw materials came from, what country or countries the materials were manufactured in, where the product was finished and packaged, and where the final product was shipped, stored, and distributed to consumers like you. Your students might be amazed to find that their favorite watch or generic razor blade traveled through five or more countries to end up on their wrist or in their bathroom. Mapping this product journey does not have to be confined to an economics class. For example, students can write creative essays from the point of view of that product or solve real-world math problems, such as calculating distance or comparing prices of raw materials and human labor in different countries, to understand why a company might choose one country over another.

Contribute to the global community. There's no better way for students to see their impact on the planet and its people than to take action and document the changes they see. This could include starting campaigns on issues that students identify as affecting them or communities in different parts of the world, creating a community garden, engaging in a "no plastic" challenge, or participating in projects that turn waste into useful resources or artwork. For example, when middle school teacher Carol introduced her students in the Bronx to the Convention of the Rights of the Child, a set of universal rights for all children that the United Nations ratified in 1989, her students were angered to find out that the United States had not ratified them. They were quick to point out areas where they saw those rights being violated in their own communities and for people in different parts of the world. Carol supported her students as they collected paper hearts from people all over the world who had experienced violence, organized a march outside the White House, and presented at the United Nations (Tichnor-Wagner, 2017). Through these actions, students demonstrated how global issues of human rights and violence affect them personally and their local communities and how actions they take (e.g., presenting to the United Nations) can have a global impact.

Think critically. "How" and "why" questions are critical to understanding globalization and its impact. Globalization is not inherently good or bad; therefore, it is important to carefully consider its pros and cons. When learning and teaching about issues that illustrate global interconnectedness—whether it's a U.S. shipping company opening a facility in Ecuador, an immigration reform passed by the European Union, fiber optic cables laid down for the first time in a remote village in India, or an oil spill in Russia—ask questions, such as "Who benefits? Who doesn't? What are the intended purposes? What are the unintended consequences? Who is affected? In what ways?"

Conducting root cause analyses can further lead to understanding why global inequities exist. Activities such as the "Five Whys," where you ask "why" five times to drill down to the root cause of a problem, can reveal underlying phenomena behind current global inequities. For example, asking why there are so many Karen refugees from camps along the Thailand-Burma border can ultimately lead to the legacy of British colonialism as a root cause.

The following are implementation tips on global interconnectedness specific to your developmental level along the GCLC.

Nascent

Do preliminary research on how the community where you work or live is connected to places around the world via the population, economy, and education system. As one place to start, the U.S. Census Bureau has town-level information on foreign-born residents, languages spoken, and businesses and industries. Likewise, the Mapping the Nation website (https://asiasociety.org/mapping-nation) provides state- and county-level data on foreign-born populations, imports and exports of goods, foreign-owned companies, international student economic contribution, number of high school students enrolled in world language programs, and participation in study abroad programs.

Have some fun and create your own "passport" to explore international restaurants, markets, shops, community centers, and more in your greater community, and reflect on the impact these places have had on your local economy, culture, and civic institutions. For example, Melissa, a Washington, DC, kindergarten teacher, runs an enrichment club where students visit the globally connected places in their neighborhood and stamp their passports every time they visit a restaurant, store, or embassy connected to a new country.

Beginning/Progressing

Use topics that align with the content areas you teach to illustrate to students how global issues affect you and how your actions affect communities in other parts of the world. In science, for example, topics might include the effects of global warming on ecosystems, animals, and people in different parts of the world; the spread of diseases such as Zika and Ebola; and the effect of scientific discoveries and technological advances made in one country on different parts of the world. One science teacher did a research project with her students on plastic pollution, examining different countries' recycling practices, including what types of materials are recycled, how often, and where the materials go. From the information they gathered, students came up with ideas on how to reduce their plastic use and created awareness campaigns on the harm their use of plastic does to the local environment and ecosystems around the world. Math teachers can use data points associated with these topics to graph trends and create models. For example, an Algebra 2 teacher had her students create a model using data on the spread of the Ebola virus and discussed the consequences for different countries.

Reading materials in numerous language arts and social studies classes are ripe for identifying global interconnectedness. Select books with a focus on immigration, natural disasters, or cross-cultural interactions (e.g., *Things Fall Apart, Esperanza Rising*). (See Figure 4.2 for more examples.)

Follow age-appropriate local and international news stories, and probe students to ask why that story might affect themselves and their local community and how it could also affect people living in other communities and nations. During a unit on teaching argumentative essay writing, high school ELA teacher Alyssa asks students to consider whether local news headlines are also global issues—and provide evidence to justify their arguments. One student, for example, argued that the Boston Marathon bombing had a global impact because of the bombers' connections to terrorist units outside the

United States, because it could change other countries' perceptions of the United States as being a vulnerable place to visit, and because citizens of other countries were victims of the bombings.

Figure 4.2 | Books That Highlight Global Interconnectedness

Book Title and Author	Grade Level
Inside Out and Back Again, Thanhha Lai	3–5
Home of the Brave, Katherine Applegate	3–8
A Long Walk to Water, Linda Sue Park	6–8
I Am Malala, Malala Yousafzai	6–9
Esperanza Rising, Pam Muñoz Ryan	6–8
Things Fall Apart, Chinua Achebe	9–12

Simulations are another way to drive home global interconnectedness. For example, middle school social studies teacher Mike presented students with a hypothetical global problem they had to solve, with the dual goal of illuminating how different countries rely on one another and instilling critical and creative thinking skills. He identified on a map the Latin American countries that are the world's biggest coffee producers and then labeled the countries with the greatest coffee consumption. He shared that cartels are holding the coffee producers hostage and the coffee-consuming countries are not happy. He then assigned students the task of avoiding a war (where the consuming countries invade) and restoring the coffee farms to their rightful owners.

Proficient/Advanced

At this level, you should feel comfortable articulating the influence that global issues have on your own local context and other communities around the world—and vice versa—and be able to think critically about how actions taken at local and global levels can contribute to or combat global inequities. Engage students in examining global supply chains by tracing the farm-to-table journey of the food they ate for breakfast, the clothing they are wearing, even the technology they are using.

For example, dissect the ingredients of favorite snacks that students like to eat (e.g., candy bar, bag of chips). What are all of the ingredients in the snack? What countries are those ingredients coming from? How much do those countries rely on exports of those ingredients for their economy? What would happen to those countries if we stopped importing those ingredients from them? What would happen to all the players involved in the production chain if different parts of the chain got disrupted by weather events or foreign government tariffs?

To demonstrate, a 5th grade teacher had her class simulate the global supply chain that results in a kid favorite: chocolate. She assigned students different roles within the chain (e.g., cacao bean grower, shipping merchant, government official who oversees export and import tariffs, factory worker, factory owner, store merchant), then distributed Hershey kisses based on how much wealth each player accrues within the chain. This sparked discussion about the "fairness" of current practices and what could be done to reduce inequities across the chain.

Work with students to calculate the environmental impact of their own actions and the actions of others—for example, they can track what happens to plastic bags after they are thrown out, calculate their carbon footprints, keep a journal of daily water usage, or conduct studies of endangered species that examine the root causes and future effects. Then have students identify actions they can take to address those issues to make a positive impact on local and global communities.

As one example, a 1st grade ESL teacher taught a unit on rainforests that introduced students to the concept that "there is a problem in a different part of the world that affects me, and I can either add to that problem or help find a solution to the problem." Students identified items in the classroom that came from trees, discussed what would happen to these items if all of the trees in the rainforests disappeared, and identified ways they could help reduce the amount of trees cut down (e.g., by using fewer paper towels, using both sides of a piece of paper when drawing, being a conscious consumer when shopping).

To highlight global inequities, work with students to identify social justice issues that personally resonate with them and their life experiences (e.g., gender equality, police brutality, treatment of refugees), and compare similarities and differences of those issues as they have played out across temporal and geographic contexts. For example, a high school English language arts teacher connected the United Nations Declaration of Human Rights to students, the people they know, and people in other countries. She showed students pictures of the Holocaust, slavery in the United States, the British Empire in 1600s, and tribes of Indian nations. Students observed details from the pictures to draw inferences about how these photos from different places and eras related to one another and connected back to students' present realities. The 17 U.N. Sustainable Development Goals (SDGs)—including no poverty, zero hunger, high-quality education, gender equality, clean water and sanitation, affordable and clean energy, and decent work and economic growth—are another source to jumpstart your thinking on current inequities that manifest for you, your students, and the world.

Though these conversations aren't easy to have, don't shy away from thinking deeply about underlying causes of current inequities, such as racism, capitalism, European colonization, and U.S. hegemony. As Bigelow and Peterson (2002) portend, "As we teach and organize around these matters, it's vital that we emphasize the centrality of race. The development of European colonialism was sheathed in theories of white supremacy which sought to justify the slaughter of indigenous peoples, the theft of their lands, and the enslavement of millions of Africans. Today's system of global inequality builds from these enormous crimes and is similarly legitimated, albeit more subtly, by notions of white supremacy" (para. 9).

Special Considerations for Elementary School Teachers (PK–5)

- For our youngest learners, picture books illustrate how the actions we take influence other people. Some examples include *The Lorax* by Dr. Seuss, *Because a Little Bug Went Kachoo* by Rosetta Stone, *The Day the Crayons Quit* by Drew Daywalt, and *The Kid Who Changed the World* by Andy Andrews.

- Introduce students to the concept of global inequities through roleplaying. For students as young as kindergarten and 1st grade, simulations where you hand out snacks or tokens unequally (e.g., based on where in the room students are sitting, the color shoes they are wearing, or their gender) can concretely illustrate the basics of how resources such as food, water, electricity, and wealth are unequally distributed throughout the world.

Special Considerations for Secondary School Teachers (6–12)

- Make explicit the relevance of global issues to students' lives. Have students bring in issues they see in the news—whether that be the imposition of new trade tariffs, the refugee crisis in Europe, gang violence in Central America, the results of U.S. government elections, or the next World Cup host—as fodder for debate about what the implications of those headlines will be for them personally, the community in which they live, and communities in different parts of the world.

- Use a variety of writing genres (e.g., persuasive and argumentative essays, informative essays, compare/contrast essays, poetry, creative writing) as vehicles for exploring topics that illustrate global interconnectedness, whether that be immigration, genocide, or global warming.

- For high school students, emphasize how global interconnectedness will affect their career choices or the jobs they might one day hold. A teacher from Texas, for example, explained to her students about the global influences on the petroleum market since oil companies are some of her region's biggest employers.

Element 4 in Action:
Teaching about Global Energy Consumption

Eighth grade science teacher Simone used her state standards on types of energy sources and the environmental consequences of obtaining, transforming, and using those sources as a way to illuminate economic and environmental interdependence and instill the importance of promoting clean energy worldwide. As she shared, "We want everyone in the world to have clean energy because if China is using coal and fossil fuels, what's going to happen? It's going to pollute the air. The air doesn't just stay over China. It's going to go all over the place. China isn't just polluting China's air, and the United States isn't only polluting the United States' air. So it's beneficial for everyone to have clean energy. What happens in other places is going to affect us."

At the same time, Simone recognized that political, economic, social, and environmental factors might impede countries from obtaining and utilizing clean energy sources, and she provided students with the space to dig deeply into why clean energy isn't a current reality in many places around the world—and its implications. After learning about the major sources of usable energy and identifying the pros and cons of each type in terms of things such as their environmental impact, cost, and availability, students in small groups were assigned a country and had to conduct research on which energy source would work best based on the country's population size, natural resources, and price of production and consumption.

Students presented their recommendations to the class and highlighted the effect on their country as a result of that decision. Based on their conclusions, the class debated whether environmental conservation or access to energy was more important and whether developing countries should have the same standards for clean energy as developed countries. As a conclusion to the mini-unit, students wrote a letter to the president about whether and how the United States should address access to clean energy worldwide based on their research. For Simone, engaging students in these discussions shed light on why global inequities regarding clean energy exist and the actions individuals and nations can take to combat those inequities.

Further Developing This Knowledge

- Conduct a scavenger hunt in your community for examples of ways that local residents, the local economy, the P–20 education system, and civic organizations are interconnected with the rest of the world. Adapt this as a classroom research project with the final product being a report that can be used as a classroom resource (e.g., *How [Your Town/ City] Is Connected to the World*). To extend the activity, reach out to organizations with global connections to forge relationships that will improve your own authentic understanding and provide opportunities for students to engage in international and intercultural conversations and partnerships (see Chapters 10 and 11).

- Keep a glocal diary for a week to track all the ways you personally interact with people, services, and goods from around the world. Map where all these interactions come from to illustrate local/global connections in your everyday life.

- Review the 17 Sustainable Development Goals (https://sustainabledevelopment.un.org/sdgs) and select two or three you feel are not being realized in your own community or a community you care about. For each goal you select, reflect on the root causes of that inequity, how global interconnectedness has contributed to and/or could combat that inequity, and come up with actions that you and others could take to address those causes.

Continuing the Journey

Explore the following resources on your journey toward understanding how the world is interconnected.

❯ *Rethinking Globalization: Teaching for Justice in an Unjust World* (www.rethinkingschools.org/books/title/rethinking-globalization): This book, geared toward teachers with students in grades 4–12, raises critical issues surrounding globalization and its impact on the planet and its people. It also includes an array of readings, role plays, interviews, poems, and classroom activities.

◉ UNESCO: Teaching and Learning for a Sustainable Future Module
(www.unesco.org/education/tlsf/mods/theme_c/mod18.html): This free multimedia online education module provides teachers with an introduction to globalization through six activities and reflections that address growing connections around the world; basic concepts, processes, and trends associated with globalization; drivers of globalization; and evaluating the impact of globalization.

◉ Mapping the Nation
(https://asiasociety.org/mapping-nation): This interactive website contains maps, data points, and infographics that show how local counties and states in the United States connect to the world via the economy, population, and education.

◉ East West Center
(www.eastwestcenter.org; www.asiamattersforamerica.org): Established by the U.S. Congress in 1960, this organization promotes better relations and understanding among the people and nations of the United States, Asia, and the Pacific. The Asia Matters for America project include data points, news articles, and more that show how Asia and the United States are interconnected via people, education, the economy, diplomacy, security, and tourism.

◉ Sustainable Development Goals
(https://sustainabledevelopment.un.org/sdgs): Declared by the United Nations in 2015 to target areas of critical importance for humanity and the planet by 2030, the Sustainable Development Goals (SDGs) outline 17 goals and associated indicators that focus on people, the planet, prosperity, peace, and partnership, and they provide data points on the extent to which these goals are being achieved. This website houses all 17 goals but also includes relative facts, targets, and additional resources.

5

Experiential Understanding of Diverse Cultures

Parker Palmer (1998) writes that "we cannot see what is 'out there' merely by looking around. Everything depends on the lenses through which we view the world" (p. 27). He further points out that "knowing my students and my subject depends heavily on self-knowledge" (p. 3). In other words, to gain an understanding of others requires us as teachers to first develop an understanding of ourselves and our experience of the world.

The culture(s) with which we identify often form the lens through which we come to understand and experience the world. A culture is composed of the shared values (e.g., judgments of what are good, bad, desired, undesirable), norms (e.g., standards of behaving), beliefs, and knowledge of a people or group, categorized based on collectives grouped together by race, ethnicity, religion, region, nation, social class, ability, or sexuality. Some aspects of culture are easily observed, such as language, clothing, rituals, and certain behaviors. Other aspects of culture—particularly beliefs and values—can be invisible to the untrained eye (Hall, 1976).

For example, Hofstede (2011) identified six dimensions of culture: individualism/collectivism, masculinity/femininity, power distance, uncertainty avoidance, long-/short-term orientation, and indulgence/restraint. If a new student entered your classroom who just immigrated from a different country, you wouldn't be able to observe whether his or her cultural orientation was more individualist or collectivist, masculine or feminine, or had more equal or unequal distribution of power. Yet these culturally embedded understandings of how society should function will shape the student's interactions in the classroom. For example, if the student moved from a large power distance country, he or she might not feel comfortable in a student-centered classroom where the teacher facilitates the generation of knowledge rather than transmitting right versus wrong answers. To avoid misinterpretations of our students' visible behaviors, developing an understanding of multiple cultures is paramount.

What Does It Mean to Develop an Experiential Understanding of Multiple Cultures?

We enter classrooms with our own cultural practices, beliefs, and values that consciously and subconsciously shape our actions. James Gee (1989) posits that we all have certain Discourses we inhabit that drive our interactions in the world. As Gee defines them, "Discourses are ways of being in the world; they are forms of life which integrate words, acts, values, beliefs, attitudes and social identities as well as gestures, glances, body position and clothes.... A Discourse is a sort of 'identity kit' which comes complete with appropriate costume and instructions on how to act, talk and often write" (pp. 6–7). Formed through direct interactions and observations in particular cultures, Discourses often become unconscious to the individual. Just as fish may not be aware of the water in which they swim, so too are we not aware of the Discourses we embody.

Similarly, much of the reasoning behind the choices we make in teaching becomes routine and unconscious once we've been at it for a little while. The examples we share, the books we read aloud (or those we assign), our choice of assignments, even the way we interact with our students in the classroom are necessarily influenced by our Discourses. For example, when Jocelyn was supervising a student teacher in an English class in early December, the teacher asked his students to write about their favorite Christmas memory. In some ways, the assignment was innocuous. Surely his students had favorite memories of that time of year. However, what about those students who did not celebrate Christmas? In constructing the assignment the way he did, prompted by what he had come to know in his own experience of the world, this teacher had unconsciously left some students out.

Bringing all students into the fold requires teachers to develop an understanding of their own cultural backgrounds and how they have shaped their perspectives and beliefs. Teachers then, or simultaneously, need to develop an understanding of who their students are (Armstrong, 2008; Dantas, 2007; Eslami, 2005; Marx & Moss, 2011). As of 2015–2016, 80 percent of teachers in U.S. public schools were white (Taie & Goldring, 2018). By contrast, 47 percent of the student population was students of color, a percentage set to exceed 50 percent in the next few years (National Center for Education Statistics, 2016). Knowing students' cultural backgrounds—their Discourses—enables teachers to better meet their students' needs and connect teaching to students' lives.

However, knowledge of diverse cultures is not a simple process, especially if this knowledge moves beyond a surface understanding (e.g., Jews celebrate Hanukkah, Muslims pray in mosques). Teachers can develop an experiential understanding of multiple cultures through authentic immersion and engagement opportunities in diverse communities. In order to teach for global competence, teachers must reflect on how different cultures compare to their own and to one another. In doing so, teachers must also resist making assumptions or stereotypes and avoid ignoring the complexities inherent within cultures (Merryfield, 2002). Globally competent teachers use their knowledge of diverse cultures to teach in culturally responsive ways that take into account and recognize the importance of positively embedding elements of students' cultures and experiences into their teaching (see Chapter 8 for specific examples).

Self-Reflection and Implementation Tips for an Experiential Understanding of Diverse Cultures

Look at Figure 5.1 and rate yourself along the GCLC for the element "Experiential understanding of multiple cultures."

1. Where do you rate yourself and why?
2. What steps do you need to take to move along the continuum?

The following implementation tips will help you think through the next steps you can take to strengthen your understanding of diverse cultures. Coming to know oneself—the "self-knowledge" that Palmer (1998) references—is a necessary precursor for coming to understand other cultures. Just as you need to develop self-understanding, so too is it critical to learn about cultures different from your own through real-life experiences. This allows you both to teach students who are themselves part of these different cultures and to teach about diverse cultures in authentic and trustworthy ways.

Beginning/Progressing

How can you come to recognize unconscious patterns of teaching that may be influenced by your own lived experiences? How can you unpack the Discourses that make up who you are? Become aware of your own cultural practices, values, and norms. The first step is to figure out the ocean in which you are swimming. Step back and consider mind mapping a day in your life. Consider questions such as the following:

- Where do I wake up in the morning? Why do I live where I live? In what ways does where I live reflect my Discourse(s)?
- If I eat breakfast, what do I have for breakfast and why? In what ways do my choices about breakfast (even choosing not to eat breakfast) form part of my Discourse(s)?
- What clothes do I put on in the morning? Why these clothes? In what ways are these clothes markers of my Discourse(s)?

Continue to ask these sorts of questions about all of your interactions during the day, including the transportation you use to get to school, what

Figure 5.1 | Experiential Understanding of Multiple Cultures

Element	Nascent ⟶	Beginning ⟶	Progressing ⟶	Proficient ⟶	Advanced ⟶
Experiential Understanding of Multiple Cultures	• I have not yet reflected on my own cultural values and norms. • I have not yet considered experiencing other cultures.	• I am aware of my own cultural practices, values, and norms in relation to other cultures. • I am interested in experiencing other cultures.	• I understand differences in practices, values, and norms across cultures. • I understand that multiple perspectives exist within and across cultures. • I seek opportunities to experience other cultures.	• I demonstrate knowledge of various cultures through cultural immersion experiences (e.g., study abroad and local immersion). • I reflect on the immersion experience in relation to my own cultural constructs, perspectives, and educational practices.	• I critically relate multiple cultural immersion experiences to one another and to my own perspectives and practices. • I modify my educational practices and/or advocate for changing educational policies and practices based on immersion experiences and an understanding of multiple perspectives.

you do after school, what language you use when you greet your students, what sort of lunch you eat, and so on. This conscious unpacking of your daily practices prompts some initial realizations about the ways your Discourses—including your class, race, gender, sexual orientation, religion, and language patterns—guide your actions. In some cases, you make conscious choices about your actions based on your own lived experiences. In other cases, these actions are unconscious. The goal is to make you aware of the moves you make and be able to consider why you make them.

Another way to unpack your own cultural norms is by carefully looking—and listening—to your own teaching. Record a few lessons. Then sit down and watch the video, paying close attention to the actions you take as teacher. Again, ask yourself questions about your practice:

- Who did I call on today? Is there anything about this choice that may be guided by my own Discourse(s)?
- Did I act differently toward different students? What did that look like? Is there anything about this choice that may be guided by my own beliefs, values, and norms?
- What sorts of examples did I use today? Why did I use these in particular? Did I make an assumption that everyone would be familiar with the examples I chose? Is there anything about these choices that may be guided by my own culture, beliefs, values, and norms?

These sorts of questions will prompt you to pay close attention to your own teacher moves and come to understand how these moves may be guided by your own cultural norms and expectations. If you feel comfortable doing so, this would be a great activity to do with a trusted colleague who can provide another perspective on the lesson.

Keep in mind that this process of coming to know and recognize your own cultural patterns, norms, and values is a long-term effort. Our Discourses are not all necessarily stable (Gee, 1989). They shift, depending on a number of things, such as if we become part of a different community (e.g., moving to a new region or country where different norms, values, and practices may be present). Those shifts lead to an accumulation of new values and norms. Therefore, reflecting and learning about oneself must be an ongoing effort.

Proficient/Advanced

Seek out opportunities to learn about and experience diverse cultures in and beyond your classroom. Travel is one way to experience other cultures. However, just because you travel to a different country does not necessarily mean that you truly experience that context or the cultures found there. It is quite easy to remain in a bubble when you travel—staying in U.S. chain hotels, traveling on a tour bus, or only visiting sites and restaurants that cater to tourists. Your experiences need to move beyond "surface-level tourist encounters" (Cushner, 2012, p. 49) and into authentic immersion experiences that provide the opportunity to engage in the daily practices and traditions of those who live there. Such experiences should also provide space to critically reflect on, discuss, and deconstruct the perceived realities of the community in which you are visiting (Alfaro & Quezada, 2010). Without structured time for reflection, you run the risk of reinforcing existing stereotypes or inflating your perception and understanding of the culture with which you are engaging (Willard-Holt, 2001).

Therefore, consider travel opportunities that enable you to learn from and with those who live in the place you are visiting. Stay with a host family, teach in a local school, or volunteer in a local community center. Consider reaching out to a school in the area you will be visiting and finding a teacher who might be willing to show you around for a few days. Teachers enjoy connecting with other teachers. Plus, this is a great opportunity to establish a connection that may ultimately support student virtual exchanges (described in further detail in Chapters 10 and 11).

There are many international travel opportunities specifically geared toward practicing teachers, some at low or no cost. The Fulbright Distinguished Awards in Teaching Program, Teachers for Global Classrooms, National Geographic Grosvenor Teacher Fellowship, and National Education Association Global Learning Fellowship are some programs for which teachers can apply and be part of a cohort that includes an international experience alongside global professional learning. Many teacher preparation programs now provide international opportunities to observe school settings and teach. Research touts the positive impact of these teaching abroad programs on preservice teachers' dispositions toward embracing diverse cultures and perspectives, awareness of self and others, and adaptability (e.g., Heejung, 2016; Parkhouse, Turner, Konle, & Rong, 2016; Pilonieta, Medina, & Hathaway, 2017). From our own experiences teaching and volunteering abroad, along with the experiences of tens of teachers whom we have interviewed (and who participated in immersion experiences for teachers), we have found that the experience of being an "Other" while immersed in a new culture allows educators to better empathize with immigrant students and English language learners—and to change teaching practices accordingly.

Understandably, international travel may be too expensive or not feasible due to scheduling conflicts or family obligations. However, you can still gain the same cultural insights by seeking out experiences in and around the community where you live. Are there people in your community, even your colleagues, who might be willing to share information about their culture? Because a single conversation will be limited (plus, a single story does not reflect a whole cultural experience), try to find a number of people who might share information about the same culture. If you live near a university, think about connecting with their foreign student groups, perhaps through the study abroad office, international student program, or the language programs on campus.

Seek out opportunities for "local" exchanges as well. Visit nearby communities with different demographics or a unique cultural immersion experience. For example, you could visit various places of worship to get a sense of how prayer is practiced in different religions. One high school history teacher in a Washington, DC, suburb created a weeklong summer professional development program on religious literacy for teachers of all subject areas that had them visit various houses of worship in the DC area, including a Buddhist temple, Jewish synagogue, African American church, Muslim community center, Unitarian meeting house, Church of the Latter Day Saints, and Seventh-Day Adventist church. Again, these experiences will not provide you with the whole story, but they will provide a glimpse into a world that may be very different from your own.

Seek out opportunities to regularly engage with others across cultures. Travel is one way to do this, but you can also look within your own school community. For example, to better understand the experience of the refugee students who were recent immigrants to her school community, 4th grade teacher Sarah, with the support of her principal, organized home visits four times during the school year to meet the families of her refugee students. Through these experiences, she began the process of learning more about the experiences of her students and their families, and she was able to reflect on the ways her own daily experience—her window to the world—differed.

To complement these experiences, explore additional resources that can further deepen your understanding of diverse cultures. There is an endless array of books and websites to read, conferences to attend, and TED talks to listen to. Literature is another way to gain insight into diverse cultures. Select stories with protagonists who have different cultural backgrounds than your own and books written by authors who represent an array of countries and cultures. If you can, connect with other educators to talk about these resources and gain additional insights from their perspectives.

Melissa, a middle school language arts teacher in a large, culturally diverse middle school, sought teachers throughout the school to begin a book club. The teachers, from a range of disciplines, met every six weeks to discuss books that highlighted the experiences of diverse adolescents, including *The Hate U Give* by Angie Thomas, *American Street* by Ibi Zoboi, and *The Absolutely True Diary of a Part-Time Indian* by Sherman Alexie. Though the books provided an opportunity for the teachers to learn more about the experiences of others, the book club discussions themselves provided an opportunity for the teachers to share different perspectives with one another. Melissa reflected on the ways the experience regularly allowed her to see things through the eyes of her diverse colleagues. This experience provided her with additional confidence to support her students in exploring diverse cultural perspectives. (If you are a movie lover, you can apply the same process to watching foreign films!)

If you are not comfortable or feel like you don't have the time to reach out to colleagues for a book club, then reading diverse books with your students is a great place to start. Resources to find diverse books include We Need Diverse Books (https://diversebooks.org), The Tutu Teacher (www.the-tututeacher.com), Global Lit Project (https://globallitproject.com), and Queen of the First Grade Jungle (http://queenofthefirstgradejungle.blogspot.com). Events such as the Global Read Aloud (https://theglobalreadaloud.com) and World Read Aloud Day (www.litworld.org/wrad) provide further opportunities for students to essentially join an international book club and learn how fellow students from different cultures and countries interpret the same books they are reading.

Regardless of the number of ways you immerse yourself in diverse cultural experiences, it is important to remember that your understanding of that culture is necessarily guided by your own lens. Even though we often use the metaphor, you can never truly "step into another's shoes." This brings us to our next suggestion.

Consider your own perspectives relative to others'. As we stated at the beginning of this chapter, our experiences in the world are necessarily influenced by our Discourses. Our perspectives on various topics are necessarily colored by our own personal experiences in the world. Therefore, as you immerse yourself in the cultures and experiences of others, it's important to step back and consider others' perspectives relative to your own and how their cultural orientations play a role in shaping their views. This is often easier said than done.

Guided reflection before, during, and after your immersion experience—whether it be a summer teaching abroad or immersing yourself in a series of books with culturally diverse characters and settings—can help this process. Reflections can take any number of forms (e.g., journaling, blogging, making videos or audio recordings, engaging in critical conversations). Preimmersion questions might include "What cultural practices, values, and norms do I hold as they relate to my understanding of how students learn and how teachers should teach? Communicating with students, parents, supervisors, and colleagues? Work-life balance? Family structures? What preconceived notions do I hold about the culture that I am about to immerse myself in? Why do I think this?"

Throughout the experience, continue to ask yourself—and document the answers to—reflective questions such as "How are my preconceived notions about this culture being challenged? How do the cultural experiences in which I am engaging differ from or complement my own cultural practices, values, and norms?" After the experience, ask yourself "How has this experience reshaped my personal perceptions? How has this changed my educational practices?" Importantly, reflection shouldn't stop a week or a month after you return home; it should occur throughout the following school year as a way to self-monitor the ways in which you are modifying your teaching in light of the cultural understandings you developed.

Provide students with opportunities to explore different cultural perspectives. After participating in immersion experiences, how can you bring your experiences of the world back into the classroom and help your students develop an understanding of different cultural perspectives? Indeed, there are many ways you can do this. High school ELA teacher Alyssa, who taught a homogenous population of African American students, created a slide show documenting her experience teaching in India, which she shared with colleagues and her students. Alyssa explained how that presentation opened her students' eyes to a different culture they otherwise would not have known about, catalyzing their curiosity with all sorts of questions about the structure of the school she taught in, the food she ate, and even the racial composition of the group she traveled with.

First grade teacher Shauna, who has traveled on numerous international trips for teachers, constantly seeks out ways to apply those experiences across the content areas she teaches. For example, after traveling through Norway, she incorporated her experience traveling to a seed vault into her science unit on plants. Likewise, middle school math teacher Chris applied his experience working with teachers in a rural mountain community in Guatemala to word problems he created on area and perimeter focused on family farms.

Special Considerations for Elementary School Teachers (PK–5)

- As you fill your classroom library, make sure that your books represent a healthy mix of windows into different cultures and mirrors that reflect the culture of your students (Bishop, 1990). The act of reflecting on whether a book is a "window" or "mirror" for each of your students is an opportunity to unpack the cultures within your own classroom and how they may be different or similar from your own.

Special Considerations for Secondary School Teachers (6–12)

- If your school has exchange programs for students, volunteer to be a chaperone. Even if the trips are geared toward a content area you don't teach, it will provide you with a unique opportunity to experience a new culture that can inform your teaching practices.

Element 5 in Action:
Various Entryways to Experiencing Multiple Cultures

What does it look like for a teacher to engage in this important work of gaining an experiential understanding of multiple cultures? Maddy, a 2nd grade National Board–certified teacher, shares her story here.

"I started to reflect on my own culture when student-teaching 4th grade in Kingaroy, Australia. This small town, known for its peanut farming, was the place that helped me appreciate my own culture and those around me. As a white American woman, I did not fully understand my own cultural norms until I was immersed in another culture. I think it is important that educators realize we do not live on an island. Teaching can be a lonely profession if you do not use each other as a resource. Yes, we are expected to work with our colleagues and collaborate to meet the needs of the students at our school, district, and across the state, but why does it have to stop there?

"Why are we not collaborating with teachers from around the world to also guide our profession? Education is a cultural norm of its own. Through this student teaching experience, I realized that maybe the way I was taught in my U.S. schools was not the 'only' way, and it is not necessarily the only right way. When in Australia, I came to learn the cultural norms of the school and the way in which a regular school day was defined in that particular place.

"I think the most powerful way to learn about other cultures is to connect. Connect with other educators, students, and authors. We live in an age when connecting with others occurs on a daily basis, whether we realize it or not. Making connections is so accessible and tangible that there is no excuse to not be digitally connected in order to learn from other educators. An easy way to connect with others and learn about other cultures is through Twitter. I have a classroom Twitter account in which I share thoughts and ideas from my own classroom and follow many other educators. Just scrolling through my Twitter feed, I can see what other educators around the world are doing and connect with them to create authentic cultural experiences for my students.

"For example, last year, I participated in the Global Read Aloud—the premise of which is 'one book to connect the world.' Through this program, you connect with other educators through Twitter or Facebook. Once you have made a connection with another educator, the possibilities are endless. You read the same book at the same time as the other connected classroom. You then have literature discussions about the book with the other class through various digital platforms. Last year, my class and the one we connected with read different books by the author Mem Fox. My students then connected with the other students through a blog we set up. The students had conversations about the stories and the cultural differences in the books with students outside of our classroom.

"Connecting with educators from different cultural backgrounds can also help you confidently create lessons that center around the global world on a daily basis. To help create these lessons, I use TeachSDGs. TeachSDGs is an international organization created for and by educators that informs educators on the United Nations' 17 Sustainable Development Goals. I use these global goals as the foundations for my lessons. For example, Global Goal Six is 'clean water and sanitation.' I connect this to the Common Core State Standards I must teach in my own classroom. But I don't do that work alone. I seek out resources from other teachers around the world who I follow on Instagram and Twitter. In the case of my focus on clean water and sanitation, I sought out blogs of teachers who use diverse literature to teach global concepts. This led me to the book *The Water Princess* by Susan Verde, a book about a young girl who seeks to bring clean drinking water to her African village. I then created literature discussion questions aligned to the course of study and used the book as the center of the unit I was teaching, highlighting Global Goal Six."

Further Developing This Knowledge

- Reflect on the traditions, values, and norms of your culture and how they have shaped your perspective on what a high-quality education looks like.
- Engage in a book or film study to learn about education in different parts of the world. Compare with the school where you teach.
- Research and participate in authentic immersion experiences overseas or in local communities outside the cultural group with which you identify.

Continuing the Journey

Explore these additional resources as you continue on your journey to develop experiential knowledge of diverse cultures. Note that this is just a sampling of short- and long-term programs that provide structured opportunities for PreK–12 teachers to learn through international experiences.

❯ Fulbright Distinguished Awards in Teaching Program (www.fulbrightteacherexchange.org): This U.S. Department of State exchange program offers short-term and semester opportunities for K–12 educators to study, teach, and research abroad.

❯ Teachers for Global Classrooms

(www.irex.org/project/teachers-global-classrooms-program-tgc): Run by the U.S. Department of State and IREX, this year-long, fully funded professional development opportunity helps U.S. elementary, middle, and high school teachers become leaders in global education. The fellowship includes an online course, a global symposium, international field experience, a capstone project, and alumni support.

❯ The National Education Association Global Learning Fellowship

(www.neafoundation.org/for-educators/global-learning-fellowship): This 12-month professional development program includes in-person workshops, online coursework, webinars by leading experts, peer learning, and an international field study experience.

❯ National Geographic Grosvenor Teacher Fellowship

(www.nationalgeographic.org/education/programs/grosvenor-teacher-fellows): Open to PreK–12 educators, this selective opportunity funds teachers to go on Lindblad Expeditions' voyages for a field-based experience and supports them as they complete a series of deliverables that enable them to transfer their onboard experience into new ways to teach students and engage colleagues.

❯ World View Global Study Visits

(https://worldview.unc.edu/professional/global-study-visits): This organization, based out of the University of North Carolina at Chapel Hill, conducts international study visits for K–12 and community college educators. These visits focus on learning about the culture, key issues, and educational practices of specific countries and include seminars, an orientation, and a follow-up workshop to design relevant curricula and initiatives that are based on teachers' experiences. The goal is to stimulate global learning in teachers' classrooms, schools, and districts.

❯ Away Games

(http://awaygames.org): This is a television series and educational platform that helps one learn about culture and cultural differences through an exploration of sports.

❯ International Children's Digital Library

(http://en.childrenslibrary.org): This resource provides a free online collection of books from various cultures.

❯ SIMA Classroom

(https://simaclassroom.com): SIMA Classroom provides over 100 award-winning short documentaries and virtual reality experiences, bonus features, and lesson plans focused on global human rights issues, the Sustainable Development Goals (SDGs), social innovations, and entrepreneurship, giving users insight into different cultures via virtual technology.

6

Intercultural Communication

During her year teaching abroad in Athens, Greece, 1st grade teacher Linda found herself in an uncomfortable situation during a faculty meeting. She recounts her story: "I felt like the teachers were just yelling at each other. And I almost felt like just crawling under the table. But I had one teacher talk to me afterwards and say, 'We weren't mad. We were just talking to each other. That's just how we talk here in Greece.' Suddenly, I realized maybe we were perceived as timid! So I learned the importance of talking to people and sharing my feelings and my potential biases and having them either clarified for me or challenge me."

By becoming aware of the differences in communication styles in Greece and the United States, Linda learned a valuable lesson in intercultural communication. Like the other elements of global competence, an understanding of intercultural communication is needed to be sensitive to the diverse students within our classrooms and to help those students develop their own intercultural competence for an ever-globalizing world.

First, teachers need a deep knowledge of the ways in which students from linguistically diverse backgrounds may communicate differently—in terms of not just the words and phrases used but also the nonverbal elements of communication, such as physical proximity, gestures, intonation, turn-taking, degree of directness, punctuality, and dress. Teachers need to be aware that certain modes of communication are valued more than others and that biases exist toward nondominant features of communication. For example, in U.S.

classrooms, teachers may expect students to maintain eye contact while a teacher is speaking with them individually, but in some cultures the expectation for respectful listening is that eyes should be gazing downward. A teacher without an understanding of cultural differences in nonverbal communication may misinterpret a lack of eye contact as a sign of disrespect, when the student may actually be working to show respect by looking away.

Second, to develop students' skills in intercultural communication, teachers need to model the skill so students see examples of how they can navigate differences in communication styles. Students will undoubtedly interact with people from various cultural backgrounds during their lives, and many intercultural communication skills (e.g., resisting the natural inclination to interpret a gesture or tone from our own cultural lens) do not come naturally. In the previous example, even a teacher who is proficient in intercultural communication skills may still *initially* feel frustration or discomfort with a student who avoids eye contact during a one-on-one conversation. What makes the teacher proficient, however, is that he or she checks that initial reaction against knowledge that some cultures view eye contact in this context as confrontational rather than respectful. This is the kind of unnatural reaction we want our students to be able to summon, based on their own knowledge of variations in communication styles.

What Does It Mean to Understand Intercultural Communication?

Intercultural communication, also referred to as cross-cultural communication, is concerned with how we communicate when we interact with people from different cultures, whether that be people from different countries or those who identify with different cultural groups (regional, ethnic, religious, or otherwise) within the same country (Kotthoff & Spencer-Oatey, 2008). Intercultural communication consists of several elements. First, and perhaps most obvious, is awareness of cultural differences in verbal and nonverbal communication and the effect they have on cross-cultural interactions. Nonverbal elements of communication are especially important, as up to 90 percent of a message's meaning is transmitted paralinguistically (Samovar & Porter, 2002). For instance, in Japanese culture, laughing or smiling may not only accompany happiness or humor but also sadness, embarrassment, or anger (Hayakawa, 2003). Someone proficient in Japanese American intercultural communication would not only be aware of this but also know how to reduce tensions in conversations that might arise as a result of the speakers' distinct uses and interpretations of laughter. This might involve the American speaker smiling to make the Japanese speaker feel more at ease.

A second element of understanding intercultural communication is an awareness of the relationship between language, communication, and identity. Language is not just how we make ourselves understood—it is also how we express love and forge connections with others. It is how we establish ourselves as part of a group and develop a sense of belonging. In other words, language makes up a huge part of our identity. Imagine if you could no longer speak your primary language but could speak only a different language. How would your identity be affected? Lily Wong Fillmore (2000) has studied the impact of U.S. schooling on immigrants' loss of their family languages. Whereas historically, many second-generation immigrants were bilingual, second-generation immigrants today often learn English *at the expense of* their home language—rather than in addition to it. Fillmore argues that this loss of the ability to speak with one's grandparents and even parents has devastating consequences for immigrant children's sense of self and belonging. Teachers need to be aware of the role of language not only in communication but also in identity development and stability.

Finally, educators proficient in intercultural communication must also understand the relationship between power and language, particularly how some forms of communication are valued over others—or even considered the *correct* way to communicate. As the great thinker and writer James Baldwin put it, "Language is also a political instrument, means, and proof of power" (1979, para. 4). We tend to think of dialects as aberrant variations of a language, but as the adage goes, "A language is a dialect with an army and a navy" (Lippi-Green, 1997, p. 43). In other words, dialects are not inferior forms of a more proper language; they are languages in their own right. They merely lack the benefit of state power to establish them as the *correct, standard,* or *proper* language.

One important example for U.S. educators is African American English (AAE), also referred to as Ebonics or African American Vernacular English. This was and continues to be perceived as incorrect English, a dialect, or a bastardization of English (Lippi-Green, 1997). In fact, AAE has internal consistency and a rule-governed structure just like any other language. It is a language without an army. Teachers conscious of this fact can be explicit with students who speak AAE that learning standard academic English, as it is often called, is essentially teaching them a separate—not superior—language, as opposed to the "correct form" of their own language. Bilingual education scholars have also pushed back on dominant ways of thinking about the "correct" way to be bilingual. Ofelia García and Li Wei (2014) developed the concept of *translanguaging* as a more accurate way to depict the fluid ways in which multilingual students simultaneously draw on all of their linguistic resources—versus the more simplified understanding of multiple monolinguals existing in one person.

Self-Reflection and Implementation Tips for Understanding Intercultural Communication

Look at Figure 6.1 and rate yourself along the GCLC for the element "Understanding of intercultural communication."

1. Where do you rate yourself and why?
2. What steps do you need to take to move along the continuum?

The following implementation tips will help you think through the next steps you can take to improve your understanding of intercultural communication and how you can apply it in your role as an educator.

Do some homework. Intercultural communication skills are not typically something one is born with or that can be easily acquired simply by interacting with people of different backgrounds. Conversing with others may alert you to some variations in communication styles, such as the divergent uses

Figure 6.1 | Understanding of Intercultural Communication

Element	Nascent ➞	Beginning ➞	Progressing ➞	Proficient ➞	Advanced
Understanding of Intercultural Communication	I am not yet familiar with cultural differences in communication.	I am aware that different cultures may have different ways of communicating (e.g., differences in language, gestures, and norms for communicating).	• I can identify strategies that enhance intercultural communication. • I can explain the relationship between language, communication, and identity.	• I can use strategies to navigate intercultural interactions effectively. • I understand that learning languages has social, emotional, and cognitive aspects.	• I critically reflect on how particular languages and modes of communication are valued more than others and the effect this has on identity. • I can help others navigate the social, emotional, and cognitive aspects of intercultural communication.

for laughter, but it may not help you know what to do in such cases. Even learning how to listen, speak, read, and write in another language may not make you proficient in intercultural communication.

The strategy most likely to help in this regard is to read about intercultural communication and specific features of communication in the various cultures you encounter. Then practice what you read as much as possible. Two books that can help you learn more are *Cross-Cultural and Intercultural Communication* (Gudykunst, 2003) and *Intercultural Communication: A Reader* (Samovar & Porter, 2002). These books provide information about cultural variations in perceptions of time, destiny, space, silence, age, eye contact, and physical gestures, among others. They also describe how culture modifies interactions in specific settings, including education contexts.

It would be impossible to memorize every communication norm in every culture. However, it is helpful to know some general ways in which cultures vary in verbal and nonverbal communication patterns and some of the specific features of communication in the cultures of your students and their families.

Avoid generalizing. Keep in mind that communication styles vary within countries and even within cultural groups. Gender, class, race, ethnicity, generation, and other affiliations often influence communication patterns. For example, researchers have found generational differences in how people of the same cultural group use language, with youth constantly "fashioning new linguistically and culturally dexterous ways" of being a part of their cultural group that draw upon long-standing and emerging practices (Alim & Paris, 2017, p. 9). The most important thing to remember is that whatever you learn about another culture is true *on the average*—not across the board—and therefore, you should avoid making assumptions about any *particular person* within that group based on these averages. To continue with the previous example, you should not assume a Japanese person you meet will necessarily smile for the same purposes. And if they don't, this does not mean that what you learned was false—only that it is not true in 100 percent of cases. Most groups will have a wide variance on any particular trait.

What follows are implementation tips specific to your developmental level for understanding intercultural communication on the GCLC.

Nascent

Whether you live in a relatively homogenous community with few opportunities to practice intercultural communication or a multiethnic community with considerably more opportunities, you may not be aware of cultural patterns in communication. It can be hard to know which elements of our own communication are universal (e.g., smiling to convey pleasure or approval) versus cultural (e.g., using a thumbs-up to signal that everything is fine) versus personal (e.g., preferring to close meetings by expressing appreciation to attendees). The only way to learn which category may best characterize a behavior is to learn more about other cultures. If we learn that other cultures do not use the thumbs-up gesture in the same way we do, we can infer that this is a culturally specific (not universal) element of communication. This is a fairly obvious example, but there are many others that are not so obvious. Do people in all cultures frown when angry? One study suggests this is not the case (Jack, Garrod, Yu, Caldara, & Schyns, 2012). Is it culturally specific to use a vertical head movement (i.e., a nod) to indicate agreement and a horizontal movement to indicate disagreement? The answer is no. In Bulgaria, these are reversed (Andonova & Taylor, 2012). We may never ask ourselves these questions if we do not first notice how other cultures' patterns are different from our own.

The best way to uncover these differences is to immerse yourself in another culture or interact regularly with people from different cultures. If you don't have the ability to travel and you live in a homogenous area, find out if there are any local agencies or faith-based organizations that need volunteers to work with refugee families or provide ESL tutoring. If you want to acquire a new language and experience firsthand the social and emotional aspects of learning a language, take classes or find a language exchange partner who wants to practice English while you learn his or her primary language. Try to spend half of your time together speaking English and half speaking your partner's primary language so you both equally benefit. (See Chapter 7 for more ideas on language learning.)

You can also learn about communication in other cultures through reading, television, and films. Keep in mind that you will have to be careful to distinguish between stereotypes and reliable representations. Films produced in other countries or created by members of the cultural community you are interested in learning about may provide more nuanced (i.e., not stereotypical) representations of the culture. Select films that relate to the cultures of the students in your classroom. While watching, pay attention to variations in communication styles. Once you notice a few, do some research to determine whether these are indeed culturally influenced norms versus traits of fictional characters, and then dig deeper to learn how these norms fit into the larger culture. For instance, the use of laughter in varying contexts is a way to show cooperative intentions—a behavior that is particularly important in more collectivist cultures such as that of Japan (Hayakawa, 2003). By learning about this single feature of communication, you can learn broader lessons about Japanese culture.

Beginning/Progressing

At these stages, appreciate the importance of patience, open-mindedness, and flexibility in intercultural communication and strive to embody those characteristics. Monitor your speech and nonverbal cues in cross-cultural interactions. For instance, consciously avoid slang and idioms and anticipate how someone from another culture might interpret your tone, body language, and word choice. Become a keen observer of subtle distinctions in verbal and nonverbal elements of communication, such as rate of speech, formality, volume, whether the speaker is standing or sitting, and hand movements (or lack thereof) during speech.

By these stages, you may be attending to another important element of intercultural communication: *communicative burden*. Rosina Lippi-Green (1997) described communicative burden as the work each party does to understand and be understood by the other in cases where there is a language barrier. Ideally, two members of a conversation equally share the communicative burden. However, if one person has what is perceived as a non-mainstream accent, the other person often expects that person to do more conversational work to help him or her understand. Someone with intercultural communication skills, on the other hand, would strive to carry at least the fair share, if not more, of the communicative burden. If you work with young students or English language learners, you may be accustomed to putting forth additional effort to make meaning of what your students say. If so, pay attention to whether you're bearing an equal amount of the communicative burden for all your students. If not, make a concerted effort to bear more of the burden in interactions where a language barrier is at play.

Proficient/Advanced

At these stages, one moves beyond awareness of the skills necessary for effective intercultural communication to a more sociocultural awareness of the unequal status of languages in society and the influence of language on identity. Explore which version of the primary language of your country is considered proper and which varieties or accents are considered inferior or dialects. In U.S. schools, those who don't speak Mainstream American English (MAE) are often viewed as having a language deficit that needs to be addressed, rather than as having the asset of emerging bilingualism (García & Wei, 2014). This includes Spanish as well as African American English, even though both languages have been common in the United States since before its founding and both are just as rule-governed as MAE (García & Wei, 2014; Rickford, n.d.). As a result, students who speak these languages are often made to feel like they are not speaking the correct or appropriate language for school, which disparages not only their cultures but also their very identities.

You might notice that villainous cartoon characters are more likely to have nondominant accents than heroic characters. A study of accents in full-length animated Disney films found that while 20 percent of U.S. English speakers are portrayed as evil, 40 percent of nonnative speakers of English are bad or evil (Lippi-Green, 1997). You might even lead your students to pay attention to these differences and reflect on the effects this has on the population's perception of various accents. If unintelligent fictional characters speak with southern accents, what does this teach children about people who have this accent? How does it make children with this accent feel about themselves and their families? Teachers can help undo the harm done by media representations by helping students critically examine the misconceptions these representations promote. Teachers can emphasize that languages and language varieties are not better or worse than one another (or more or less correct)—they are just different.

Help others navigate the social, emotional, and cognitive aspects of intercultural communication. This means recognizing that intercultural communication not only may be cognitively demanding but also can take a toll on a person's emotions. The feeling of not being understood or of being surrounded by a language we do not fully understand makes us feel alone. It makes us feel like outsiders who may never be accepted into the group we wish to join. Students can even feel less intelligent or that others perceive them as dumb because they cannot fully express themselves in the mainstream language. Teachers have a responsibility to students from linguistic minority backgrounds to help them navigate these emotionally taxing situations. Teachers can support students by celebrating their linguistic capital, allowing students of the same language background to speak in their home language and allowing multilingual students to translanguage—in other words, flow freely between and through multiple languages rather than viewing them as completely separate (García & Wei, 2014)

Teachers can also create learning activities in which all students can fully participate regardless of their proficiency in the language of instruction. For instance, design activities that require students to respond through body movement, drawing, or manipulating objects. Though this is not feasible for all instruction (or desirable, given that students also need to develop language skills), it can serve as a comforting break for students who are tired of spending a majority of the school day navigating intercultural communication challenges.

Special Considerations for Elementary School Teachers (PK–5)

- Young children are learning how to make friends in general, so having peers with a different way of communicating might initially be frustrating. Modeling gestures and behaviors and teaching simple words or phrases in another language when students are trying to make friends can help them learn to interact appropriately and begin to build a foundation of intercultural communication skills.

- Reading aloud a book about children from different places and discussing how they communicate is a great way for students to begin to understand different communication skills. This can also be extended into a writing activity in which students reflect on how they communicate with their own families. Recommended children's literature on intercultural communication include the following books:

  - *Carmen Learns English* by Judy Cox
  - *I'm New Here* by Anne Sibley O'Brien
  - *My Language, Your Language* by Lisa Bullard
  - *No English* by Jacqueline Jules
  - *Yo! Yes?* by Chris Raschka
  - *Yoko Writes Her Name* by Rosemary Wells

- Ask your students, "How would you communicate with someone if you do not speak the same language as that person?" Have them brainstorm ideas and then practice in pairs or small groups how they might respectfully work to convey or receive a message. Discuss the different strategies they can use to share the communicative burden and help their interlocutor understand or be understood.

Special Considerations for Secondary School Teachers (6–12)

- Developmentally, young people between the ages of 11 and 18 are generally very interested in the social realm of life. They are forming many new relationships during these years and noting differences in social behaviors among groups and individuals. Thus, it is an opportune time of life for learning intercultural communication skills. Youth at this age are interested in this topic, and their brains are primed for learning it.

- Rather than allowing students to select their own partners or group members for collaborative learning activities, assign groups so you can give students opportunities to work with peers from different backgrounds. Before starting a collaborative activity, give a 5- to 10-minute minilesson on some of the skills essential for effective communication, such as active listening, displaying interest, paying attention to equal turn-taking, and requesting clarification when a statement is confusing or appears to be erroneous. If you have the privilege of teaching in a culturally diverse classroom, you can include elements specific to intercultural communication, such as taking on more of the communicative burden and monitoring reactions for cultural assumptions or biases. At the end of the collaborative activity, spend another 5–10 minutes guiding students to reflect on their strengths and weaknesses in active listening and the other elements of communication you taught. Have them identify a personal goal they want to work on the next time your class uses collaborative learning.

- High school students may be entering the world of work for the first time. They are likely to have coworkers, customers, and clients with different communication styles than they have encountered in their schools or neighborhoods. This may help them to see the relevance and real-world application of lessons on intercultural communication skills, as well as to have a bank of life experiences to bring into classroom discussions of this topic.

Element 6 in Action:
Comparing Idioms from Different Countries

Kate teaches 6th grade English language arts in a diverse urban, public middle school. She teaches a unit on idioms in order to help students understand that communicating across cultures is challenging not only because the languages may differ but also because many cultures use figurative language that cannot be interpreted literally. Idioms can only be understood if you know the figurative meaning that is understood within the culture.

She begins the unit by showing students how the meaning of the idiom "It's raining cats and dogs" is expressed differently in different countries. In Norway, the phrase translates to "It's raining female trolls," and in Ireland "It's throwing cobblers' knives." She then provides examples of various idioms from other countries and asks students to use their skills in making inferences to guess which country each example is from. Next, she asks students if they know where the common expression "let the cat out of the bag" originates. She explains that the origin is from medieval marketplaces in which people would purchase livestock and other animals and be advised to check the contents of their bags before returning home in case an animal was erroneously placed in it. Finally, students have the opportunity to create their own idioms for a project on literature around the world.

Kate explains that she had several goals in mind when designing this unit, which reflect Kate's understanding of intercultural communication. One is to help students understand figurative language, which is one of the standards in her standard course of study. Another is to spark students' interest in learning about other cultures by exposing them to the unique and imaginative ways in which various cultures express similar ideas. This also helps them value cultural differences because they add such richness to our lives. At the same time, students can also see how cultures are more similar than they may at first appear because they express ideas through figurative language.

Kate also wants her students to empathize with people who are learning a new language, including classmates who may be learning English as a second or third language. For language learners, idioms can pose a challenge because their intended meanings may be quite different from their literal meanings. Kate's students begin to understand that immigrants or visitors to a new culture must learn a lot more than how to translate words—they must also learn the multiple meanings words can have depending on the context in which they are used. In doing so, her students see that intercultural communication is about much more than translating words—and that learning a language is about more than cognition; it has social and emotional components as well.

Further Developing This Knowledge

- Immerse yourself in a setting where you are a linguistic "other," and reflect on how it made you feel. What cognitive demands did you face as you attempted to understand and be understood? What emotional challenges were involved? What strategies did you use to overcome the language barrier? How can you use the lessons you learned to help others navigate those challenges?
- Volunteer to tutor immigrant students who are learning a new language, if you do not already work with any in your classrooms. Use the opportunity to develop the intercultural communication skills described in this chapter.
- Reflect on the linguistic power dynamics within your community, state, or country. What is the dominant language within the government, school, and business? How does that match with the language(s) spoken by residents? Where do nondominant languages appear in public spaces, if at all? What social and emotional impact might this have on residents who speak those languages? A list of readings on the interactions between language, identity, and power is provided in the next section.

Continuing the Journey

Explore these additional resources as you move forward in your understanding of intercultural communication.

◗ **Lessons on Communication from The Asia Society** (https://asiasociety.org/china-learning-initiatives/many-ways-world-communicates): This lesson plan develops understanding that languages follow a system of rules, are not static, and are made up by much more than words alone.

(https://asiasociety.org/china-learning-initiatives/create-language): This lesson plan gives students an opportunity to create their own language and helps them take into account others' perspectives when choosing how to express themselves.

❂ TED Talk on the Relationship Between Language and Thought
(www.ted.com/talks/lera_boroditsky_how_language_shapes_the_way_we_think): Cognitive scientist Lera Boroditsky draws on research with different cultures to show how the language a group speaks shapes the way they think.

❂ International Children's Digital Library
(http://en.childrenslibrary.org): Teachers and students can access scanned copies of international books in English and other languages.

Readings on Language and Identity

- Fillmore, L. W. (2000). The loss of family languages: Should educators be concerned? *Theory into Practice: Children and Languages at School, 39*(4), 203–211.
- Lippi-Green, R. (2011). *English with an Accent: Language, ideology, and discrimination in the United States.* New York: Routledge.
- Ogbu, J. U. (1999). Beyond language: Ebonics, proper English, and identity in a Black-American speech community. *American Educational Research Journal, 36*(2), 147–184.
- Perry, T., & Delpit, L. (Eds.) (1998). *The real Ebonics debate: Power, language, and the education of African-American children.* Boston: Beacon.

Readings on Bilingualism and Biculturalism

- Darder, A. (2012). *Culture and power in the classroom: Educational foundations for the schooling of bicultural students.* Boulder, CO: Paradigm.
- Flores, B. M. (2005). The intellectual presence of the deficit view of Spanish-speaking children in the educational literature during the 20th century. In P. Pedraza & M. Rivera (Eds.), *Latino education: An agenda for community action research* (pp. 75–98). Mahwah, NJ: Lawrence Erlbaum.
- Valdés, G. (2001). *Learning and not learning English: Latino students in American schools.* New York: Teachers College Press.

SECTION III

SKILLS

The elements within the dispositions and knowledge domains of global competence are broad enough to apply to a variety of professions and settings, but the elements in the skills domain are specific to the classroom. Globally competent teaching skills refer to the ability to promote students' growing interest in and knowledge about the world through the classroom environment and instructional experiences. Specifically, the six globally competent teaching skills elaborated on in this section are an ability to

- Communicate in multiple languages. (Chapter 7)
- Create a classroom environment that values diversity and global engagement. (Chapter 8)
- Integrate learning experiences for students that promote content-aligned explorations of the world. (Chapter 9)
- Facilitate intercultural and international conversations that promote active listening, critical thinking, and perspective recognition. (Chapter 10)
- Develop local, national, or international partnerships that provide real-world contexts for global learning opportunities. (Chapter 11)
- Develop and use appropriate methods of inquiry to assess students' global competence development. (Chapter 12)

These six skills emerge out of the dispositions and knowledge presented in the first two sections of this book. Globally competent teaching skills are grounded in empathy, a commitment to promoting equity and considering multiple perspectives, knowledge of global conditions and the ways the world is interconnected, and an understanding of multiple cultures and intercultural communication.

From these foundations, one can develop the skills for fostering such dispositions and knowledge in students. For instance, a teacher cannot promote global engagement and an appreciation for diversity without valuing those things himself or herself. Likewise, to design learning experiences that promote explorations of the world requires personal knowledge of global conditions, current events, and the ways in which local and global forces interact. Developing your own knowledge in these areas will provide examples you can use to make the case to students that global awareness matters for their lives. Therefore, educators may find that they advance in each of the skills simultaneously as they advance in the dispositions and knowledge elements of global competence. As teachers become more committed to acting on issues of global concern, they may emphasize this more in their classrooms, moving them closer to the advanced level of creating a classroom environment that values diversity and global engagement.

The six skills presented here also reflect research-based, effective teaching practices for general purposes. Leading class discussions or small-group activities that require active listening, critical thinking, and perspective recognition is a high-leverage instructional practice (Ball & Forzani, 2011). So too is using frequent, authentic, and differentiated assessments to provide feedback to students and inform subsequent instruction (Chappuis & Stiggins, 2017). Thus, as you develop globally competent teaching skills, you are also becoming a more successful teacher overall. Moreover, you are helping your students adopt not only a lifelong love of learning but also a commitment to understanding and acting on issues of global importance.

7

Communicating in Multiple Languages

Our world is not monolingual. Neither are our countries, states, cities, towns, and classrooms. There are roughly 7,000 languages spoken throughout the world. In the United States, the number of languages spoken exceeds 330. Nigeria, India, China, Mexico, Brazil, and others have hundreds of languages—both indigenous and immigrant—spoken on their shores (Anderson, 2010; Simons & Fennig, 2018). Approximately one in five U.S. residents speaks a language other than English at home. A school community might serve 75 or more languages or as little as 3. Alternatively, it might serve a student population where a majority of students are nonnative English speakers or only a handful are. Regardless of whether 1 or 100 percent of your students speak a language other than English, it is a worthwhile and urgent task to expand your linguistic repertoire.

For some educators, speaking multiple languages is second nature—it's a part of their upbringing, life experiences, or (in the case of world language teachers) their profession. However, despite the increase of nonnative English speakers in our classrooms and communities, a majority of U.S. teachers are monolingual. Indeed, only 20 percent of adults in the United States have knowledge of a second language, as compared to 66 percent of adults in the European Union (American Academy of Arts & Sciences, 2017).

This is not to say that teachers must become perfectly fluent in another language or learn every language their students speak. Rather, it is imperative to be *willing* to pursue basic conversation and fluency skills in a language other than one's home language in an effort to communicate with students and families effectively. Even if all students and their families are native English speakers, it is still important for teachers to model multilingualism so students will value language diversity and be inspired to learn additional languages. This embodies an assets-based, or additive, approach to language development, wherein the acquisition of the official language of school (e.g., English) is viewed as a new set of tools to be incorporated into students' existing linguistic repertoires—rather than replace them (Gibson, 1988, 1998).

Your school may already have specific programs in place that embrace multilingualism. World language classrooms have traditionally served as the home of language diversity in schools, with the most common being Spanish, French, German, Chinese, Latin, Arabic, Greek, Japanese, Korean, Portuguese, and Russian (American Councils, 2017). These take an array of forms, from core courses that are a part of students' daily schedules to elective courses that students rotate through once a week or on a quarterly basis. World language courses for heritage speakers have also grown in popularity. These are designed specifically for heritage language speakers—in other words, someone who has some proficiency in or a cultural connection to a language other than English, including immigrant, indigenous, and colonial languages (Center for Applied Linguistics, 2016). (See, for example, North Carolina's Spanish for Native Speakers Standard Course of Study at www.ncpublicschools.org/curriculum/worldlanguages/resources/spanish).

Bilingual education programs also promote the importance of speaking multiple languages in a globalized world and can serve as vehicles to communicate with students who speak a language other than English at home. This is especially true with programs that aim to develop bilingualism and biliteracy (e.g., developmental and dual immersion programs) rather than transitional bilingual programs that use students' home language solely as a stepping stone toward developing English (García, 2009). Developmental bilingual programs target heritage language speakers, with 90–100 percent of instruction in students' native language in early elementary school and half of instruction in English by upper elementary school. Dual immersion programs serve a mix of native English and native target language speakers and have a 50-50 split of instruction between students' target and native language.

Importantly, in a world where cultural and linguistic heterogeneity is the norm, the responsibility of communicating in multiple languages extends to all teachers, not just those with bilingual or world language endorsements. For starters, both world language and bilingual education programs are still on the periphery of instruction in most U.S. schools and districts. Only 20 percent of students are enrolled in a second language course, and only 11 states explicitly have foreign language as a graduation requirement (American Councils, 2017). For example, only 58 percent of middle schools and 25 percent of elementary schools (and just 15 percent of public schools) teach languages other than English (American Academy of Arts & Sciences, 2017). Furthermore, both types of language programs often have a shortage of qualified teachers and lack sufficient resources in terms of funding for staff and curricular materials. In addition, for schools with heterogeneous linguistic populations, bilingual education programs only serve a small subset of linguistically diverse students when it comes to heritage language instruction and communicating in the languages that students' families speak.

To address these issues and refrain from placing the responsibility of family communication solely on the language department, every teacher— regardless of who, what, or where they teach—can infuse multilingual communication into their classroom. As Agirdag (2009) argues, "To move toward a supportive school setting for all students, educators can create a linguistically plural learning environment, even without bilingual instruction" (para. 11).

What Are the Benefits of Learning to Communicate in Another Language?

On more than one occasion when reviewing the GCLC, educators have pushed back on the notion of having to learn to communicate in a language other than English. Common refrains include "English is our official language," "Everyone else around the world is learning English," and "Artificial intelligence can translate everything for us." However, as a report by the American Academy for Arts and Sciences (2017) argues, "While English continues to be the lingua franca for world trade and diplomacy, proficiency in English is not sufficient to meet... the needs of individual citizens who interact with other peoples and cultures more than at any other time in human history" (p. viii). In addition, the true value of learning another language is so much deeper than translating a sentence word for word. It allows you to better connect with others' ways of seeing the world. As Nelson Mandela is credited with saying, "If you talk to a man in a language he understands, that goes to his head. If you talk to a man in his language, that goes to his heart." This is particularly important for educators who interact with culturally and linguistically diverse students every day.

Communicating with students and their families in their native language benefits their social-emotional development, English proficiency, and academic achievement. Language and identity are largely intertwined (Agirdag, 2009). Therefore, when you validate a student's home language by using it in an official public setting such as school, you are validating an important part of who they are, which helps support positive identity formation and overall social-emotional and cognitive development (Spencer, Noll, Stoltzfus, & Harpalani, 2010; Steele & Cohn-Vargas, 2013). Long-standing research also confirms that being proficient in your first language increases language proficiency in a second language (Cummins, 1979). Therefore, when nonnative English speakers feel supported in maintaining their heritage language, it can increase their English language proficiency.

Furthermore, students' academic achievement also improves when they are in additive linguistic learning environments. Decades of research on the efficacy of dual immersion programs have concluded that bilingualism leads to higher levels of academic achievement in core subject areas (Collier & Thomas, 2004; Steele et al., 2017). By contrast, cultural discontinuity between students' school and home experiences can adversely affect students' sense of belonging and academic achievement (Gay, 2000). In sum, supporting multilingual environments helps educators knock down language barriers and build two-way bridges between home and school that support students' overall development.

Second, pursuing a second language can also build empathy, as it puts you in a similar situation as your nonnative English speakers and their families are experiencing when they are immersed in an unfamiliar language setting. As TESOL's *Principles of Language Learning* (2017) argues, "The more experience you have as a language learner, the more you will know about what does and doesn't work in language learning" (p. 5). Even if you aren't learning Mandarin, Tagalog, Arabic, or any other language your students speak, you can still transfer your own experiences with learning languages to better accommodate your students' needs (e.g., giving ample processing time and using nonverbal cues).

Third, making the effort to learn additional languages can lead to a greater appreciation of cultures. Language is a ticket to another person's culture, and the increase in cultural awareness that comes from learning a new language can lead to greater understanding of different perspectives and cultural values. In fact, research suggests that language learners develop a more positive attitude toward speakers of the language they are learning (American Council on the Teaching of Foreign Languages [ACTFL], 2018; Merrit, 2013). This in turn can result in better relationships between yourself, your students, and your students' families.

Benefits to learning new languages extend well beyond the classroom as well. Research has found correlations between bilingualism and improved cognitive development, the ability to multitask, memory skills, problem-solving abilities, and improved verbal and spatial abilities (ACTFL, 2018; Merrit, 2013). Cognitive research has also found that the brains of multilingual speakers have a higher density of gray matter, which contains all your neurons and synapses. On top of that, studies suggest that multilingualism can offset age-related cognitive decline, including delaying the onset of dementia and Alzheimer's disease by as much as five years (ACTFL, 2018; Merrit, 2013).

On a grander societal level, learning nondominant languages helps pre-serve cultures. Though our world is replete with languages, about one-third of languages today are endangered with fewer than 1,000 speakers remaining (Simons & Fennig, 2018). Thirty-five years ago, the Hawaiian language was on the brink of extinction, with fewer than 50 people under the age of 18 able to fluently speak it. Through a grassroots revitalization effort that introduced Hawaiian immersion preschools (Pūnana Leo) using Hawaiian as the medium of instruction (an act that was illegal as late as 1983), the first graduates of the Hawaiian immersion program are now raising their own children in Hawai-ian and sending their students to the same Hawaiian schools they graduated from. As the number of immersion schools increased to more than 20 across the state, the number of people who can speak Hawaiian has risen to 18,000 (Neason, 2016).

In sum, learning another language will help your emerging bilingual stu-dents while simultaneously expanding your worldview. It's never too late to begin the journey.

Basics of Learning Another Language

Language is fundamental to what it means to be human, as it is the primary mode through which our species communicates with one another. That we appear to develop our first language almost naturally out of basic instinct belies the complexity of phonology, morphology, syntax, semantics, and pragmatics—the major components of language—and the various modalities through which we receive and produce language. Luckily, educators don't need a degree in linguistics to learn to communicate effectively in a new lan-guage through listening, speaking, reading, and writing.

TESOL (2017) published the basic principles of language learning that apply to educators as they pursue learning another language:

- First, language is a communicative tool to foster human interactions. Therefore, the more practice you have communicating with real people about real things and thoughts in another language, the more moti-vated you will be to continue to pursue that language.

- Second, language learning should be viewed as the acquisition of an applied skill as much as it is knowledge of vocabulary and grammar. As such, language learners need repeated practice to hone in on listening, speaking, reading, and writing in a new language.
- Third, emotions play a role in language learning, particularly because language learning takes a prolonged effort over long periods of time. It is important not to become discouraged when you don't become fluent overnight or don't seem to hit the communication milestones you want.
- Fourth, as with learners generally, language learners don't all learn the same way. You might be a visual, auditory, kinesthetic, or tactile learner; introverted or extroverted; or cognitively or affectively oriented, all of which affect the modes through which you acquire a new language. For example, an extrovert might prefer learning language through social engagements and an auditory learner might find language podcasts particularly useful. Therefore, adapt your language learning process to best accommodate your learning preferences.

Self-Reflection and Implementation Tips for Communicating in Multiple Languages

Look at Figure 7.1 and rate yourself along the GCLC for the element "Communicating in multiple languages."

1. Where do you rate yourself and why?
2. What steps do you need to take to move along the continuum?

The following implementation tips will help you think through the next steps you can take to improve your communication in multiple languages, regardless of your linguistic background or proficiency.

Focus on person-to-person communication. For educators of culturally and linguistically diverse student populations, communicating across languages is not about perfect verb conjugation or memorized grammatical rules. Don't get hung up on past participles or an *A*-quality oral exam performance.

Figure 7.1 | Communicating in Multiple Languages

Element	Nascent	Beginning	Progressing	Proficient	Advanced
Communicating in Multiple Languages	I speak one language and have not yet pursued learning another.	I am pursuing or have pursued learning a language other than my native language.	I can have a basic conversation in two languages (including my native language).	• I am proficient in at least two languages (including my native language). • I can effectively communicate with students and families in at least two languages.	I am fluent in at least two languages and seek opportunities to use them in schools and communities.

It's about using language to get across important ideas and form relationships. For starters, you might focus on vocabulary and phrases that would be useful when talking with your students and their parents. For example, *The Essential Spanish Phrase Book for Teachers* (Perez-Sotelo & Hogan, 2008) provides classroom and school-specific phrases, expressions, and vocabulary to improve communication between Spanish-speaking students and families and school teachers and administrators. Another resource, the *Spanish for Educators* audiobook (Kammerman, 2006), also teaches essential Spanish phrases used in a school setting to improve communication with Spanish-speaking students and parents, covering topics such as classroom management, parent conferences, first aid, and praise.

Integrate multiple languages throughout the classroom environment. Celebrate language diversity in all of the verbal and written ways you communicate with students and families, from posters on the walls to books displayed in your classroom library to the language you use when greeting students and parents. Similarly, make sure your communications to families go out in the language they speak. If you don't feel confident translating newsletters, notices, and flyers, draw upon translation services that your school, district, or community organizations provide. Also, be careful not to make assumptions about what languages parents speak. Though not required under federal law, most states require that schools send out a home language survey to identify students who may qualify for language support services. This can be a good place to start gathering data about your students' home language(s). However, be aware that in some states, the questions asked may not drill down to the specific language(s) that students speak (e.g., "Is a language other than English spoken at home?") (Bailey & Kelly, 2013). You may need to create a classroom survey of your own that captures all the languages spoken at home and the primary language spoken by students and their parents.

Use families and communities as learning resources. Languages are best learned in real-world settings, which you can easily access by tapping into the linguistic diversity in your school community. For example, a kindergarten teacher with students from all over the world, including Ethiopia,

Vietnam, Central America, and Serbia, invites parents in to teach about their language during an "Around the World" unit. She shares that having parents teach their home language not only enhances her own linguistic toolbox—"I now know more Spanish through contact with families"—but also helps students feel excited about where they and their friends are from and the languages they speak.

The following are implementation tips on communicating in multiple languages specific to your developmental level on the GCLC.

Nascent

You can make diverse languages visible and audible without being able to speak or write in a second, third, or fourth language. Hang posters on the wall that have words in different languages. Play music from around the world when students walk into class in the morning and in the background during worktime. Encourage students to speak with one another in their native languages, and ask students to teach you words in their native language. Even if you can't understand or speak the home language(s) of your students, allowing students to freely switch between English and their native languages—a practice referred to as "translanguaging" (García & Wei, 2014)—creates opportunities for students to easily use all the tools in their linguistic toolbox as they digest content.

Beginning/Progressing

Start by learning a few key phrases you can regularly use with students. Take advantage of the plethora of free language learning apps, such as Duolingo and LingQ. Subscribing to a language podcast is another free and easy way to expose yourself to the basics of a new language (and that can easily be done during your commute to work or when you're out walking the dog). You can also invest in fee-based language programs, such as Rosetta Stone or Glossika, that allow you to progress in your own time and at your own pace.

Another way to pick up on basic conversational phrases in another language is by immersing yourself through culture: reading books, watching movies, and listening to music in the target language. To improve listening and speaking skills, explore opportunities to converse with native speakers. For example, through tandem language learning, you team up with a partner who speaks the language you want to learn who also wants to learn your native language. You take turns having conversations in both of your languages so you both mutually benefit. Depending on where you live, you might be able to find a tandem partner through programs run through local cafés or universities for face-to-face meet-ups, or you can find a tandem partner through various online communities.

Spending time abroad is another avenue for learning a language via immersion and real-world practice. For example, the majority of 5th grade teacher Taylor's students spoke Spanish at home. Having only taken a year of introductory Spanish when she was in college, she spent three weeks of her summer in an intensive language program in Peru, taking Spanish classes, meeting regularly with a tandem partner, and living in a homestay. She returned with the confidence to speak Spanish with her students and their parents in daily greetings and meetings.

As you develop a basic understanding of a second language, begin incorporating it informally and formally throughout the school day. For example, middle school band teacher Nelson had been working on improving the Spanish he learned in high school, and he had conversations in Spanish with three students who didn't speak, read, or write Spanish proficiently. Together, they collectively worked on learning new vocabulary. During lessons, he incorporated songs from Latin America and took time to go over the lyrics and decipher their meaning.

Proficient/Advanced

At these levels, teachers may have studied or been immersed in a language for years or they may be a heritage speaker. During informal interactions with students and their families, teachers chat in their students' native language. High school Spanish teacher Marlene shares that when she talks to her native-Spanish-speaking students in the hallways and cafeterias in Spanish, it builds a rapport that translates into the comfort they feel in the classroom.

When applicable, use your language skills to help translate school resources for families. This could include flyers, notices, newsletters, classroom and school websites, and school social media feeds. Serve as your own translator at parent-teacher conferences, IEP meetings, and back to school night, and check in with families to make sure they are getting linguistic access to the resources they need and answers to the questions they have surrounding the education of their child.

Finally, include parents, community members, and community organizations as language learning resources both inside and outside the classroom. Partner with parents to translate books and other curricular resources into their native languages. For example, early childhood educator Laura Linda Negri-Pool (2017) shared how she worked with the mother of a student from the Marshall Islands to translate their morning greeting song into Marshallese and then recorded a version of a favorite class book into Marshallese that her daughter could listen to at the listening station.

Help with school-based supports such as parent training programs, ESL classes, or literacy nights and use your language skills in the community. For example, libraries, nonprofit ethnic services, religious organizations, or ethnic businesses and language schools are all places where families convene for formal and informal educational experiences (Zhou & Li, 2003). Finally, seek out participation in community events where the heritage languages of students and their families are spoken. For example, the Hawaii Department of Education sponsored a Hawaiian language event at the state fair, attracting thousands of families who stayed for hours.

Special Considerations for Elementary School Teachers (PK–5)

- Decorate preK and early elementary school classrooms in multiple languages. For example, buy bilingual reading rugs or floor mats that have colors, numbers, shapes, or school supplies in both English and another language. You can also label classroom items (e.g., window, chair, table, cabinet) in both English and the home languages your students speak.

- Build a bilingual or polylingual classroom library. Prominently display picture books in different languages—making sure to include the languages your students speak at home—and incorporate them into class read-alouds and independent reading time.

- When teaching social studies or ELA units focused on other countries or on indigenous or immigrant cultures, take time to research the relevant languages and introduce them to students. For example, when 4th grade teacher Leah taught a social studies unit on Western Europe, she displayed flags of Spain, Portugal, France, and the United Kingdom with phrases such as *hello* and *How are you?* translated to Spanish, Portuguese, and French.

Special Considerations for Secondary School Teachers (6–12)

- Invite speakers from non-English-speaking backgrounds, including students' parents, and encourage them to incorporate their native language into their presentations. For high school Spanish teacher Marlene, this includes having presenters from various Spanish-speaking countries present on where they are from so students are exposed to different dialects across the Spanish-speaking world.

- Create a translingual learning environment that encourages students to speak, write, and present content in the language or languages of their choice. For example, the School Kids Investigating Language in Life and Society (SKILLS) program is a university-school partnership that works with K–12 public schools to "support and develop the full repertoire of cultural and linguistic practices that young people engage in with their communities, families, and peer groups" (Bucholtz, Casillas, & Lee, 2017, p. 48). The program gives students space to identify and valorize the cultural linguistic practices that are a part of their lived experiences through activities such as giving public presentations, serving as language brokers at parent-teacher conferences, and advocating to change school policy for graduation speeches to be in multiple languages.

Element 7 in Action: Bilingual Read-Aloud

First grade teacher Shauna took Spanish in high school, but she hadn't felt a need to put her language skills to use until she started teaching at an elementary school where many of her students came from Mexico and Central America. Motivated by the desire to "communicate with students and parents beyond just *hello*," she began working on improving her Spanish to feel comfortable with basic conversations. She used the Duolingo app to refresh her Spanish because it's available on her phone and she could practice anywhere and anytime she had a few minutes.

Bilingual Spanish-English books were an effective vehicle Shauna used to drive home the importance of multilingualism in the classroom and simultaneously practice her Spanish. She filled her classroom library with bilingual books and often chose them for her daily class read-aloud. For example, one afternoon she selected the book *The Empanadas That Abuela Made* by Diane Gonzales Bertrand. She read the English and then the Spanish translation. After she read the first line in Spanish, one of her native Spanish-speaking students said excitedly, "*¡Español!*" Another said, "*Muy bien, muy bien!*" applauding Shauna for her efforts in pronouncing Spanish words.

Shauna and her students continued to highlight Spanish vocabulary throughout the story. One student raised her hand and pointed out, "They keep saying *calabaza*. That means a pumpkin."

"What is *milk* in Spanish?" Shauna asks, pointing to a picture in the book.

Students call out in response: "*Leche!*" As a result of her approach, Shauna's students became extremely engaged in the story and were able to showcase their Spanish expertise and see their culture valued during official learning time.

Further Developing This Skill

- Conduct a home language survey for all your students. (Alternatively, if your school already conducts home language surveys, request access to them.) Use that data to run a needs assessment. What resources do you already have and what do you need to communicate with families in their respective languages? How can you incorporate those languages into the classroom?

- Download and start using language learning apps and software to begin familiarizing yourself with a language spoken by your students.
- Research opportunities to immerse yourself in a setting where you are a linguistic "other"—either through travel abroad or in cultural spaces within your city or community (e.g., ethnic markets and restaurants, places of worship, civic organizations). Reflect on how you felt and how you sought to understand an unfamiliar language.

Continuing the Journey

Explore these additional resources as you move forward in your development of communicating in multiple languages.

⊙ 4 Reasons to Learn a New Language

(www.ted.com/talks/john_mcwhorter_4_reasons_to_learn_a_new_language): This TED talk by linguist John McWhorter provides a compelling argument for learning new languages.

⊙ The Benefits of a Bilingual Brain

(www.youtube.com/watch?v=MMmOLN5zBLY): This five-minute video explains how the bilingual brain works and what its cognitive benefits are.

⊙ Duolingo

(www.duolingo.com): This is a free website and app that provides bite-sized lessons in 32 different languages.

⊙ LingQ

(www.lingq.com): This is an online language learning website and app that includes 18 languages and allows you to read and listen to content in the language you are learning, track and save vocabulary, and connect with native speakers in a global online community.

❍ Language Lizard

(www.languagelizard.com): This resource sells bilingual children's books in more than 50 different languages. It also sells multilingual posters and provides lesson plans on multiculturalism that celebrates the diversity in our communities.

8

Creating a Classroom Environment That Values Diversity and Global Engagement

Creating the right classroom environment for global learning is the foundation for building global learning experiences and cultivating international collaborations. Such activities emerge more organically and produce more fruitful results if you first develop students' curiosity and desire to learn about the world. When students have this motivation, they will beg you to find global examples to bring into the curriculum. They may even draw their own connections and find their own examples, which makes your work easier!

In other words, creating a classroom environment that values diversity and global engagement is about fostering in students the motivation to acquire global skills and knowledge. Some of your students may already have this inclination. Many already possess a deep curiosity about different places and cultures or have firsthand knowledge from traveling or living in other countries or living in a multicultural home. Those students can help spark the interest of peers who may not initially find these topics exciting or relevant to their lives. Alternatively, students who may not have considered engaging with diverse people and perspectives might be enticed by your excitement and the ways in which global awareness can help them in their personal and future professional lives. This chapter provides ideas for piquing your students' interest in learning about diverse perspectives, cultures, and global issues.

What Does a Classroom That Values Diversity and Global Engagement Look Like?

What do teachers do to create a classroom environment in which students are interested in learning more about diverse cultures and engaging in discussions about global issues from a variety of perspectives? They model culturally responsive and sustaining teaching practices, fill their classrooms with resources that represent the diversity of places and people around the world, and guide students to collaborate with those who hold different ideas and worldviews.

Teachers often spend a considerable amount of time preparing their classrooms. They buy borders, colorful posters with inspirational quotes, and various other supplies for their students. However, many of the ingredients needed for creating an environment that is welcoming to diverse learners cannot be purchased in a store and do not involve the aesthetics of a classroom. Rather, this kind of environment must be accomplished through the tone teachers set. This includes establishing a classroom management plan that is flexible and inclusive, and one that is centered around openness, respect, and consideration of others. That tone is set by teachers' instructional strategies and their ability to respect and value all students.

When students' cultures differ from the school's dominant culture, either teachers can encourage students to adapt or conform to the dominant culture, *or* they can actively sustain the home cultures of students in order to affirm their identities and draw on the many benefits of a multicultural classroom. The former approach is grounded in the deficit orientation that students of nondominant backgrounds are at a cultural disadvantage and need to adopt mainstream norms in order to succeed in life (Ladson-Billings, 1995). Global classrooms, however, take the latter approach. This approach recognizes the harm done to children when their culture is treated as inferior and in need of replacement and instead embraces culturally sustaining pedagogy, which "seeks to perpetuate and foster—to sustain—linguistic, literate, and cultural pluralism as part of the democratic project of schooling" (Paris, 2012, p. 93). This means that students are not expected to adopt a shared culture but rather take pride in who they are and how their uniqueness makes the classroom, and the world, a richer place.

Whereas some teachers have the privilege of working with culturally and linguistically diverse students, other teachers may have more homogenous student populations. There are still plenty of ways to bring the diversity of the world into the classroom, such as through virtual and in-person partnerships. (See Chapter 11 for concrete examples.) Regardless of the cultural composition of students, globally competent teachers are intentional about modeling their appreciation of diverse people, places, and perspectives.

Self-Reflection and Implementation Tips for Creating a Classroom Environment That Values Diversity and Global Engagement

Look at Figure 8.1 and rate yourself along the GCLC for the element "Create a classroom environment that values diversity and global engagement."

1. Where do you rate yourself and why?
2. What steps do you need to take to move along the continuum?

The following implementation tips will help you think through the next steps you can take to foster conditions that will help your students value diversity and global engagement.

Celebrate and sustain the diversity within your own classroom. Your classroom should not simply tolerate diversity; it should do much more. It should actively sustain students' cultural and linguistic competences and cultivate students' pride in their heritage. At the same time, several precautions should be taken. First, remember that cultures are not static but dynamic and adaptable to new contexts and circumstances (Paris, 2012). Second, it is important not to assume students of a particular background will have particular interests, knowledge, or characteristics. Thus, getting to know every

Figure 8.1 | Create a Classroom Environment That Values Diversity and Global Engagement

Element	Nascent ——→	Beginning ——→	Progressing ——→	Proficient ——→	Advanced
Create a Class-room Envi-ronment That Values Diver-sity and Global Engagement	I do not yet consider global issues or diverse perspectives and cultures in my classroom.	I discuss global engagement and the value of diverse perspec-tives and cultures in my classroom.	• I engage students in learning about other cultures by emphasizing the relevance of global issues to students' lives. • I teach my stu-dents to respect diverse per-spectives and cultures. • My class-room contains resources that represent multiple global perspectives.	• I teach my stu-dents to respect and learn from diverse per-spectives and cultures. • I provide opportunities for students to collaboratively discuss global issues. • I consistently encourage students to use resources in my classroom for global learning.	I help my students develop a concern for global issues, an interest in learning more about diverse cul-tures, and a desire to take action.

student as a unique individual, not just a member of a cultural group, is essential. From these one-on-one relationships, you can learn about each student's cultural traditions and how they may converge or diverge with others' traditions. Finally, be careful not to ask students to speak for an entire culture, even if it is a culture with which they identify. Putting them on the spot in such a way can evoke anxiety and a fear of misrepresenting a whole group of people. Let students volunteer to share what they know. If you have created an environment that values diversity, students will be eager to do so.

One way to sustain students' home cultures is to draw on their funds of knowledge. *Funds of knowledge* refers to "historically accumulated and culturally developed bodies of knowledge and skills essential for household or individual functioning and well-being" (Moll, Amanti, Neff, & Gonzalez, 2001, p. 133). Create opportunities for students to share the knowledge and skills they have learned in their homes and neighborhoods and that may not typically be valued in a school setting. One 1st grade teacher shared that, during her lesson on the life cycle of plants, several of her Latinx students were excited to share the wealth of knowledge they had gained from helping in their families' gardens. Other students may have math skills from helping their families grocery shop or an ability to manipulate fractions from cooking and working with recipes.

Ethnomathematics examines the connections between math and culture by having students study mathematical concepts they utilize as part of their everyday cultural practices. Examples include traditional units of measurement common among Bedouins (Amit & Abu Quoder, 2017) and exploring the Navajo *hooghan*, or traditional building, to teach spatial geometry from a Navajo worldview (Pinxten, 1994). Doing so affirms the cultural dignity of students, particularly students of color who have often felt marginalized in Eurocentric math classrooms (D'Ambrosio, 2001).

Model respectful interactions and excitement around global issues. Model to students how interested you are in learning new things about the world and its kaleidoscope of people. By valuing the diversity in your classroom community, children will be more motivated to learn about cultures, languages, and people that differ from their personal backgrounds and experiences. Students will also look to you to set the standard of how to respond to challenges or disagreements around topics discussed in class. (Indeed, when students feel comfortable enough to vocalize divergent opinions, that is a sign you have created a classroom environment that values a diversity of perspectives!)

If a student disputes a statement you have made, use it as an opportunity to model how to appropriately respond during a disagreement. Don't say, "You're wrong" or "That's incorrect"; such statements reinforce a singular, teacher-is-always-right perspective. If the dispute was done in a respectful manner, thank the student for having the courage to push back against you. This will help foster an environment in which students feel comfortable practicing the important democratic skill of speaking up when they have a different viewpoint. After thanking the student, you could ask him or her to expand on their thought process (for example, say, "That's a really interesting point you made. Why do you say that?" or "Say more about why you said that").

Another good habit to model is paraphrasing what students say so you can demonstrate how to check with a speaker to ensure you have interpreted the message correctly. The student will either confirm that your interpretation was correct or clarify his or her statement. Only then should you proceed to share your response to the dispute. The class may not realize you are modeling how to respectfully disagree, so you will want to draw their attention to what you are doing and ask follow-up questions to ensure they understood the practice you were attempting to model. Doing so will contribute to an atmosphere in which disagreements are viewed as avenues for learning rather than uncomfortable interactions that should be avoided.

Don't shy away from controversial discussion topics. When considering how to create an environment that welcomes diversity and global engagement, a great place to start is the news—both local and global. What are some topics you can use to increase students' global awareness and help them see an immediate relevance to their lives? Human rights protections, environmental conservation, migration, and food security are all good places to start. Some of these topics, such as migration or global warming, may spark controversy. Strong emotions can emerge in class discussions and teachers may fear they won't know what to say if a potentially hurtful or provocative comment is made. As such, many teachers postpone bringing up controversial topics until they have a more thorough knowledge of the issue, or they may avoid such topics altogether out of fear of parent response or a discomfort with political issues (Avery, Levy, & Simmons, 2013; Hess, 2011).

However, preparing informed citizens who have practice with the democratic process requires teachers to facilitate discussion of controversial issues (Hess, 2011; National Council for the Social Studies, 2016). In fact, discussing difficult issues can help students "clarify and justify their opinions about social and historical events, can improve students' ability to think, increase their awareness of social, political, and environmental issues, be actively engaged in the curriculum, and develop critical decision-making skills" (Byford, Lennon, & Russell, 2009, p. 166). Thus, educators dedicated to developing global citizens who are engaged in the world around them must give students opportunities to practice debating, deliberating, and discussing within a setting that prioritizes respect and openness to new ideas and to revising one's own opinion.

Barton and McCully (2007) offer several recommendations for guiding discussions of sensitive issues. The first is to avoid attempting to suppress students' emotions and instead give them a chance to wind down at the end of a discussion. The second relates to the fact that teachers are often wary of sharing their viewpoints. Be aware that students are likely to infer your position on an issue even if you attempt to remain neutral. Therefore, disclosing your position may not impede students from forming their own opinions independently. Sharing your own uncertainties can be particularly helpful to students who may have doubts and questions themselves but not realize these are normal and even desirable as they keep their minds open to alternative perspectives. Finally, find and activate the diversity within your classroom so a full range of views are available for exploration and consideration.

One popular instructional strategy for doing this is called Four Corners. A variation of this activity involves labeling the four corners of your classroom: *Agree, Disagree, Neutral,* and *Need More Information.* Read a statement and have students move to the corner that best represents their position on the issue. This allows students to see the diversity of opinions existing in the class that may not be visible through class discussions in which only one student speaks at a time. Students can then share their reasoning within and across corners so a variety of views are expressed and compared.

The following sections include implementation tips specific to your developmental level on the GCLC.

Nascent

Encourage students to think beyond themselves and pursue knowledge about different cultures around the world. One way to help students take an interest in the world around them is to have them examine international news articles on a topic they are interested in. Michael, a 7th grade English teacher, has his students investigate the news on a weekly basis to ensure they are engaged in the world around them. After students determine what news story they connect with, they are placed into groups with others who picked the same story. The students then dig deeper into the stories to gain more background information, and, finally, they discuss all aspects of the story as a group. Michael explains that sometimes the conversations can get a little heated, but he allows his students to go through this process to better understand other people's experiences and the diversity of perspectives around any particular issue. By going through this process, his classroom environment truly becomes a place that values others.

You can also encourage dialogue that engages diverse perspectives by taking advantage of the teachable moments that happen within the classroom. These may arise out of students' natural conversations. For example, students may be discussing their plans for the weekend or a holiday break. Insert yourself into the conversation by bringing in information about what students from other places do during holidays or over school breaks. If you don't have such knowledge, prompt your students to consider the possibility that school breaks may occur at different times of the year in other parts of the world. Ask, "I wonder when students in [fill in a country, ideally one the class has studied] have their school breaks and how they use their time off?" or "Why do school breaks differ by country?" Question like these may pique students' interest, inspiring some independent explorations of student life in other parts of the world.

Beginning/Progressing

Begin by designing lessons with the specific goal of relating students' interests to global topics. For instance, many young people are interested in fairness, equality, and human rights. Use these as hooks to spark interest in how people in different parts of the world think about these ideas. You could begin with warm-up questions, such as "Do you think all people deserve the same rights? Why?" or "Do you think societies should strive for equality? Why?" You could talk about how different cultures hold different perspectives on what equality means and how equal rights is sometimes secondary to other values such as the stability of the community or maintaining patriarchal family structures. Students may enjoy the challenge of trying to imagine societies with entirely different value systems than their own.

If students are interested in sports or music, bring in relevant examples that relate to sports or music played in other countries and cultures. High school physical education teacher Marcus provides students with the historical and cultural context of the sports and skills he teaches. During a swimming unit, he shared that the origins of the backstroke came from the Amazon, and during a lesson on surface diving, he explained how it was a leisure sport in West Africa throughout the 19th century. If students are interested in family life, bring in examples of how families are structured differently or engage in different traditions based on cultural values and norms. Students may also be interested in what life is like for kids their age in different countries. Encourage them to ask questions and research the answer. Prompt them to ask questions such as "Do they also take a bus to school? Do they take the same classes? What kinds of foods are served in their school cafeterias? Do they play the same games and sports after school? What kinds of chores do they have to do around their house?"

For resources that help students answer these questions, *The Barefoot Book of Children* (Strickland & DePalma, 2016) is a beautifully illustrated picture book that shows similarities and differences of life for children across cultures. For older students, the PBS documentary *Time for School* follows students from Afghanistan, Benin, Brazil, India, Japan, Kenya, and Romania throughout their educational journey for 12 years. By starting with your students' interests, you can make global perspectives less foreign and detached from their everyday lives.

Exposing misconceptions about other countries can surprise and intrigue students as well. Take advantage of this by having students brainstorm words or ideas that come to mind when they hear about a particular country or continent. Then reveal differences between popular conceptions versus reality. For instance, try having them imagine or sketch images of Africa. Then show photographs of the metropolises of Lagos, Nigeria, or Dar es Salaam, Tanzania, and see how these contrast with ideas students may have had about safaris, poverty, and villages without power or running water. Ask why these misconceptions exist, what the potential negative consequences of these misconceptions might be, and what students can do about them. Can they help inform their peers about the realities of life in other countries? Can they help spread global awareness to others?

Fill your classroom with as many resources as you can find that represent the diversity found in your classroom, community, country, and world. Maps, flags, newspapers, and artwork from different countries; literature by diverse authors; even photos of yourself and your family in different places around the world expose students to the world and can spark informal conversations that pique interest in the wider world. Ensure that your classroom library is representative of diverse people by race, gender, religion, culture, language, and sexual orientation. One resource that can help educators create a diverse learning library is the National Network of State Teachers of the Year

(NNSTOY) social justice booklist. (See Continuing the Journey later in this chapter.) This list covers a variety of books that educators can introduce to their students from PreK to adult.

Proficient/Advanced

Don't let the global resources you bring into your classroom rest on shelves to collect dust or atrophy on walls. Design activities that prompt your students to put these resources to use. Have them compare pieces of art, literary texts, math problems, or scientific projects from two different countries or cultures and analyze how they reveal similarities and differences between the two. Make sure you have reference books in your room and access to computers so students can explore their emerging global interests. Allow students the freedom to come to your room any time they think of a question to research that could expand their global awareness—and maybe even your own! Giving students free rein over your classroom resources will give them a sense of ownership over their global learning, and ownership often yields motivation and engagement.

Help ignite a desire in your students to take action by exposing them to a range of global issues. Such issues could include the environment, child health, working conditions, education for girls, famine, conflict, or animal protection. (See Chapters 1 and 3 for additional examples of global inequities, conditions, and events that might resonate with students.) For example, design a project in which students choose an issue and create an action plan for addressing it, using the skills they are learning in your class. The key here is giving students the time and space to explore cultural concepts and global issues in which they are personally vested, and feeling comfortable going off-script to let those projects morph into innovative ways that students engage with the world.

I know there are those who think, "Where on Earth do I find time in my overloaded schedule for an unplanned three-week inquiry?!" Don't despair. You do not have to create elaborate projects to spark students' desire to act. Merely modeling your own commitment to take action and address global inequities (e.g., climate change, conflict mining, sweatshops, famine, migration) can show students how important these problems are and how people all around the world can do something to address them. Remind them of the phrase "Think globally, act locally." Talk to students about the effects of their purchasing decisions and the power of petitions, letter-writing campaigns, contacting representatives, and of course voting when they are old enough. You've reached your goal if whenever your students learn about a new global issue, their first response is to ask themselves, "What actions, however small, can I take to address this problem?"

Special Considerations for Elementary Students (PK–5)

- Build a positive classroom community as one of the first things you do at the beginning of the school year. The first few weeks of school is a great time to get to know your students and allow them to get to know one another. A powerful way to get to know your students and their families is by doing home visits before or at the beginning of the school year. According to teachers who conduct home visits, home visits help them build stronger relationships with parents and students and contribute to students' improved attendance and achievement (Ernst-Slavit & Mason, n.d.) During the first weeks of class, plan activities that encourage students to share information about themselves, their culture, and their family life. Have them create posters, write autobiographies, or interview a classmate and present what they learn to the class. Emphasize that diversity in cultures and family life add to the richness of your class and that the more different we are from one another, the more we can learn from one another.

- Have students bring in items for show-and-tell that their families allow you to keep displayed in your room for the remainder of the year. Examples include family photos, magazine or newspaper pages, flags, currency, recipes, or articles of clothing. You can also post your own photos of the class so every student sees his or her image proudly displayed in the room.

- Incorporate student-friendly news resources into your language arts or content-area instruction, such as *Time for Kids*, *National Geographic Kids*, or Newsela. Each contains a variety of illustrated articles on global topics, such as current events, the environment, people, and animals, making them a great starting point for global conversations.

Special Considerations for Secondary Students (6–12)

- Get to know your students at the beginning of the year by having them fill out personal interest sheets. You can ask questions about their hobbies, goals, favorite films and musical artists, the topics they like to read and learn about, or anything else that may help you learn more about the unique characteristics of each of your students. Remember to review these throughout the year so you can continually draw connections to students' funds of knowledge and areas of interest.

- Because secondary students are typically quite social and enjoy learning about their peers, even if they live on the other side of the planet, introduce a global issue from the perspective of a young person in another country. How are Cambodian or Indonesian youth affected by working conditions in garment factories? How is air pollution affecting youth in Beijing or migration affecting youth in Jordan? Students might feel greater empathy for strangers of different cultures when they realize they all share some universals of adolescence, such as first loves and rites of passage into adulthood. To help students arrive at these realizations, intercultural conversations such as those described in Chapter 10 can be used as opportunities to compare and contrast experiences.

- Research on youth political engagement suggests that young people are more interested in local issues than national or global ones (Levine, 2007). Therefore, motivate students to take an interest in global issues by showing how they have local effects. Give students concrete examples of how global patterns affect local conditions and how local actions can affect global events. For example, 8-year-old Ryan Hickman was recognized as one of the 2017 CNN Young Wonders for his achievement of engaging his community to recycle 275,000 cans and bottles (CNN Staff, 2017).

Element 8 in Action:
Comparing Music Genres in Spanish-Speaking Countries

Nelson teaches music and band for middle and high school students at an urban, global studies–focused, public magnet school. The school's approximately 700 students are 57 percent black, 27 percent Latinx, and 8 percent white. Nelson continually strives to create a classroom environment that values diversity and global engagement by sharing his own travel experiences and inviting students to share experiences from their own travels or from growing up in other countries. For instance, Nelson tells stories from his time in Costa Rica attending a professional development program, which then prompts many of his students to describe how his observations are similar to or different from what they experience in their own homes and cultures.

Nelson explains, "The students heard about Costa Rica the first three months of school. There is so much that I learned that they could appreciate. We had dialogues for extended periods of times. They, especially the Hispanic students, were able to relate, and the Hispanic students were able to educate their neighbor who did not have a similar background as to how their family sometimes operates."

Nelson also exposes students to musical resources that represent cultures in different parts of the world. For example, he has students sing and play songs in Spanish so they are exposed to world languages while advancing their musical performance skills. This familiarity with a new language has sparked students' interest in learning more about new languages and culture. Students ask questions about what the words in the song mean. To respond to students' queries, he teaches the difference between *un* and *una* in Spanish, for example, and how the noun gender determines which article to use.

Nelson further expands his curriculum beyond the content of musical compositions to encourage students to take an interest in global cultures. For instance, whenever he introduces a new musical genre, he provides background knowledge of the geographic location of the country of origin and the history and politics of that country's music education systems. His students have learned about Mexico, Paraguay, and Venezuela, to name just a few. During one lesson, he taught about Venezuela's *El Sistema*, a program that provides free classical music lessons to children living in poverty. Learning that the Venezuelan government provides much of the funding for El Sistema created an opportunity for the class to discuss the ways in which politics and music sometimes interact. Through this conversation, students developed an interest not only in Venezuelan music but also in learning more about the politics of Venezuela and other countries in general. As the imaginary boundaries between music class, social studies, and other subjects gradually faded away, so too did the boundaries between what students found interesting and what they didn't.

Further Developing This Skill

- Learn about the cultural backgrounds of your students' families through writing assignments, student surveys, and home visits. Then work with this information and your students' families to find ways to incorporate their cultural knowledge into the classroom.
- Conduct a resource inventory of your classroom and/or school to see how many different countries/cultures are represented. Invite your colleagues to help create a visual display of this diversity on a hallway bulletin board or another public space. For example, represent each country with a flag or each culture with artwork from an artist of that culture. Have students help you decide how to represent the information. Consider having them create pieces of the display themselves.
- Design a project that allows students to think globally and act locally. Collectively come up with a list of global issues students want to address based on discussions you've had during the year. Then help them brainstorm local actions they can take to affect their global issue of choice (e.g., letter writing, boycotting, creating public service announcements).

Continuing the Journey

Explore these additional resources as you move forward in your development of creating a classroom that values diversity and global engagement.

❯ Asia Society: Children's Literature Builds Global Competence
(https://asiasociety.org/education/childrens-literature-builds-global-competence): This site provides lists of children's books and online interactive books, as well as guiding questions to help students develop global perspectives.

❯ Smithsonian Center for Folklife and Cultural Heritage
(https://folklife.si.edu/education#resources): This center provides resources to help educators teach about cultural heritage through various subject areas. The website includes online exhibits, lesson plans, and videos about cultures from around the world.

❯ CNN 10
(www.cnn.com/cnn10): Formerly known as CNN Student News, CNN 10 is a daily digital video that presents international news stories and their significance from multiple viewpoints.

❯ TeachUNICEF
(https://schools.unicefkidpower.org): TeachUNICEF is a portfolio of global education units, lesson plans, stories, videos, and other multimedia components covering a variety of global issues and topics ranging from the Millennium Development Goals to poverty and water and sanitation.

❯ Curriculum21 Global Partnership Resource Hub
(www.c21hub.com/globalpartnership): The Global Competence Resource Hub provides links to projects, initiatives, books, and other classroom activities that engage students with the world.

❯ National Network of State Teachers of the Year (NNSTOY) Social Justice Booklist
(www.nnstoy.org/wp-content/uploads/2017/08/NNSTOY-Social-Justice-Book-List.pdf): This list of books related to equity, equality, and fairness is divided by early elementary (PK–3), elementary (4–6), middle (7–9), and high school (10–adult). There are also books for teachers.

9

Integrating Global
Learning Experiences

"I would love to engage my students in global learning, but I don't have the time because of standards and curriculum requirements." This common refrain, which is often recited among educators, propagates the misconception that teachers must choose between the content they are mandated to teach and global learning experiences for students. This could not be further from the truth. The two are not mutually exclusive. Students may need to master state standards and take a specific sequence of courses to check off the requirements for graduation, but educators truly committed to preparing students for college, career, and citizenship can create opportunities to develop global competence while simultaneously meeting subject-specific standards.

The skill of integrating global learning experiences that promote content-aligned explorations of the world plays an integral role here. This skill allows educators to infuse learning opportunities that foster global competence into what they are already required to teach, including dispositions and knowledge related to global inequities, global conditions and current events, global interconnectedness, and multiple cultures. This ensures that all students, regardless of the courses in which they are enrolled, have an opportunity to develop global competence.

Educators' plates are already full. Rather than trying to squeeze an extra scoop of mashed potatoes on top of an overcrowded dinner plate, integrating global learning into the standard course of study is akin to drizzling gravy over the turkey, stuffing, and potatoes. It provides a richer, more enticing learning experience for students.

What Does It Mean to Integrate Global Learning Experiences?

Educators who integrate learning experiences that promote content-aligned investigations of the world incorporate global learning into everyday instruction and connect students to the world beyond the classroom. They do not see global learning as an add-on—a special elective course for a select group of high-achieving students, a unit tacked on to the end of the school year, or a lesson taught the Friday afternoon before spring break. They understand that global learning is a way to teach the standard course of study that looks at content-area objectives through a global lens. When integrating global learning experiences, educators align global connections, content, and perspectives to rigorous content-area standards and use a constructivist approach to learning that allows students to explore the world beyond their school, community, and country.

First, global learning can—and should—occur across content areas (Kirkwood, 2001b; Mansilla & Jackson, 2011; O'Connor & Zeichner, 2011). As Vivian Stewart (2010) argues, "Every discipline can be given a global perspective. International education is not a separate subject but an analytical framework that can transform curriculum and instruction in every discipline and provide rich content for interdisciplinary work" (p. 105). Consider the following examples:

- A social studies teacher tasked with teaching the foundations of American constitutional government plans a lesson in which students compare the formation and fundamental principles of the U.S. Constitution to constitutions in different nations.
- The collection of literature that a language arts teacher selects to use throughout the year represents authors and settings from an array of

countries and covers global themes such as civil rights, human trafficking, refugees, immigration, and revolutions.

- To teach the standard of multiplying fractions and mixed numbers, a 4th grade teacher asks students to investigate recipes from different countries that are associated with popular holidays from those regions. They are then asked to double, triple, and quadruple the recipes.
- A high school algebra teacher provides students with data on the spread of the Ebola and Zika viruses to practice creating models.
- A music teacher uses different musical genres from Central and South America to teach music method standards, such as developing tone and discerning pitch, using expressive elements, and interpreting standard musical notation.

As these examples show, global learning directly aligns with state standards.

Global learning explorations can also take place through interdisciplinary study. A 6th grade language arts teacher and a social studies teacher coteach a unit on media bias, during which students explore a current event of their choosing from multiple media sources across and within countries; examine the connotations of authors' word choice; and identify the political, cultural, and social factors that may have shaped authors' biases from different outlets. Before students learn a new song from a different region or country, a band teacher builds background knowledge on the geography of where that piece of music originated, its historical context, and the language in which it is sung. Though it requires more time and energy to plan, and oftentimes takes dedicated coordination across departments, interdisciplinary explorations most accurately depict the world as a system and global issues as multifaceted phenomena (O'Connor & Zeichner, 2011). As students make connections across content areas, the potential for knowledge building expands (Selby & Pike, 2001).

Second, a constructivist teaching philosophy is at the heart of global learning explorations. Constructivism posits that learners actively build knowledge of the world through subjective experiences and interactions with their environment. Instructional practices, based on constructivism, include student-centered, inquiry-based, problem-based, and project-based learning. They follow these general principles: learning is anchored to a challenging problem or question; students engage in authentic tasks that have relevance in the world beyond the classroom and have meaning to students' lives; students feel ownership over the learning activity; students socially construct meaning through collaborative group work that forces them to test ideas against alternative views and contexts; and students reflect on the learning process and outcomes (Larmer, Mergendoller, & Boss, 2015; Wilson, 1996). This stands in direct contrast to a transmissive instruction, or what Paulo Freire (1970) categorized as a "banking" concept of education, wherein teachers transmit or "deposit" knowledge to students.

In the context of global learning, constructivist pedagogy allows students to build knowledge about global issues they consider important through the lens of various countries, cultures, and perspectives (Merryfield, 1998; O'Connor & Zeichner, 2011). When empowered to guide their own learning, students learn about issues that resonate with them; as a result, this leads to increased engagement and enlightenment. As Selby and Pike (2001) explain, "Children learn best when encouraged to explore and discover for themselves and when addressed as individuals with a unique set of beliefs, experiences, and talents" (p. 11).

Self-Reflection and Implementation Tips for Integrating Global Learning

Look at Figure 9.1 and rate yourself along the GCLC for the element "Integrating learning experiences that promote content-aligned explorations of the world."

1. Where do you rate yourself and why?
2. What steps do you need to take to move along the continuum?

The following implementation tips will help you think through next steps you can take to improve how you integrate content-aligned explorations of

Figure 9.1 | Integrate Learning Experiences That Promote Content-Aligned Explorations of the World

Element	Nascent	Beginning	Progressing	Proficient	Advanced
Integrate Learning Experiences That Promote Content-Aligned Explorations of the World	I do not yet include global learning experiences aligned with content standards.	I can identify global learning experiences that align with content standards.	I integrate into my instruction global learning experiences aligned with my students' interests and content standards.	I regularly integrate real-world and challenging global learning experiences aligned with my students' interests and content standards.	• I reflect on my students' global learning experiences and revise my teaching accordingly. • I support the school community in integrating global learning experiences.

the world into your classroom, regardless of what grade levels and subject areas you teach.

Know your students and the issues that affect them. Students are more likely to be engaged in learning when they know their teachers care for them (Valenzuela, 1999) and when the learning has direct relevance to their lives and future (Bridgeland, Dilulio, & Morison, 2006; Marks, 2000). Getting to know students by forming caring relationships with them can provide rich insights into the issues they care most about. Such relationships are built through open, ongoing dialogue wherein teachers listen and respond to the circumstances and needs of their students (Noddings, 2005; Valenzuela, 1999). Caring teachers are able to foster such dialogue by asking students about their academic, social, and home lives; opening up to share information about themselves; making themselves accessible to students outside class; offering academic and social-emotional guidance; reaching out to students' families; and staying attuned to the political, cultural, and social realities of the communities where students live (Tichnor-Wagner & Allen, 2016).

For example, a group of boys in 5th grade teacher Taylor's class in a Title I elementary school in Phoenix, Arizona, came to school every day with baseball gloves, quick to share stories about their exploits in the previous day's game. At the same time, students were murmuring with worry about SB1070, a recent immigration law in Arizona that threatened to detain and deport many students' family members who had immigrated from Mexico and Central America. When selecting novels for students to use for their next book group, Taylor provided *In the Year of the Boar and Jackie Robinson*, the story of a girl who emigrates from China to New York after World War II, as an option. Students gravitated to the book, which allowed them to explore questions related to immigration, such as why families move to new countries and the challenges kids face when they have to adjust to a new culture.

You can also gather information about student interest in specific global topics through formal activities. At the beginning of the school year, have students fill out a survey about their hobbies and interests to keep on file throughout the year. Before embarking on a new literature or math unit, have students rank their interest in global themes the class might explore through words or numbers. Place a suggestion box in your classroom where students can submit topics they want to explore. Surveys and suggestion boxes shouldn't be symbolic. Students should see that you use the information they provide in shaping classroom instruction.

Know your content area. Global competence is grounded in disciplinary and interdisciplinary study (Mansilla & Jackson, 2011). The traditional content-area disciplines (e.g., science, English language arts, math, history, arts) provide concepts, thinking tools, and methods through which one makes sense of the world. Take, for example, the topic of immigration. From a mathematics lens, you could graph ebbs and flows of immigration rates from different countries to understand change over time and the push-and-pull factors that may have influenced the direction of the graph. From a language arts lens, you could read a series of stories with protagonists who immigrate to a new country and then compare the similarities and differences in their perspectives and experiences. From a social studies perspective, you could explore the rights of immigrants and refugees along with the process of naturalization in different countries.

Having a firm grasp of the scope and sequence of the discipline(s) you teach makes it far easier to determine where and how to insert global content and perspectives. For example, when students in Justin's 3rd grade class expressed concern about water shortages due to the drought in their home state of California, Justin made the connection to math standards about estimation and measurement. When that unit came up in his district's curriculum map, Justin incorporated an exploration in which students estimated and measured their own water use and devised ways to conserve it.

Knowing your content area can help with interdisciplinary units based around a global theme, as it allows you to more easily determine the connection points between the theme of interest and the standard course of study. For example, a language arts teacher, social studies teacher, and math teacher might team up for a unit on immigration and refugees. The language arts teacher could incorporate standards on informational text as students read news and opinion articles about the refugee crisis in Europe that reflect different points of view. The social studies teacher could tie in content related to how geography plays a role in migratory paths and the historical antecedents leading to the current influx of refugees to Europe. The math teacher could have students use descriptive statistics to understand the ebbs and flows of migration patterns over time.

As a practical note, schools typically organize instruction by discipline. The same goes for government-mandated standards. Therefore, integrating global learning into the content you are already required to teach solves the perennial issue of time. You don't need to add global learning onto an already packed curriculum. It is aligned with what you are already required to teach.

Wear a global lens when planning for and conducting instruction. When planning lessons, ask yourself where global content and perspectives naturally fit into what you already teach. Does an earth science unit on volcanoes lend itself to explorations of volcanoes in different regions of the world? Can a math lesson on exponents lead to an investigation of population growth? What if, when teaching a unit on persuasive text, students take a stand on an issue they deem globally important? Don't be shy about unleashing your creativity! To keep global integration at the forefront of your mind when planning, it can be beneficial to place a "global connections" section into whatever template you use to lesson plan. Figure 9.2 provides specific examples of how you can infuse a global lens in different content areas.

Veronica Boix Mansilla (2016) of Harvard's Project Zero further suggests that teachers insert global thinking routines into any lesson to provide students with a global lens to wear. One such global thinking routine, The Three Whys, prompts students at the beginning of a lesson to ask, "Why does this topic matter to me, the people around me, and the world?" These questions motivate students to explore a new topic in depth while aiding them in the discovery of local-global connections. Another routine, How Else and Why, prompts students to reflect on what it is they want to say and multiple other ways they can say it and why. This is a means of fostering students' ability to communicate with diverse audiences.

Figure 9.2 | Global Integration Across Content Areas

Content Area	Examples of Global Integration
Math	• Use real-world data sets on population, wealth, trade, and disease as the basis for practicing arithmetic and algebraic skills. • Learn techniques for various numerical skills used in different cultures. • Explore geometry, patterns, and symmetry through artwork, architecture, and traditional clothing across cultures.
Science	• Examine advantages and disadvantages of different means of energy production. • Explore the effect of climate change on ecosystems around the world. • Examine water pollution and usage around the world.
Language Arts	• Read books, stories, poems, and plays written by authors from diverse cultures around the world. • Use literature to explore global themes and diverse perspectives. • Analyze nonfiction text (e.g., news stories, textbooks) for examples of stereotyping and bias of global themes.
Social Studies	• Explore political, social, and economic trends across different countries. • Read articles on the same current event from newspapers around the world. • Examine the effect of colonization from immigrant and indigenous perspectives. • Compare various world maps and the underlying assumptions they hold.
Music	• Teach songs from musical genres that represent different cultural traditions. • Play musical instruments from different countries. • Examine how different musicians from around the world discuss a particular topic in their music, and consider how this music enables students to understand the topic from different perspectives.
Art	• Virtually visit art museums in different parts of the world. • Connect pieces of art created in different time periods and regions to their cultural, social, and political contexts. • Examine paintings or photographs from around the world that reflect each artist's rendering of school (for example), and compare those images with students' own renderings of school.
Physical Education	• Incorporate physical activities popular in different parts of the world (e.g., cricket, tai chi). • Explore the origins of team sports and their spread around the world. • Consider what it means to play a favorite sport in another country (e.g., playing soccer in Syria versus the United States versus Brazil).

Source: Examples compiled from Asia Society (2009), Pike and Selby (2001), and various teacher interviews.

Reach out to colleagues. Seek out your grade-level or departmental team to map out lessons and units with global connections. The power of collaboration is mighty, as each of us has unique global experiences and perspectives to contribute. For example, Shauna, a 1st grade teacher in an ethnically diverse urban school, explained that working with four other teachers on her grade-level team during weekly planning sessions created more opportunities for her students to make connections between the curriculum and the world. The team came up with resources and knowledge from their personal and professional international experiences that enhanced every lesson with global perspectives.

Work with colleagues across departments to share resources or plan interdisciplinary units of inquiry. When planning a global book study unit that included a book report and exploration of the country where the book was set, middle school language arts teacher Kate reached out to her media specialist. Together, they compiled an annotated list of books in the school library set outside the United States. Kate's students could then use this list to choose books they want to read.

The following are implementation tips specific to your developmental level on the GCLC.

Nascent

Identify areas in your course of study where you can plug global content and perspectives into existing lessons. Elementary, middle, and high school math teachers have created word problems related to current events or that take place in a different country. One 4th grade teacher described how she turned a standard math lesson on converting fractions into decimals and percents into an exploration of population demographics and languages spoken in different countries. Each answer was in response to a question, such as "What percent of the population in China speaks Cantonese?"

First grade teacher Shauna regularly provides examples from different parts of the world when introducing new units. To introduce a unit on bridges, she showed her class pictures of bridges in different countries. During a unit on plants, students compared rice, corn, and wheat seeds; mapped their origins;

and reflected on how those seeds influenced the food eaten in different cultures. For a unit on rocks, she showed beaches all around the world. Students were amazed to see that some beaches had black sand, which opened up a line of student questioning on why sand is different colors in different locations. Eighth grade science teacher Simone similarly makes sure to insert lots of global examples into her lessons. As she explains, "When I teach oceans, I talk about oceans around the world and how different cultures use their ocean resources."

Think about what units make the most sense for the first steps into content-aligned global learning experiences. If you teach all subjects in an elementary school classroom, an obvious and easy entryway into global content might be through social studies geography standards. If you teach middle school language arts, use a book such as *A Long Walk to Water* or *I Am Malala* to teach key ideas and details of literature. If you teach high school biology, you might determine that it makes the most sense to begin talking about global issues in units on ecology. You will find that the more you plan lessons with a global lens, the easier it will be to incorporate global learning into different subject areas and units.

Global education experts Homa Sabet Tavangar and Becky Mladic-Morales (2014) remind us, "As simple tweaks or new ideas are infused into existing lessons, a global mindset—like a muscle that's always been there—will get stronger and be used more often. Students and teachers will create more extensions to the larger world and diverse cultures, more naturally, particularly as experience grows" (p. 68).

Beginning/Progressing

Design a unit of inquiry around a global issue that interests students and can be taught within the confines of your content-area standards. Familiarize yourself with guidelines of effective project-based, inquiry-based, or student-centered instruction to guide the planning and execution of the unit. A number of frameworks and professional development resources are available that can help you and your school in this process:

- Project-based learning can be used as a tool for global learning as it directly engages students in the world around them while focusing on complex issues, problem solving, and taking action (Miller, 2017). The Buck Institute for Education's (2015) framework for Gold Standard Project Based Learning includes eight essential project design elements: (1) key knowledge, understanding, and success skills; (2) challenging problem or question; (3) sustained inquiry; (4) authenticity; (5) student voice and choice; (6) reflection; (7) critique and revision; and (8) public product. (See www.bie.org for more information.)

- The Asia Society and Council of Chief State School Officers created a checklist for teaching global competence alongside examples of how teachers can engage students in learning explorations that require them to investigate the world. These explorations frame significant problems around which students can conduct research, recognize their own and others' perspectives, communicate ideas to diverse audiences, and take action based on their findings (Mansilla & Jackson, 2011).

- The International Baccalaureate programs (www.ibo.org) focus on "structured, purposeful inquiry that engages students actively in their own learning." The Primary Years Program incorporates six interdisciplinary global themes that students explore across the curriculum: who we are, where we are in place and time, how we express ourselves, how the world works, how we organize ourselves, and sharing the planet. The Middle Years Program organizes the curriculum around teaching and learning in a global context; conceptual understanding of personal, locally, and globally significant issues; approaches to learning; service as action; and language and identity.

Proficient/Advanced

Allow students to design and implement global explorations based on authentic issues they want to understand and help solve. Instead of thinking about how you can plug global topics into your content areas, start with a global topic of interest to your students, and explore how it can be studied through disciplinary lenses. Seventh grade social studies teacher Mike, who teaches at a suburban IB middle school, ends many of his units with a final assignment on something that affects them now or will affect them in the future. In one instance, students were asked to update or create an invention in a field of their choosing—farming, education, medicine, film—in order to make improvements on the future.

Work with other teachers in your school to create interdisciplinary global explorations. When students in a Florida high school expressed concern about the spread of the Zika virus, a high school biology and statistics teacher joined forces to create an interdisciplinary unit on the spread of virus- and bacteria-driven diseases. Students researched the cellular biology to learn how specific diseases such as Zika and Ebola spread, and they then used publicly available datasets to create models for how those diseases spread transnationally.

Take time to share with colleagues the success and challenges you've faced when implementing global learning experiences for students. Sixth grade language arts teacher Kate emphasized the importance of supporting colleagues who have not yet begun implementing global learning explorations. She shared, "I was pleasantly surprised last year when I presented a project on clean water that teachers really were receptive to it and wanted to participate. The main thing that we can do is actually give teachers resources and ideas because if you don't really know where to start with global learning, it can be really intimidating."

Spiral this learning across the school year. After each exploration, reflect on the learning process and outcomes that took place, individually and together with the teachers with whom you planned or cotaught the unit of inquiry. Reflective questions you might ask yourself include "How well did our students meet the learning objectives? In what ways did our students expand their global awareness? What areas provided some challenges for them? How could we address these challenges in future units?" Use your reflections to revise how you facilitate the next global exploration.

Special Considerations for Elementary School Teachers (PK–5)

- Students are never too young to build the foundational mindsets, knowledge, and skills of global citizenship. We have witnessed enlightened discussions of 1st and 2nd grade students articulating the importance of learning about natural disasters in different parts of the world and the need to recycle and reduce waste. At the same time, it is important to be mindful of what is developmentally appropriate for younger children when teaching about sensitive global topics.

- While it may seem easiest to use social studies as the sole subject for global learning, remember that student learning is enhanced when integrating global topics into all subject areas.

- Create interdisciplinary units across the content areas you teach or introduce a monthly theme on a global topic that permeates across different content-area lessons. For example, a unit on protecting the environment might include reading books on environmental protection, creating math problems that require data gathering on environmental topics (e.g., creating tables and graphs of how much plastic is consumed by individual students), learning about threatened ecosystems in science, and writing a story from the perspective of an endangered species.

Special Considerations for Secondary School Teachers (6–12)

- Particularly when teaching tested subject areas, clearly articulate the specific content-area standards your global explorations address.

- Lobby your principal for time to collaborate with teachers in other departments. Cross-departmental planning can both create cross-disciplinary units to deepen student learning and provide you with an additional set of eyes and experiences to help create robust global learning opportunities for your students.

Element 9 in Action: Global Math Stories

Chris teaches 6th–8th grade math at a K–8 school of predominantly white, affluent students in a small southeastern city. As he was simultaneously teaching and working toward a graduate degree in mathematics education, he came upon ethnomathematics—the study of the intersection between mathematics and culture and how people practice mathematics in their native communities. He shared, "One of the very first things I read about was Brazilian street vendors. These boys could do amazing calculations instantly in their heads selling food and goods on the street—better than I could. But in the classroom, you ask them what is 7 – 6 and they say –42. This made me realize the importance of connecting to their real world. The numbers start to dance when you do that."

Chris first introduced ethnomathematics lessons with his students using the example of Brazilian street vendors. Students learned about what life was like for child street vendors in Brazil and set up their own vending booths. Chris recalled, "I would see these kids light up in my classrooms. So that's how I got started with making global connections."

Chris now regularly weaves global connections into math lessons. For five minutes at the beginning of a lesson, he builds background knowledge of a global context—dubbed a "global math story"—to which students apply a recently acquired math skill. Students then spend the bulk of the class solving problems situated in that context. As the lesson comes to an end, Chris asks students to reflect on what their answers reveal about the context. He makes sure that global connections do not come at the cost of students mastering math skills. "[I am] judicious about the concepts that I want to have the story connected to," and he balances these applied lessons with time for students to conceptually understand and practice specific skills. Chris also notes that global math stories are a great way to teach real-world problem solving, which the Common Core State Standards emphasize.

To give students opportunities for ownership over global connections to mathematics, he also asks students to write their own stories based on their unique cultural and intercultural experiences and create math problems based on that context. Chris notes that it is important for students to write stories based on their own culture to teach them that global learning is not just about other people in other countries. Rather, global math stories are a way to showcase that we all have a culture and that each of our cultures is a part of the rich tapestry of humanity.

Further Developing This Skill

- Survey students to see what types of global issues are important to them, and brainstorm how those issues could be incorporated into classroom instruction. Consider providing students with a list of global issues and asking them to rank them in order of importance/urgency.
- Examine your content-area standards to identify areas where global learning could take place.
- Reflect on your style of teaching. Do you feel more comfortable transmitting knowledge to students, or co-constructing knowledge with students? Brainstorm some ways you can take the first steps toward gradually transferring ownership of learning to students.
- Design and implement a lesson that incorporates global explorations. What was successful? What challenges did you face? What would you do differently?

Continuing the Journey

Explore these additional resources as you move forward in your development of integrating global learning experiences.

❯ Global Math Stories

(www.globalmathstories.org): This interactive map contains stories about places all over the world, followed by a series of math questions. Students and educators can submit additional questions to any story or write a new story about anywhere in the world.

◆ iEARN Projects

(http://us.iearn.org/projects): Plan and conduct an online collaborative project with classrooms around the world, or join an existing project, representing all grade levels and subject areas.

◆ Global Literature—Primary Source Resources

(http://resources.primarysource.org/content.php?pid=57875&sid=423830): This resource provides lists of award-winning global and multicultural literature, along with lists of global books for grades K–5, 6–8, and 9–12.

◆ Project Zero Global Thinking

(www.pz.harvard.edu/resources/global-thinking): This toolkit provides a series of thinking routines to help students develop global competence in any content area along with a framework for planning, documenting, and reflecting on the implementation of these routines in your classroom. Routines include The Three Whys, Step In–Step Out–Step Back, How Else and Why, and Circles of Action.

◆ World of Words

(http://wowlit.org): This website and collection, housed at the University of Arizona, provides book lists; culture, language, and culture book kits; and global story boxes to encourage dialogue around global literature.

10

Facilitating Intercultural Conversations

There is no better way to foster understanding, appreciation, and respect for those with different cultures, beliefs, and perspectives from our own than by engaging with them in real conversations. As one educator once shared with us, "It's very difficult to dehumanize someone and treat someone in a negative way if you make that human connection." Engaging in intercultural and international conversations is an authentic way for students to expand their understanding of the world around them and their worldviews, all while helping them develop the intercultural communication skills they need to communicate effectively with people in the communities where they live and travel, in the workforce, and in digital spaces.

Globally competent teachers provide ongoing opportunities for students to connect with individuals from diverse countries and cultures, all while teaching students to listen actively, think critically, and recognize new perspectives. Today, we are in constant contact with people from different cultures—in both physical and virtual spaces. However, contact itself doesn't translate to productive communication; it can in fact lead to the opposite when cultural misunderstandings arise. For example, international study abroad experiences can reinforce stereotypes that students hold about other cultures and peoples if programs don't provide the space for reflection and dialogue (Martin & Griffiths, 2014). As such, fostering healthy and productive dialogues among students and individuals outside their identity groups requires intentionality on the part of the teacher.

What Does It Mean to Facilitate Intercultural Conversations in the Classroom?

As defined in Chapter 6, intercultural communication is concerned with how we interact with people from different cultures. When students are engaged in productive intercultural conversations, they display an ability to engage in the following intercultural conversation skills.

Actively listen. Contrary to linguistic dichotomies that consider listening and reading to be "passive" language skills, listening for understanding is a deeply involved activity. Signs of active listening include displaying engaged body language, asking thoughtful questions based on what students have heard, and confirming or clarifying what students have heard before sharing their own responses. Active listeners do not interrupt, nor do they simply wait to share whatever comment they want to make. In addition, active listeners understand that the "communicative burden" of successful communication is a joint responsibility between speaker and listener. That is, it is equally up to the listener to help make the speaker understood and overcome barriers to understanding (e.g., accents, regional slang) (Lippi-Green, 1997).

Think critically. When engaging in intercultural conversations, students should not take everything they hear at face value or make assumptions based on their own cultural schema. Instead, they should question and analyze why and how to make informed conclusions based on evidence. Specifically, when cultural differences emerge in conversations, students question the origins of those differences and come up with hypotheses about why misunderstandings might occur, recognizing that intentions might be different from what is conveyed (Matsumoto, Hee You, & LeRoux, 2007).

Recognize perspectives. As defined by Robert Hanvey (1982), *perspective consciousness* is "the recognition or awareness on the part of the individual that he or she has a view of the world that is not universally shared, that this view of the world has been and continues to be shaped by influences that escape common detection, and that others have views of the world that are profoundly different from one's own" (p. 162). In intercultural conversations, students can articulate their own point of view and how it is different or similar from others' points of view in a way that is judgment-free. (For example, "I believe _____ because of _____, and I see that you believe _____ instead because of _____.")

Importantly, intercultural conversations should be a *dialogue*: a mutual, reciprocal process through which all participants learn from one another's unique perspectives. As the Tony Blair Faith Foundation (2015) defines it, "An encounter with those who might have different opinions, values, and beliefs to my own, *dialogue* is a process by which I come to understand the other's lives, values, and beliefs better and others come to understand my life, values, and beliefs." Students should not teach about their own culture, community, or country without learning from their conversation partners—nor should they simply listen to someone speak without sharing their own perspectives and ideas.

Teachers can foster intercultural conversations through multiple mediums: face-to-face encounters (e.g., speakers, field trips, welcoming overseas visitors or traveling overseas) or virtual encounters (e.g., videoconferencing, blogging, emails); synchronous conversations at a set date and time or asynchronous conversations (e.g., blogging; pen pals; shared videos, pictures, and other artifacts to a virtual space). The medium you choose can be based on any number of factors, including your comfort level with specific technologies, accessibility, available resources, and time zone differences.

For whatever medium you use, the Tony Blair Faith Foundation (2015) offers tips for creating an effective environment for dialogue and ensuring successful facilitation:

- Create a safe space by building trust among participants, being nonjudgmental, and including everyone's voices equally.
- Prepare ahead of time, including building background knowledge of who your students will be conversing with, having students prepare

questions and discussion points, and confirming logistics with your conversation partners (e.g., topics to be discussed, who will be facilitating, the need for translators, dates and times).

- Set ground rules that are agreed on by everyone and ensure they are observed throughout the conversation.
- Structure the dialogue. For example, begin with introductions and ice-breakers and set the ground rules before diving into meatier discussion topics.
- Monitor the dialogue and ensure that everyone has opportunities to share. Intervene when students are disrespectful or make inappropriate comments.
- Build in time for reflection before, during, and after the conversation.

For language teachers, intercultural conversations are an obvious way for students to practice speaking and listening in the target language and support the World Readiness Standards for Language Learning, which emphasize interpersonal communication, interacting with cultural competence and understanding, and using language to interact with school and global communities (ACTFL, 2015). Intercultural conversations benefit the teaching and learning that goes on in all classrooms, though—not just world languages. For example, the Common Core State Standards English Language Arts Listening and Speaking standards across K–12 require that students participate in collaborative conversations with diverse partners. Furthermore, ask any teacher who engages students in international or intercultural conversations—whether it be writing letters to pen pals or synchronous video chats—and they will tell you that intercultural conversations engage, energize, and motivate students of all ages.

Self-Reflection and Implementation Tips for Facilitating Intercultural and International Conversations

Look at Figure 10.1 and rate yourself along the GCLC for the element "Facilitating intercultural and international conversations."

Figure 10.1 | Facilitate Intercultural and International Conversations

Element	Nascent	Beginning	Progressing	Proficient	Advanced
Facilitate Intercultural and International Conversations	I do not yet provide opportunities for students to converse with individuals from other cultures or nations.	I provide opportunities during the school year for students to converse with individuals from other cultures or nations.	I provide opportunities for students to converse with individuals from other cultures or nations, in which students demonstrate active listening, critical thinking, and/or perspective recognition.	I provide ongoing opportunities for students to converse with individuals from other cultures or nations, in which students demonstrate active listening, critical thinking, and perspective recognition.	My students initiate communication with individuals from across cultures and nations, in which they demonstrate active listening, critical thinking, and perspective recognition.

1. Where do you rate yourself and why?

2. What steps do you need to take to move along the continuum?

For those new to facilitating intercultural conversations, any number of questions may understandably jump out at you. Engaging students with unfamiliar people extends beyond traditional teaching practices of engaging students with static curriculum. For example, you might ask yourself, "How do I put myself out there to even start these conversations for my students? How do I vet people? Where can I find the time amid curricular demands and an overcrowded schedule? How do I overcome language barriers?" The following implementation tips should help assuage these concerns and help make intercultural conversations part and parcel of all students' learning experiences.

Look locally. For many teachers, you don't need to search further than your class roster. Many schools are already microcosms of our diverse world, which gives educators the unique opportunity to facilitate intercultural conversations among student groups who might not otherwise interact or who may not be aware of one another's unique cultural heritage. For example, at the beginning of the school year, have students introduce their cultural backgrounds through icebreaker activities (e.g., presenting a cultural coat of arms, writing "Where I'm From" poems) and engage in Q&As with one another so they develop a deeper knowledge of their peers. These activities can serve as grounds throughout the year for appreciating one another's similarities and differences. It's important to refrain from using students as token representatives of countries, cultures, or religions you may be studying. (For instance, if your 2nd grade class is doing a unit on winter holidays around the world, don't put a Jewish student on the spot and ask him or her to explain how Jews around the world celebrate Hanukkah.) Parents can also be great resources who can share their experiences about specific cultural practices and places in the world they have lived or traveled. Reach out to school staff as well. For example, a high school art teacher in an urban district taught a unit on Día de Muertos (Day of the Dead) and reached out to the predominantly Mexican school maintenance crew to share with her predominantly African American students how they celebrate the holiday with their families.

Your community beyond the school's walls offers a trove of opportunities for intercultural conversations. As described in Chapter 5, colleges and universities often house international students and programs. Connecting with international life on college and university campuses not only benefits your own experiential understanding of multiple cultures but also can be a resource for students. As one example, North Carolina State University's cultural correspondents program paired undergraduate students traveling abroad with local classrooms across the state. The students and local class regularly Skyped to discuss a range of things related to the host country, including the culture, climate, geography, food, education, and topics related to the curriculum. An elementary school teacher who led the program in her school explained, "Some of these things about a country you don't get in textbooks and you have to find out by being there. Students get firsthand knowledge, and when you connect it to the learning in the classroom, because they are having that real experience, the information becomes something they retain a lot longer."

Other types of organizations you might want to consider for intercultural conversations include religious institutions, World Affairs Council offices, and—for those teaching in or nearby major cities—embassies or consulates. The District of Columbia Public Schools run an embassy adoption program, which facilitates a range of planned activities throughout the year and allows 5th and 6th grade students to engage with a diplomat from another country and explore other cultures, languages, history, and perspectives on international issues (https://dcps.dc.gov/page/embassy-adoption-program).

Leverage your professional connections. Take stock of the professional network you already have and actively seek to expand the number of educators and experts you can connect with your students. Reach out to colleagues you've met and friends you've made through previous study or teaching abroad experiences, conferences, and professional associations. For example, after an 11th grade ELA teacher spent the summer on a teaching exchange in India, she engaged her students in a pen pal exchange with students from the school where she taught. Her students created Prezi presentations introducing their own cultures and preferences for food, music, and the like. They also asked questions about things they wanted to learn about their Indian peers. The teacher then emailed the presentations to the school in India.

If you have not yet participated in an international experience, consider applying for fellowships and programs that fund teachers to travel abroad. (See Chapter 5 for lists of these programs.) When participating, make it a personal goal to maintain the relationships with the educators you meet on the program. You can also expand your global professional network without leaving your country—or couch. Twitter, for example, has exploded as a means for educators around the world to connect with one another. By following experts in the field(s) in which you and your students are interested, following hashtags of interest, participating in Twitter chats, and posting lesson plans or advice based on your classroom experience, your professional network and ability to find conversation partners for your students will expand (Pitler, 2017; Ray, 2012). Popular global education hashtags and Twitter chats that can connect you with other globally competent educators include #globaled, #globaledchat, and #TeachSDGs. Once you take the initial step and start making connections, they will begin to snowball. As an elementary school teacher shared, "It's amazing getting connections from places you wouldn't even dream of, and then they have connections who become your connections."

Embrace technology. Virtual exchange greatly expands access for students to engage in intercultural and international conversations. There's a seemingly endless number of platforms and tools that allow you to connect with people from all around the globe, from videochat platforms (e.g., Skype, Zoom, Google Hangouts) to messaging apps (e.g., WhatsApp, Facebook Messenger) to social media to blogging. A growing number of platforms also provide outlets for intercultural and international conversations among educators and students (e.g., Skype in the Classroom, Edmodo, Participate, Generation Global, Global Nomads Group). Research on virtual exchange programs have found them to increase participants' empathy for other cultures and perspectives, develop participants' willingness to engage constructively with peers of different backgrounds and views, and provide an experience of being heard and respected (Virtual Exchange Coalition, 2018).

Embracing technology also means embracing flexibility. As numerous educators who engage in virtual exchanges have advised, accept the fact that no matter how often you test the equipment and your Wi-Fi signal, you will inevitably run into technological snafus. Internet connections might go down or be spotty, software might not download properly, or the partners with whom you are conversing might have a different concept of time. Simply take a deep breath, be patient, and model adaptability in the face of adversity.

Of course, using virtual media to broker intercultural conversations also requires teachers to guide students in navigating digital platforms effectively and act as responsible digital citizens who understand things such as the appropriate use of digital devices, the permanence of their digital footprint, digital etiquette that considers the feelings and perspectives of others, and digital security as they engage in online platforms (Ribble, 2011). While technological proficiency is a valuable outcome of virtual conversations, remember that the core of intercultural conversations is *human* connectedness.

Avoid assumptions. Whether you are inviting a guest speaker from a local indigenous community, setting up weekly Skype chats with a class in Nairobi, or having students share their own cultural heritage with one another, make clear that a single individual is not the torchbearer for an entire culture or country. As emphasized in Chapter 8, there is not *one* Mexican, Jewish, or Arabic culture, and students should not be expected to represent an entire people. To that end, prod students to use the pronoun *I* instead of *we* when describing their own cultural practices, and avoid using *us* and *them* language (Tony Blair Faith Foundation, 2015). Furthermore, there is no need to memorize and teach the communication practices of every culture with which your students might interact. Instead, be cognizant that cultural misunderstandings might exist, and present students with critical thinking strategies to overcome anxiety, frustration, or anger that could arise out of potential cultural misunderstandings (Matsumoto et al., 2007).

Finally, it is important to remember that different dialects of the same language exist. Therefore, just because someone speaks the same language as you, certain phrases may get lost in translation. For example, in Hawaiian, *ma-make* means "to like" and "to want." So if you say, "I like your hat" as a compliment, the person you directed that comment to might interpret that to mean you want them to give you his or her hat. In Persian culture, it is common for parents to call their children "mom" and "dad" and for kids to refer to their aunts and uncles as "mom" and "dad" as a way to express endearment. To help students avoid frustration if their conversation partner gets confused by what they are saying, make them aware that differences in interpretation might arise and that their conversation partner might use different jargon or slang—even if they both speak the same language. For example, English language arts teacher Alyssa had students proofread the presentations they sent to their peers in India to identify local slang they might not understand.

The following are implementation tips specific to your developmental level for facilitating intercultural conversations on the GCLC.

Nascent

Begin exploring tools that can catalyze intercultural and international connections. Skype in the Classroom is one easy jumping-off point. Mystery Skype is a global guessing game that teaches students about geography, culture, similarities, and differences of children around the world. Two classes are paired together, and over Skype, students ask one another *yes* or *no* questions to see who can first guess the other school's location. Twitter can be another starting place for connecting students with people in different countries. A rural elementary school teacher regularly reaches out to international experts via Twitter, and more times than not they reply with a willingness to speak to his class. For him, it's always worth reaching out, because the worst thing that happens is they say *no* or don't respond.

Invite guest speakers or take students on field trips that will provide them with an opportunity to interact with people from different cultures. Before these interactions take place, build background knowledge and ask each student to brainstorm some questions they would like to ask the speaker, which they can add to or change throughout the talk. When planning the schedule, build in enough time for a Q&A so students have an opportunity to share their questions and comments.

For example, high school Spanish teacher Marlene brings in guest speakers from different Spanish-speaking countries and territories—including Peru, Puerto Rico, and Costa Rica—to discuss basic information about their place of origin, education experience, upbringing, economy, geography, foods, and other things related to that place. She taps into the school community to find most of these speakers. For example, one guest speaker was a former teacher at their school, and another was a student who had recently immigrated from Costa Rica. She shares that these conversations are "better than writing a flat paper because it's something they can relate to a little bit."

Beginning/Progressing

At this stage, teachers move beyond exposing students to interactions with people from different places and backgrounds to engaging students in conversations that foster greater intercultural understanding. For example, a 5th grade teacher in Missouri has students write blogs online, international students then comment and ask questions, and her students reply to those comments and questions. Not only are students excited that they have an audience of peers as far away as Israel and Germany, but they are intentional in their writing to make sure it can be understood by nonnative English speakers and that it avoids cultural assumptions.

It is also important to provide scaffolds for students so they actively listen, think critically, and recognize perspectives during these conversations. To foster active listening and critical thinking skills across her racially and culturally diverse student population, one 4th grade teacher has a poster of sentence frames on the wall that reminds students how they can communicate with one another respectfully and reasonably. Before students engage in discussions about controversial topics, she refers to the poster and asks, "What question could you ask if you aren't sure about something or if you disagree with something?" Her students immediately recite, "Where did you find the evidence? Why do you think that?" Likewise, a high school social studies teacher prods his students to ask lots of questions during conversations to recognize where others are coming from and to deepen their understanding of people's beliefs, intentions, and actions and not jump to unsupported conclusions. See Figure 10.2 for how to scaffold active listening, critical thinking, and perspective recognition into daily classroom conversations.

Figure 10.2 | Sample Sentence Starters to Promote Active Listening, Critical Thinking, and Perspective Recognition

I think _____ because _____.
I like what you are saying because _____.
I agree/disagree with _____ because _____.
I'm uncomfortable with _____ because of _____.
I hear you saying _____, but I disagree because _____.
If I understand what you are saying, _____.
Can you share more about _____?
I used to think _____, but now I think _____ because _____.

Give students time to reflect before and after the conversation. Before the conversation, ask them to reflect on their own beliefs, behaviors, assumptions, biases, and expectations about the conversation. After, ask students to reflect on what they learned. "What similarities and differences were revealed between yourself and the person you conversed with? What surprised you? What assumptions were proven wrong? What new insights did you gain?" K-W-L charts or dialogue journals are examples of ways that students can document these reflections and show growth in their global learning.

Proficient/Advanced

At this stage, teachers support students in sustaining intercultural and international conversations. Lead the charge to find a sister school in a different part of the country or world for your school to stay in constant communication with. If you can't get the administrative support for forming a sister school partnership, you can always adopt a sister classroom for weekly or monthly video chats.

Although virtual exchanges provide more equity of access, face-to-face exchanges can forge even deeper connections. Whether hosting students or going to a host country (or both), the ongoing interactions that students have within that short period of time can lead to prolonged virtual interactions long after the exchange ends. As research from the District of Columbia Public School Study Abroad Program found, participants placed a higher value on making friends across Washington, DC's diverse landscape, and their relationships with peers from different socioeconomic and racial-ethnic backgrounds persisted long after the trip ended (Engel, 2018).

Numerous local, national, and international organizations (e.g., EF International) can help you plan exchanges so you don't have to do it on your own. Finally, keep in mind that face-to-face exchanges don't have to be limited to high school. An elementary Spanish teacher's school hosted a group of students from Mexico who performed music, after which the performers and her students had a potluck lunch where they had rich conversations about one another's cultures. Following their visit, her class sent postcards to the Mexican students, and the two groups continued to exchange letters about their lives.

Once you've laid the groundwork for your students, encourage them to initiate their own intercultural conversations. For example, select virtual tools that allow students to initiate conversations on their own time. When international visitors come in, provide time for students and the speakers to exchange information. Multiple high school educators have said that their students will maintain weekly—if not daily—conversations with the peers they meet through school visits or through social media and messaging apps. For example, after high school students in Raleigh, North Carolina, and Suzhou, China, participated in an investigation of water ecology, they took it upon themselves to create their own international club. They meet online once a month to talk about cultural traditions, norms, and values (Spires, Himes, & Wang, 2016).

Special Considerations for Elementary School Teachers (PK–5)

- Engage your class in an "object exchange." For example, the Flat Stanley Project allows classes to send any flat object to a classroom in a different part of the country or world and receive a journal and souvenirs of the object's visit (www.flatstanleyproject.com). Similarly, the Teddy Bear Project matches classes together to exchange teddy bears or other stuffed animals, and students write weekly diary messages from the perspective of the stuffed animal as it experiences the new culture (https://iearn.org/cc/space-2/group-94).

Special Considerations for Secondary School Teachers (6–12)

- Let students drive the discussion. Adolescents are social creatures and will most likely jump into conversations without much prompting.
- Connect intercultural conversations to your content areas. Speaking at the U.S. Department of State Global Teaching Dialogue in 2017, a math teacher shared, "These conversations make my students more engaged in math content."
- Encourage students to participate in exchanges beyond the classroom and share these resources with them. They may already have an international following through their own social media accounts, messaging apps, or blogs. Particularly as they advance to high school, more curricular and extracurricular programs will be available that give them the opportunity to interact in intercultural dialogues. Examples include international extracurricular organizations (e.g., Key Club, Model UN), summer abroad programs focused on volunteering or language immersion, and the hosting of exchange students.

Element 10 in Action: Connecting North Carolinian and Indonesian Students

Every Friday, Ally and her 1st grade students in rural North Carolina Skype with a class in Indonesia. Students learn about each other's cultures as they share songs, show artifacts, and ask questions. Before each call, Ally taught a miniunit on Indonesia in which students learned basic facts about the country, language, and culture. Each student wrote a list of questions he or she could ask, and as a class they reviewed what appropriate questions might be. Ally pointed out that this is a helpful scaffold to make sure introverted students have an opportunity to ask questions (i.e., they can read from the list of questions if they feel shy).

The conversation always begins with a greeting of both classes animatedly welcoming one another. Students take turns walking up to the camera to introduce themselves and ask questions. After the Indonesian teacher translates what the student says, the class in Indonesia waves and responds, "Hi, [student name]!" One boy asks, "Why do all the girls have to wear hoods over their heads?" A student from the Indonesian class comes up to the camera and responds. Then an Indonesian student asks if students in their school have to wear uniforms. A different student comes up to the camera, introduces himself, and answers, "In our school, we don't have to wear uniforms."

Ally shares how through this experience, her young learners demonstrate knowledge of Muslim traditions such as Ramadan and eagerly share the information they learn during their calls with one another and their families.

Further Developing This Skill

- Create an inventory of guest speakers to bring into your class either virtually or in person, drawing on personal, professional, and community resources that represent an array of cultures and global experiences.
- Review three tools for intercultural conversations cited throughout this chapter (and listed under Continuing the Journey). What are the strengths and weaknesses of each, as it specifically relates to the resources you have in your school, the students you teach, and the content you cover?

Continuing the Journey

Explore these additional resources to help you initiate intercultural conversations. Note that this is not comprehensive or inclusive of the many platforms and programs out there, but it is a place to get started.

Asynchronous Platforms

❯ Edublog
(https://edublogs.org): This site provides a WordPress platform for your class with the ability to invite students, moderate content, and participate in conversations with other classroom blogs around the world.

❯ Edmodo
(www.edmodo.com/): This resource offers a communication, collaboration, and coaching platform to K–12 schools and teachers.

❯ ePals
(www.epals.com): This is a community of collaborative classrooms engaged in cross-cultural exchanges, project sharing, and language learning.

❯ Kidblog
(https://kidblog.org/home/): Kidblog provides a blogging platform for your class that allows you to moderate activity and connect students with authentic audiences in over 70 countries.

❯ Participate
(www.participate.com/mktg/find-your-community): This site provides online communities of practice for educators around the world focused on specific topics, such as Teaching the Global Goals and New Global Citizens.

Guest Speakers

❯ Peace Corps World Wise Schools
(www.peacecorps.gov/educators): The Peace Corps' World Wise Schools program connects classrooms with current and returned Peace Corps volunteers.

❯ Pulitzer Center

(https://pulitzercenter.org/education): This site connects journalists with K–12 schools to speak about the international locations and stories they cover.

Videoconferencing

❯ Empatico

(https://empatico.org): This is a free tool that connects classrooms around the world for students age 7–11 through live video and research-based activities.

❯ Generation Global

(https://generation.global): Geared toward 12- to 17-year-olds and with over 20 countries, Generation Global provides students with opportunities to learn and practice the skills of dialogue, engage in videoconferences with another classroom in a different part of the world, and continue the conversation online in small groups focused on prearranged topics.

❯ Global Nomads Group

(https://gng.org): Videoconferencing, virtual reality, and other interactive technologies bring young people together across cultural and national boundaries to examine world issues and learn from experts in a variety of fields. This website includes lesson plans, videos, and other resources.

❯ Skype in the Classroom

(https://education.microsoft.com/skype-in-the-classroom/overview): This site gives access to virtual field trips, Skype lessons, Skype collaborations, guest speakers, and Mystery Skype, a global guessing game that connects classrooms around the world.

11

Developing Glocal Partnerships

A group of scientists in Florida wait excitedly around a computer. The Skype phone rings. It's their counterparts in Brazil. Both groups have been tracking the spread of mosquito-borne illnesses in their cities. Today's meeting is to present findings on interviews they conducted with community members to better understand the root causes of the spread of such diseases before they devise joint solutions. These scientists don't have PhDs or even high school diplomas. They are middle school students working in partnership with peers a hemisphere away to examine a problem of global significance (the spread of disease) that affects each of their communities in localized ways.

Teachers can create these global learning experiences for students that have them acting on real issues in the real world through local, national, or international partnerships. Partners can include classrooms or schools from different places or organizations, such as universities with international students, cultural institutions, businesses, and nonprofits. Whether an elementary school halfway across the world or an NGO three blocks down the road, partners bring added value to student learning. Partners can provide new perspectives as they engage in collaborative inquiries around shared goals or by creating authentic settings that expose students to real-world experiences, such as field trips, service activities, internships, or job shadowing (Eslami, 2005; iEARN, 2014; Merryfield, 2002; Sanders & Stewart, 2004). Partnerships for global learning are actually *glocal* in nature. They are globally connected and locally rooted, tapping into the intersecting local, national, and international affiliations with which students themselves identify (Tichnor-Wagner, 2017).

Partnerships also provide students with firsthand involvement as global citizens who assume responsibility for and actively participate in the global community by taking individual and collective action on behalf of humanity and the planet. Working with partners provides students with authentic contexts in which they can collaborate across physical and imagined borders, wherein "students solve problems like those faced by people in the world outside of school" and can "have a real impact on others" (Buck Institute for Education, 2015, p. 3). In short, the authentic global experiences offered through partnerships expand students' worldviews and open doors to opportunities for them to engage with the wider world throughout their lives and careers.

What Is the Value of Glocal Partnerships?

Developing local or global partnerships doesn't happen with the snap of your fingers or the click of a mouse. As with any relationship, partnerships take time to cultivate and sustain. Furthermore, when it comes to incorporating global learning into a partnership, it can take time to plan and redesign the curriculum (Lindsay, 2016). The payoff is well worth the time investment, though, as forming partnerships for global learning benefit students in a myriad of ways.

First, partnerships help students develop all domains of global competence, including examining issues of local, global, and cultural significance; understanding the perspectives of others; engaging in open, appropriate, and effective interactions across cultures; and taking action for collective well-being and sustainable development (Colvin & Edwards, 2018). Partnerships also provide students with a way to practice collaboration skills with diverse peers. Not only is collaboration a skill that employers consider essential, research points to a range of social, psychological, and academic benefits associated with collaborative learning, including higher self-esteem, lower anxiety, a greater understanding of diversity, deeper relationships, and enhanced critical thinking, problem solving, and motivation for learning (Laal & Ghodsi, 2012; Panitz, 1999a). As Vygotsky's (1978) theory of social development portends, collaborative learning experiences aid in the learning process as social interactions play a vital role in cognitive development. Because learning is a social phenomenon, students are motivated by the community in which they are interacting. Partnerships expand students' learning community and therefore motivate students beyond what a traditional classroom lesson could.

Self-Reflection and Implementation Tips for Developing Glocal Learning Partnerships

Look at Figure 11.1 and rate yourself along the GCLC for the element "Developing local, national, or international partnerships that provide real-world contexts for global learning opportunities."

1. Where do you rank yourself and why?
2. What steps do you need to take to move along the continuum?

The following implementation tips will help you develop and sustain meaningful partnerships for glocal learning.

Emphasize equal parity among partners. A partnership is a two-way street where all of those involved have equal status and learn from and with one another by engaging in inquiries related to shared, collaborative goals around global topics that have meaning and relevancy in their lives. As global educator Julie Lindsay (2016) argues, "A successful global collaboration is where all members work hard to share knowledge and understanding in order to propel the learning" (p. 149). In mutually beneficial partnerships, students are learning *with* their collaborators, not learning about or teaching to. Therefore, all parties should codevelop the collaborative learning goals around relevant global topics they aim to achieve (Merryfield, 2002; Roberts, 2007).

As students learn with glocal partners, keep in mind that the central premise of collaborative learning is the process of working together, where consensus is built by team collaboration and shared authority and responsibility

Figure 11.1 | Develop Local, National, or International Partnerships That Provide Real-World Contexts for Global Learning Opportunities

Element	Nascent	Beginning →	Progressing →	Proficient →	Advanced →
Develop Local, National, or International Partnerships That Provide Real-World Contexts for Global Learning Opportunities	I do not yet create opportunities for my students to communicate with local, national, or international organizations or individuals.	I present students with an opportunity to participate in a global learning experience with local, national, or international organizations or individuals.	I present students with opportunities for short-term collaboration with local, national, or international organizations to learn about the world.	I develop local, national, and/or international long-term partnerships that allow my students to learn about the world with diverse communities.	I guide my students to develop local, national, and international partnerships; direct their own communication with these partners; and develop their own global learning opportunities.

(Panitz, 1999b). Specifically, teachers from "developed" countries who partner with schools or organizations in "developing" countries should refrain from taking responsibility for the other (i.e., "to teach the other") and instead adopt a responsibility toward the other (i.e., "mutual accountability") (Andreotti, 2006).

For example, rather than have your students donate money or goods, "which places the givers in a superior or more powerful role" (Merryfield, 2002, p. 20), emphasize that students and communities in both places have an equal role in developing and participating in activities. One high school English language arts teacher explained that as she embarks on service learning with her students, she defines it as "service learning to each other" and seeks to ensure that the learning that takes place is both a service to her students and to the community with whom they are working.

As with intercultural conversations, teachers should place themselves on equal footing with their students. Rather than transmit knowledge, teachers should take on the role of flexible facilitators who pave the way for students to construct knowledge and understanding with their partners (Vygotsky, 1978).

Start with the learning, not the location. To create real-world learning opportunities for students around global issues doesn't mean you have to collaborate with a classroom halfway around the world. More often than not, global issues manifest themselves locally. It can be just as powerful for students to connect with a local organization combatting human trafficking, monitoring water quality, or sustaining biodiversity. This allows students to see for themselves what global issues look like "on the ground," to engage in a global issue that personally resonates with them, and to understand the interconnectedness of their community with communities in different parts of the world.

To figure out what learning areas you want to focus on, start with the standards and topics you already have to cover in your curriculum. For example, a high school biology teacher looked at her curriculum sequence for the year and determined that the unit on infectious diseases was a logical place to engage in global learning partnerships because the spread of diseases transcend borders. From there, she reached out to local health clinics since HIV/AIDS was an ongoing epidemic in her city. The Sustainable Development Goals (SDGs) are a great starting place for mapping global issues to the curriculum (see Chapter 1). For connecting with other educators around the world focused on specific SDGs, TeachSDGs is a teacher-powered organization that connects educators around the world with resources, projects, and one another to collaboratively bring the global goals into their classrooms. (Follow them at www.teachsdgs.org or on Twitter at @TeachSDGs). Note that many organizations that support global online collaboration allow you to search for existing projects by content area and grade level.

Explore multiple modes of cultivating partnerships. There is no single playbook for cultivating partnerships for global learning. Rather, design a partnership experience that matches the needs and interests of your students, the resources you have available, and your own comfort level. As with intercultural and international conversations, partnerships for global learning can take the form of face-to-face or virtual exchanges (Gallavan, 2008; Merryfield, 2002; Roberts, 2007). You can take a DIY approach, reaching out to fellow educators in the Twitterverse or across your global professional learning network, codeveloping a series of lessons, and setting up the logistics of the technology tools your students will use to collaborate (e.g., Skype, Google Hangouts, Ning, Padlet, Flipgrid). Alternatively, you can sign up for programs that do the partner matching and curriculum development for you with a built-in platform for connecting classrooms. You can also select the pedagogical approach, whether it be service learning or project-based learning.

Cultivate your own cross-cultural collaboration skills. Developing partnerships also requires you to apply cross-cultural collaboration skills. For students to actually participate in collaborative learning activities with peers in Finland or a sustainable farming co-op the next county over, a lot of behind-the-scenes collaboration needs to occur (e.g., developing a relationship with partners, scheduling, coplanning). Along with navigating time differences and language considerations (depending on your partner), you may encounter cultural differences that, if unaddressed, could impede collaborative planning.

Many of these cultural differences may be undetectable from the surface. The cultural iceberg metaphor suggests that, like an iceberg, only a fraction of culture is visible (Hall, 1976). A vast majority of culture is hidden below the surface, and much of this—notions of time, gender roles, body language, etiquette, leadership styles, problem-solving approaches, collectivist versus individualist orientation, value of education—can affect what your partner perceives to be the value of the partnership, the ways in which they tackle collaborative planning, and how rigidly your partner sticks to the schedule. Being cognizant that such differences may exist can help ameliorate frustrations and false assumptions. For example, a North Carolina elementary school teacher who co-led a partnership with a school in Mexico shared, "We would have a planning call at 7 in the morning, and all of us teachers would be right on time, waiting 20 minutes before the teachers in Mexico called in. We learned that it wasn't because they were being rude, but they interpreted the time to mean *around* 7, not *exactly at* 7 as we interpret it in the United States."

The following are implementation tips on developing local and global partnerships specific to your developmental level on the GCLC.

Nascent

Take the adage "the journey of 1,000 miles begins with a single step" to heart as you embark on glocal learning partnerships. Start incrementally by forging an initial relationship with your partner through emails, messaging apps, videoconferencing software, or an in-person visit (Stewart, 2012). Another way to build rapport with partners is through empathy interviews, which evoke stories and feelings with interviewees to build an understanding of their motivations, desires, and needs. Importantly, make sure that you and your partner are ready for learning. For example, after 1st grade teacher Alyssa connected her class with a class in Indonesia via Skype through a series of getting-to-know-you intercultural conversations, she wanted to start coteaching lessons with the partner class. However, the partner teacher said, "We can't do that yet. We still have more questions we want to ask!" This points to the value that your partner might hold of building relationships before diving into collaborative lessons and the need to practice patience as you get activities off the ground.

You can also get your feet wet through one-time learning events such as field trips, hosting guests, service days, or virtual global learning events. For example, the Global Read Aloud (https://theglobalreadaloud.com) has taken place every October since 2010. Created by a teacher for teachers, the Global Read Aloud allows K–12 classes all around the world to read the same book and connect with other classes to discuss and collaborate on projects. The Global Monster Project (www.smithclass.org/proj/Monsters/index.htm), designed for elementary school students, has classes around the world request a monster part (e.g., head, ears, feet), write a description, and submit it online. Each class then builds a monster using everyone's descriptions. The World's Largest Lesson (http://worldslargestlesson.globalgoals.org) encourages teachers all around the world to teach about the Sustainable Development Goals during one day in September.

Beginning/Progressing

At this stage, global learning experiences with partners focus on more structured learning outcomes (e.g., studying endangered species in the rainforest, conducting language exchanges, arranging music performances) and extend for a few days or a few weeks (Stewart, 2012). Short-term collaborations include face-to-face experiences such as traveling for or hosting overseas exchanges for a week or two and online collaboration.

Global educator Julie Lindsay (2016) argues that over the last few decades, online global collaboration has transformed from information exchange to information and artifact exchange to information and artifact cocreation, where partners can build knowledge together and share it with the world. To do this, educators must "carefully design global collaborations that are implemented and managed with a view to effectively join classrooms together to enhance learning and support co-created outcomes, have common assessment objectives between global partners, provide student autonomy in learning and an ability to initiate online collaborations, peer-to-peer learning, online publishing and sharing" (p. 136). Steps for planning and implementing collaborative global projects include the following:

- Develop with your partner class or organization a clear vision and purpose with a driving question and delineated learning outcomes that you will address. Ideally, the driving outcome should be open ended, simple to understand, and have complex solutions (i.e., "How can we have a positive effect on our environment?") (Brody & Davidson, 1998; Lindsay, 2016).
- Prepare the logistics. Considerations include determining what online platforms you will use, ensuring that technology tools work ahead of time, arranging the timing and schedule, solidifying a plan for translation, establishing expectations for frequency of communications, and—if collaborating online—identifying whether conversations will be synchronous or asynchronous (Lindsay, 2016).
- Facilitate learning activities so all members are participating visibly, reliably, and regularly (Lindsay, 2016). Students should also not ask questions for which they already know the answers but ones that require them to investigate and cocreate knowledge (Brody & Davidson, 1998).
- Decide on collaborative final products with your students and partners, and share those products with local and global audiences. Examples include producing a joint publication, producing video documentaries, creating histories of local communities around the world, creating a photo essay to share online, conducting workshops on a global issue in the community, creating a global art gallery, conducting a public awareness campaign that addresses a shared global issue, hosting an online summit, or publishing a multimedia presentation (Lindsay, 2016).

The collaborative partnerships on which you embark can stem from an existing project or emerge from an original project based on the needs and interests of students and your community. Seek out your own project through Twitter or Skype in the Classroom, or draw upon existing relationships with sister schools or educators in different parts of the country and world that are a part of your professional learning network. Short-term collaborations of this nature might include tandem teaching with a partner class where both are contributing local knowledge of a common topic (e.g., indigenous communities in your region, the history of your town or city, extreme weather conditions, immigration policies).

Reduce your own preparation time and take advantage of organizations that match you with partners and existing collaborative learning experiences. For example, Empatico is a free video collaboration platform geared toward students ages 7–11 that matches partner classes that are 100 miles or more away from each other, emphasizing the value of connecting nationally and internationally. The platform also provides standards- and evidence-based shared learning activities that cover a range of content areas, including geography, history, science, and language arts. For example, Our Local Landmarks has partner classes research and share information about a local landmark in each of their communities, Everyday Energy has partner classes explore how they use energy in their lives, and Folktales to Learn From has partner classes read three folktales from around the world and share which ones resonate most to them. All Empatico activities include prep work, a learning activity with a partner class via video collaboration, and post-class reflections. After the first activity, teachers can choose to continue with more activities with the same partner classroom.

Citizen science projects are another source of "prepackaged" partnership opportunities, wherein scientists work together with citizen volunteers to collaborate on the discovery of new scientific knowledge—often on projects that span across a continent or around the globe. Projects in which you could involve your students include testing local bodies of water for water quality data, monitoring bird nests across North America, and measuring and mapping noise population. Lists of over 1,000 citizen science projects can be found at the SciStarter database (https://scistarter.com/citizenscience.

html) and National Geographic (www.nationalgeographic.org/idea/citizen-science-projects).

Proficient/Advanced

Sustained partnerships over the course of multiple months or a year allow students to build relationships that allow for deeper learning and for students to internalize equal parity with their partners (Merryfield, 2002). Strive to maintain partnerships through activities such as remaining in regular contact, codeveloping curriculum and other learning activities, and providing consistent opportunities for students to participate in joint projects, seminars, or discussions that connect with the curriculum and require them to identify, research, and devise solutions to shared problems (Stewart, 2012).

One example of a sustained partnership is one that grew out of a professional development exchange between upper elementary school teachers in Belize and Colorado. Initially, students researched and wrote to one another about their respective cultures and climates, which developed into lessons that students created for one another about their communities and countries (e.g., the symbols on the Belize flag, building snowmen). This evolved into joint projects where students coauthored books about their passions, fears, and hopes (Kirshner, Tzib, Tzib, & Fry, 2016).

The World Smarts STEM Challenge, a program supported by the global development and education nonprofit organization IREX, provided a year-long collaboration between students and teachers in the United States and Ghana focused on finding STEM solutions to hazardous waste and repowering communities' energy use. Throughout the year, U.S. and Ghanaian teachers received STEM professional development together, co-led equally balanced teams of secondary U.S. and Ghanaian students over the course of 10 weeks, participated with their students in a virtual STEM fair to pitch innovative solutions, and attended a finalist contest and showcase (IREX, 2018).

Draw on students' interests and inspiration to forge topics for collaboration, and allow students to drive partnership development, communication, and learning experiences. Give students autonomy in the learning activities and ability to initiate online collaborations, peer-to-peer learning, and final learning products (Lindsay, 2016). Not only does this engage and motivate students, but when students have a voice and ownership in real-world learning opportunities such as service learning, their self-concept and tolerance toward other groups improves (Morgan & Streb, 2001). Remember, deviating from the planned path can be a valuable learning experience for students, and it can further empower children to become autonomous learners (Brody & Davidson, 1998).

Special Considerations for Elementary School Teachers (PK–5)

- Start with a local project to which students have access. Look around for community organizations that would be willing to partner with your classroom (e.g., a community garden, an animal shelter, a recycling center, a city park, a fire department, a retirement home, a homeless shelter, a food kitchen). Have students interview individuals from that site, think about the needs of the area, and then brainstorm projects they could do to help. Take a field trip to complete the project and stay in touch with the organization so students can understand the lasting impact of their work.
- For a national or international partnership, try your best to incorporate videos, real-time video chats (e.g., Skype), or pictures for students to better understand who exactly they are working with.

Special Considerations for Secondary School Teachers (6–12)

- Give students the autonomy to voice what topics to study, projects to conduct, and vetted partners to reach out to. If students have multiple ideas for projects, let them break into small groups so they can pursue their interests.
- Even though teenagers spend a lot of time socializing online already, it doesn't hurt to remind them of responsible use of the internet as digital citizens as they communicate with partners and publish projects in online formats. (Whatever they post online is permanent and can be seen by anyone!)

Element 11 in Action: Fourth Grade Scientists Investigate Natural Disasters in the United States and Guatemala

Denise's elementary school in the rural southeast United States forged a sister school partnership with a school in Guatemala. The partnership arose out of a principal's visit to the school during an education exchange to Latin America and has lasted over five years. Denise connected her 4th grade classroom via videoconferencing to peers of their age at the Guatemalan school. During one of the introductory calls, the students in Guatemala shared that they lived in view of a volcano, which immediately triggered an onslaught of questions from Denise's students. What is it like living near a volcano? Have you ever seen it erupt? What would happen if it erupted? Would you have to evacuate?

Based on the rich conversation that took place and students' obvious interest in the topic, Denise and her partner teacher decided to have each of their classes create lessons on natural disasters their communities face, including the science behind the natural disaster, its potential impact on the environment and people, and how they prepare for natural disasters. Denise's students presented on hurricanes, and their Guatemalan counterparts presented on volcanoes. After each presentation, students asked additional questions they had. In the follow-up lesson, the two classes worked together to come up with a list of similarities and differences related to the extreme weather their communities face.

Not only did student interest drive the unit, but Denise saw that it aligned with the 4th grade earth science standards on weather and climate she already had to teach. This sparked further collaborative inquiries into weather, including observing and comparing cloud types and measuring rainfall in both communities. For Denise, this collaborative partnership deepened her students' learning. She shared, "You won't get this understanding from a textbook. All you get from a textbook is whether a volcano is dormant or not and the type of volcano that it is. You don't actually learn what it is like for people to live near a volcano."

Further Developing This Skill

- Identify places in your curriculum/standard course of study wherein a glocal partnership would enrich the learning experience for students.
- Create an inventory of potential global learning partners in your local community and through your professional learning network. What type of global learning experiences could those partners provide, in terms of both content (e.g., global topics/expertise) and pedagogy (e.g., service learning, internship, project-based learning)? What resources— technological, monetary, and so on—would you need to get the partnership off the ground?

Continuing the Journey

Explore the following resources on your journey toward developing partnerships that provide real-world contexts for global learning:

❯ Empatico
(https://empatico.org): This is a free tool that connects classrooms around the world for students ages 7–11 through live videoconferencing and standards- and research-based activities covering a range of disciplines.

❯ Global SchoolNet
(www.globalschoolnet.org): This site allows teachers to sign up to participate in collaborative projects with partners around the world.

❯ iEARN
(www.us.iearn.org): This is a global network that facilitates online project-based collaborative learning in classrooms around the world.

❯ Level Up Village
(www.levelupvillage.com): Geared toward students in grades K–9, Level Up Village offers schools STEAM courses that can be run through in-school, after-school, and summer programming. Each course connects students with peers in other countries through exchanging video letters and collaborating on projects with global partners. Fees vary.

❯ TakingITGlobal

(www.tigweb.org): An organization focused on student voice, global citizenship, and environmental stewardship, TakingITGlobal provides a free online classroom platform for use in developing collaborative projects. Teachers can search or post projects by subject area, grade level, and global issue.

12

Assessing Students' Global Competence Development

In today's era of test-based accountability, what we measure matters. Although global competence is not on the list of state-mandated subject areas for testing, it nonetheless deserves to be measured as a vital learning outcome. We recognize that most teachers are already inundated with assessments and evaluations, and the last thing you want to do is add more to your plate. At the same time, what we measure matters. Intentionally and explicitly assessing students' global competence shows that these are outcomes that are important to them, gives your content area significance beyond the classroom, and helps students become lifelong learners and global citizens. Furthermore, assessing students' global competence development allows you to celebrate milestones of your growth as a globally competent teacher and design goals for how to continue your growth and the growth of your students. How can you develop the capacity and creativity to measure students' global competence growth within your classroom?

Whether related to global competence or your content area, student performance assessment is most commonly referred to as the systematic collection of information to improve performance through awareness, growth, and action (AERA, APA, & NCME, 2014). This information should be collected *before* a lesson or unit to ensure that what you teach meets the needs of your students and to establish a baseline to document growth. You should also collect information *during* a lesson for formative use and to adjust your teaching along the way. Finally, you should collect information *after* a lesson or unit, either immediately or after some time, to assess growth and retention of lesson or unit goals.

In a student-centered classroom, assessments are done *with* students and not *to* students so they are actively engaged in the process. Students understand the aim of the assessment and how to track their progress. Because globally competent teaching embraces a student-centered philosophy wherein students' individual and cultural identities are valued and incorporated into curriculum and instruction, and because students are encouraged to lead their own global learning experiences, it is important to involve them in actively measuring their global competence growth. With assessment as a collaborative endeavor between teacher and student, the goal is for students ultimately to be able to evaluate their own global competence. This skill will help them both within the classroom and beyond, as it can guide their further development as global citizens.

What Does Assessing Students' Global Competence Look Like?

The ability to develop and use appropriate methods of inquiry to assess students' global competence starts with an understanding of what it means to be globally competent. Global competence is a complex construct; therefore, teachers should delineate the subelements they will be assessing (e.g., empathy; recognizing perspectives; intercultural communication; an understanding of local, national, and global issues; motivation to take action) so that tracking growth becomes more manageable for teachers and students alike. Figure 0.2 on page 9 references the specific elements of global competence teachers might measure.

Before developing your own assessments, it is best to become familiar with existing measures of global competence for K–12 students. The Asia Society developed Global Leadership Performance Outcomes and Rubrics for grades K–2, 3, 5, 8, 10, and 12. These outcomes are organized under the Asia Society's four global competence domains for students—investigate the world, recognize perspectives, communicate ideas, and take action—and written as "I can" statements (e.g., "I can share my personal perspective on an issue and provide one reason for my opinion"). Each performance outcome has an accompanying rubric divided into four levels: emerging, developing, proficient, and advanced.

The 2018 PISA (Programme for International Student Assessment) Global Competence Assessment measures students' global competence through a cognitive test of their global understanding and a self-reported student questionnaire. Cognitive questions are open ended, asking students to analyze a real-life scenario that touches on multiple global competence domains. Sample scenarios include inferences about the rise of global warming from a temperature chart printed in the newspaper and a Quechua student who posts a video that goes viral in which she sings a Michael Jackson song in her native language (OECD, 2018a). (PISA is a triennial survey of 15-year-old students that aims to evaluate education systems worldwide. Other areas that PISA has assessed include reading, scientific thinking, mathematics, collaborative problem solving, and financial literacy.)

Global certificate programs, a growing trend among schools, districts, and states, distinguishes students who take global coursework (e.g., world history, world and heritage languages), participate in global experiences (e.g., service learning, travel, internships, extracurricular activities), and demonstrate evidence of global learning through capstone projects (Singmaster et al., 2018). For example, the Illinois Global Scholar Certificate requires students to complete a performance-based capstone assessment task in which they investigate and take action to address a global concern of their choosing (https://global-illinois.org/illinois-global-scholar-certificate).

To assess students' progress in developing global competence, globally competent teachers regularly use a mixture of formative and summative assessment to provide students with feedback and inform their own globally oriented instruction. Formative assessment occurs during the learning process as a means of monitoring student learning and modifying teaching practices to improve student learning. Examples of formative assessment include observations, journal entries, entrance and exit slips, and reflective classroom conversations. Whereas formative assessment is often low-stakes, summative assessment is more evaluative in nature, taking place at the end of a unit or learning cycle (see Figure 12.1). Examples include final projects, portfolios, reports, essays, and presentations (along with traditional end-of-unit tests). As demonstrated in Chapters 9, 10, and 11, global learning activities tend to take the form of authentic, real-world activities and investigations. Therefore, authentic performance assessments—those that require students to apply the knowledge and skills learned to real-world tasks—best evaluate students' global competence growth.

Figure 12.1 | Formative Versus Summative Assessment

Formative Assessment *more frequent; low-stakes*	Summative Assessment *less frequent; higher-stakes*
• exit tickets • entrance tickets • journal entry • weekly quizzes • in-class discussions • observations	• project • presentation • final report • final essay • portfolio • end-of-unit test

Self-Reflection and Implementation Tips for Assessing Students' Global Competence Development

Look at Figure 12.2 and rate yourself along the GCLC for the element "Developing and using appropriate methods of inquiry to assess students' global competence development."

1. Where do you rate yourself and why?
2. What steps do you need to take to move along the continuum?

Figure 12.2 | Developing and Using Appropriate Methods of Inquiry to Assess Students' Global Competence Development

Element	Nascent	→ Beginning →	Progressing →	Proficient →	Advanced
Developing and Using Appropriate Methods of Inquiry to Assess Students' Global Competence Development	I am not yet familiar with how to assess students' global competence development.	I am familiar with resources to assess students' global competence development.	• I develop and use appropriate assessments of students' global competence development. • I can provide students with feedback and analyze students' global competence development.	• I develop and use frequent, authentic, and differentiated assessments of students' global competence development. • I can provide students with constructive feedback and analyze students' performance to inform subsequent instruction.	I guide students to evaluate their own global competence development.

The following implementation tips will help you as you prepare to develop and use appropriate methods of inquiry to assess your students' global competence development.

See global competence beyond knowledge. Deardorff (2018) acknowledges that educators are conditioned to focus on knowledge when developing assessments and warns that it is only one aspect of global competence, which is a multifaceted construct consisting of knowledge, skills, *and* dispositions. Take time to reflect on what effect you want to have on your students as you embark on globally competent teaching. In addition to knowing facts about world geography, global conditions, and cultural practices, consider what you want students to do with that information. What dispositions do you hope they embody? What skills do you hope they develop? Are they able to critically analyze information and identify biases? Are they able to collaboratively come up with solutions? As you are exploring, it may help to use existing global competence definitions and frameworks as an anchor, such as the Globally Competent Learning Continuum, the PISA Global Competence Framework, or others mentioned in the Introduction that address the cognitive, social-emotional, and behavioral aspects of global competence. Once you have determined the specific elements of global competence you aim to foster in your students, be explicit with your goals. Let students know that global competence is a part of your classroom mission and an important learning outcome.

Be open to a range of assessment practices. Because of the nature of global competence, much of your assessment may be more qualitative and formative in nature (Deardorff, 2006), and that is perfectly fine. As one 1st grade teacher shared, "The best way for me to gauge whether students are developing global competence is through conversations and observing how they are interacting with the lesson."

Whatever assessment methods you choose, they should match the lesson objective. If you are interested in what students know about specific global conditions, then the assessment might mirror more traditional tests where students show what they know through open-ended test questions. If your goal is for students to dispel the myth that Africa is a country, then students could label a map or name the 54 countries in Africa. If your goal is for students to apply a critical lens to the effect of colonization on countries in Africa, then the assessment will be more complex, such as an essay or a debate where students are assessed using a rubric that examines their ability to synthesize information from a variety of sources and draw conclusions. In other situations, the use of authentic and direct evidence collected during the actual learning process might be more appropriate (Deardorff, 2018), such as documented observations, guided journal entries, and written or recorded reflections.

See assessment as a co-learning opportunity. Consider assessing the development of globally competent students as an ongoing opportunity to learn from and with your students. As Deardorff (2018) suggests, the "assessment should be viewed as something done in partnership with your students, instead of to your students" (p. 2). From the beginning, provide students with opportunities to assess their own global learning and that of their peers. Before assessing their own learning, students can start with a guided assessment of their peers—a shift that embraces student-centered learning. To provide effective feedback, students must be aware of the project goal and assessment expectations. Therefore, it is helpful to create rubrics or checklists to guide the feedback that students provide one another.

Make time to reflect on your global assessment practice. Engage in reflection around your own practice of integrating global competence assessment. Deardorff (2018) suggests that you ask yourself the following questions as part of the reflection process:

- How is this assessment relevant to students?
- How will I provide feedback so they continue their own development of global competence?
- How am I using a variety of means to assess global competence (e.g., assignments, observations, self-reflection)?
- What perspectives and knowledge are privileged through the assessments I use?

Ongoing critical reflection about these types of questions will help you be more effective in your assessment strategies and in turn help your students strengthen their global competence development for lasting change.

The following are implementation tips specific to your developmental level on the GCLC.

Nascent

Start by familiarizing yourself with existing resources for assessing students' global competence. As you review these resources, find one you really like and consider the knowledge, skills, and dispositions that the assessment highlights. It is important that all three areas are highlighted, as a high-quality resource will acknowledge the multifaceted nature of global competence. The lessons and activities in your classroom should align with and provide opportunities for students to develop the knowledge, skills, and dispositions the assessment targets. For example, if you are interested in assessing students' intercultural communication skills, it would be most appropriate to have them engage in an activity such as participating in a conversation with a peer from another country to demonstrate that skill (as opposed to completing a multiple-choice assessment).

To help you do this, outline the global learning activities you're doing in your classroom and what types of learning objectives an assessment would best match. For example, if you're engaging in intercultural conversations, then assessing students' empathy, understanding of diverse cultures, and intercultural communication skills might make the most sense. If your students are conducting content-aligned investigations of the world, then an understanding of global interconnectedness and the ability to synthesize sources that represent diverse viewpoints would be logical global competence attributes to measure.

Even though some K–12 global competence assessments do exist, there are, unfortunately, few to choose from. Therefore, it is also important to familiarize yourself with different types of formative and performance-based assessments you could adapt to measure different global competence attributes.

Beginning/Progressing

After familiarizing yourself with different resources to assess global competence, these next levels emphasize using appropriate global competence assessments in your day-to-day instruction. First, consider the various ways you can gather information about student growth and decide which aligns with the global learning goals you have identified with your students. Figure 12.3 provides examples of tools, activities, and strategies you might use to assess various elements of global competence. As you review the list, think about how you could modify these examples to apply to the content area(s) and grade level(s) that your global lessons or units cover.

Figure 12.3 | Examples of Assessing Global Competence Development

Domain	Sample Learning Objectives	Sample Assessment Activities
Social-Emotional *(Dispositions)*	• Students can recognize, understand, and appreciate the perspectives and worldviews of others (OECD, 2018a). • Students can recognize, articulate, and apply an understanding of different perspectives, including their own (Asia Society, 2013). • Students can develop attitudes of empathy, solidarity, and respect for differences and diversity (UNESCO, 2015).	• Journal entries with prompts before, during, and/or after a learning activity that ask students to critically discuss topics (e.g., poverty, conflict, immigration) from multiple points of view. • Reflective conversations following a Socratic seminar, discussion, or debate assessed with a checklist. • Portfolio of assignments. • Self-reflection at multiple times to chart growth in connection with or response to an activity, such as a service-learning project or virtual video exchange. • Observations of student reactions and responses to new perspectives and cultures documented in a notebook over time. • Guided peer assessment rubrics that guide students' ability to articulate different perspectives in a debate, written assignment, or intercultural conversation.

Cognitive (Knowledge)	• Students can investigate the world beyond their immediate environment by examining issues of local, global, and cultural significance (OECD, 2018a). • Students can pose a broad question on a local or regional issue and identify the significance to the global community (Asia Society, 2013). • Students can provide an accurate summary of evidence from sources that are relevant to a global question (Asia Society, 2013). • Students can explain how multiple conditions fundamentally affect diverse global forces, events, conditions, and issues (World Savvy, 2018). • Students can explain how the current world system is shaped by historical forces (World Savvy, 2018). • Students can describe how global and local events or conditions are interconnected (OECD, 2018a; UNESCO, 2015; World Savvy, 2018).	• Report or presentation where students analyze conflicting perspectives and come up with a conclusion based on an array of evidence sources. • KWL chart. • Venn diagram or other graphic organizer. • Exit/entrance ticket. • Socratic seminar, discussion, or debate to demonstrate knowledge assessed with a rubric or follow-up reflective conversation. • Think-Pair-Share.
Behavioral (Skills)	• Students can communicate ideas effectively with diverse audiences by engaging in open, appropriate, and effective interactions (OECD, 2018a). • Students can use knowledge and their experiences to take action for collective well-being and sustainable development both locally and globally (OECD, 2018a). • Students can work in diverse teams to identify a solution to a problem. • Students can listen actively and engage in inclusive dialogue (World Savvy, 2018).	• Socratic seminar, discussion, or debate assessed with a rubric or follow-up reflective conversation. • Self-reflection at multiple times to chart growth in connection with or response to an activity, such as a service-learning project, video, issue, or current/historical event. • Peer assessment in which teacher (and eventually students) identify goals.

Because of the dearth of premade tools that explicitly measure students' global competence, if existing assessments don't match what your own goals are, you may need to develop your own formative and summative assessment questions, checklists, and rubrics. See, for example, *How to Create and Use Rubrics for Formative Assessment and Grading* (Brookhart, 2013) for how to write effective rubrics.

If you are worried about assessment overload due to the content-area objectives your students are required to master, this can be an opportunity to build specific global competence attributes into rubrics or other assessments you are already using to assess "traditional" content.

Implementing global competence assessments is only one side of the equation, however. The other side is feedback. To truly enhance student learning, feedback should be timely, specific, goal oriented, and provided to all students regardless of their proficiency level. First, for feedback to be useful, it must be timely to allow students time to revisit the concept and for the teacher to restructure the lesson, if necessary (Wiggins, 2012). It also has to be specific. General feedback (i.e., responses such as "Great job" or "Incorrect") does not provide information students need to improve. Regardless of whether students are at, above, or below target, feedback should provide language they can comprehend and point to specific ways to improve. You can do this in several ways, from written comments with further guided questions on a journal entry, rubric, or essay to face-to-face conferences where you discuss students' performance.

Questioning is one strategy you can use to help students lead their own learning as a part of the feedback process. Writing questions, instead of neutral comments, in response to students' work helps move them toward the objective and models how they can challenge their own thinking and be active in their progress. Some examples of questions are "How can this goal be achieved? Why is this goal important? What would be some barriers? Why?" Questions such as these help students think more critically about their role as global citizens and provide an opportunity for written dialogue between you and your students. Another feedback strategy is providing additional prompts for what students can do to extend their learning around a particular global competence element so they are still accountable for growth. For example, ask them to revise a piece of the assignment to better demonstrate their understanding of the element or encourage them to pursue a completely new assignment that extends the activity to a deeper level.

Proficient/Advanced

With greater experience, your use of assessments for global learning becomes more frequent, authentic, and differentiated. Initially, it may be easier to incorporate global competence assessments at the end of a project or unit. However, global competence assessment should be ongoing over time and include preassessments that allow you to make adjustments based on students' baseline performance, post-assessments, and formative assessment that checks student growth throughout the unit (Deardorff, 2006; Mansilla & Jackson, 2011). As such, it is important to determine the timing of the global competence assessments and explicitly build them into your lesson and unit plans.

For example, a middle school math teacher tied a unit about proportions to a goal that had real-world meaning and relevance to her students: understanding racial disparities by examining the racial disproportionality in incarceration rates in the United States. She shared this goal with students so they understood how learning about proportions could help them critically analyze real-world problems. To assess students' understanding of the global issue of racial disparities, she started the unit with a preassessment that took the form of a KWL chart. Students individually filled out what they knew (*K*) and what they wanted to know (*W*) about racial disparities. At the end of each lesson, she gave students exit tickets that tracked their growth on the math content by having them solve a proportion problem. She also asked students to reflect on what the numbers were teaching them about racial disparities. The unit concluded with a summative assessment that took the form of a test on which students demonstrated mastery of proportions. Students' understanding of racial disparities was also measured when they filled out what they had learned (*L*) on the KWL chart. Students were incensed by what they had learned, and they extended their learning by creating a project to share what they had learned with their school community.

To make student assessments more authentic—meaning they "require that students engage with real-life problems, issues, or tasks for an audience who cares about or has a stake in what students learn" (Martin-Kniep, 2000, p. 26)—have students apply what they learned to real-world contexts. Examples of authentic assessments include creating artwork, making a public service announcement, writing a persuasive letter to a politician, teaching a lesson to students in other classes or younger grades, acting out a play students wrote, or participating in a debate. In a project focused on access to education, rather than have students recall facts about inequitable access to education around the world, middle school teacher Jonah assigned a country and a role to students who then prepared and presented a poster to their peers during a schoolwide assembly. Students were assessed on their ability to share knowledge and devise a solution, which extended their basic knowledge of facts.

Bring in authentic audiences to which students can demonstrate their global learning. This can include peers, both within the classroom and around the world (see Chapters 10 and 11), parents, or community members. As Mansilla and Jackson (2011) explain, "When members of the community or experts are similarly invited to offer feedback on student presentations, video productions, or graduation portfolios, they can deepen students' sense of the authenticity of their studies—their engagement in topics that matter well beyond grades, exams, and classrooms" (p. 66).

As assessments become more frequent and more authentic, you will have more opportunities to gauge student learning—and therefore differentiate assessments. You can provide different types of assessments that meet students where they are developmentally, as some students may have background knowledge already needed for the learning objectives and can start with a more rigorous task. Assessments can also be differentiated based on students' strengths. As you develop and use assessments that measure global competence, reflect on how they align to Howard Gardner's multiple intelligences:

verbal-linguistic, logical-mathematical, kinesthetic, visual-spatial, musical, interpersonal, and intrapersonal.

For example, students who are more verbal-linguistic may best demonstrate their understanding of global interconnectedness through a written essay on the life of an iPhone. Students who are visual-spatial could create a poster or mural that illustrates where all the parts of an iPhone come from, where an iPhone is assembled, and where it is distributed. In other words, provide students with a menu of authentic options for demonstrating their global learning. Remember that you can design these performance tasks in such a way that students are able to achieve the same global competence goals. Giving students this choice will have the additional benefit of motivating and empowering them (Reeves, 2011).

Along with informing students of their global competence growth, assessment can be used to inform your own classroom instruction. After each lesson that incorporates a global learning goal, review your formative assessment techniques and adjust the next lesson and your approach to teaching, as needed. For example, a 1st grade ESL teacher explained that during a lesson on identifying solutions to a problem, she gave students the task of identifying solutions to the problem of pollution in the Amazon using a graphic organizer. As she walked around to check on each student, she noticed that not all students were using words in the "Solution" box that addressed a solution. She immediately knew that the next day she would reteach that aspect of the lesson. In this way, assessment becomes assessment *for* instruction. You use assessments to shape your instructional planning in ways that will best move students forward regarding the knowledge, skills, and mindsets they need as global citizens (Tomlinson & Moon, 2013).

Finally, as you become more advanced in assessing global learning, give students ownership over evaluating their global competence development. Timely, specific, and goal-oriented conversations with students about their global competence progress model how to evaluate their own learning as they work toward a goal. Give students the reins by explaining your goal or intent regarding their globally competent learning. For example, if the goal is to take action for collective well-being and sustainable development both locally and globally, have student discuss what this means for them and how they can "take action."

Then walk them through the potential outcomes of the options they identify. Compare the effect of volunteering, fundraising for a cause, and/or holding a community event. Have them think through the goals and determine if their activity achieves that. Through this process, students are learning to align outcomes and actions, and they are taking ownership over what they need to learn and the skills they need to develop. When you provide opportunities for students to evaluate their own global learning, it can help to have premade checklists or rubrics delineating clear expectations for what proficient global competence looks likes in the final products students will create. As you become more comfortable, take time to collectively design those checklists and rubrics with your class.

Just as you can use assessment to reflect on your globally competent teaching, help students reflect on their global competence learning through assessment activities. For example, have students create a global competence portfolio to which they add artifacts throughout the year. This helps them see their growth in specific aspects of global competence, such as appreciating diverse perspectives or understanding global interconnectedness.

Special Considerations for Elementary School Teachers (PK–5)

- Because existing formal assessments for global competence are few and far between for our youngest learners, observations can be a great way to document these students' global competence growth. After lessons you've taught that intentionally integrated global competence elements, write reflections on instances when students showed curiosity and cared about different people and places. Create checklists for behaviors you'd like to see (e.g., sharing two different perspectives about an issue, selecting books during independent reading that represent multiple cultures).

- Celebrate globally competent behaviors you observe! When you have classroom celebrations during circle time or at the end of the day, share instances when you heard a student modeling respectful language toward differences or observed a student devise a creative solution to a global issue. Have students recognize or award one another for demonstrating specific aspects of global competence.

Special Considerations for Secondary School Teachers (6–12)

- Include a global competence column into rubrics you already have for writing assessments, projects, and more. Because global competence transcends content areas and specific topics within those content areas, the same language can be attached to any assignment. For example, if you are interested in measuring the construct "valuing multiple perspectives," you can set criteria for students to incorporate at least three different sources or alternative perspectives in research assignments.
- For middle and high school students, formal assessments may be more standardized—and may be a source of added anxiety. As you reflect on ways you will assess global competence, keep in mind how you will incorporate assessment of global competence into the curriculum in an unthreatening way without overwhelming students.

Element 12 in Action: Using Multiple Metrics to Assess Global Learning Through a World Literature Project

Sixth grade English language arts teacher Kate utilizes both a multimetric and long-term approach to assessing her students' global competence development. A world literature project she developed and taught—Where Have You Traveled Through Books?—engaged students in an array of differentiated activities that allowed her to assess students' progress in developing an awareness, understanding, and appreciation of the diversity in the world around them.

During the project, students selected a book set in a country outside the United States to read independently. They wrote a traditional book report and conducted a research project on the country where their book was set, which they presented in a gallery walk on a trifold poster. In addition, they had to find a recipe for and bring in food from that country, which they presented along with their poster during the gallery walk. These tangible final products allowed Kate to assess English language arts–specific skills, such as reading comprehension, communication, research, use of credible sources, and writing along with global competence attributes, such as understanding culture, understanding global conditions, and developing empathy and appreciation of diverse perspectives. She broke the book reports and presentations into separate grades to allow students multiple opportunities to show their learning.

Throughout the three-week unit, Kate also used formative assessment to track student progress. She asked students to set weekly goals for themselves, and during class work time, she discussed with students whether they felt they were meeting their goals and what they were learning about the country and culture represented in their books. As Kate shared, "I can see how they're progressing mostly through conversation. It's really through their discussion, their thoughts, and what they say that I can really tell that they're developing a deeper understanding and appreciation for the wider world."

Kate also emphasized that global competence takes time to develop. She doesn't expect to see rapid changes in her students' global perspectives and understanding. She explained, "This isn't something that develops overnight. It's not like a math problem where you get it and you have the answer. It's about exposure and discussing and seeing what happens as the year goes on."

Further Developing This Skill

- Reflect on how you currently provide feedback to students on their global competence development. How frequently do you provide feedback? In what formats?

- Design a rubric or checklist to accompany a lesson you are planning on teaching that measures the aspects of global competence your lesson will address.
- Create a menu of performance assessment tasks students can choose from as a summative evaluation of their global learning. Try to ensure that the menu provides choices that covers multiple intelligences.

Continuing the Journey

These additional resources can be helpful as you continue to develop and use appropriate methods of inquiry to assess students' global competence development.

❯ **Asia Society Global Competence Outcomes and Rubrics**
(https://asiasociety.org/education/global-competence-outcomes-and-rubrics): Asia Society's Graduation Performance System is a user-friendly set of performance outcomes to help teachers prepare globally competent students. The outcomes are phrased as "I can" statements and organized by the Asia Society's four competencies that globally competent students possess: investigate the world, recognize perspectives, communicate ideas, and take action. They are available for grades K–2, 3, 5, 8, 10, and 12 in the following subject areas: leadership, mathematics, science, art, social studies, and language arts.

❯ **PISA 2018 Global Competence Framework**
(www.oecd.org/pisa/pisa-2018-global-competence.htm): The Programme for International Student Assessment (PISA) is a triennial survey of 15-year-old students aimed to evaluate education systems worldwide. This website includes sample questions across the variety of tested areas and the results and key findings from previous years. The questions are available in over 90 languages.

❯ **The Performance Assessment Resource Bank**
(www.performanceassessmentresourcebank.org): The Performance Assessment Resource Bank provides a curated collection of high-quality performance tasks and resources. Resources include performance tasks delineated by content areas, tips on how to develop performance tasks and rubrics,

professional development tools, and examples of how schools, districts, and states have integrated performance assessment into their assessment systems.

Conclusion

Supporting Teachers' Professional Learning Journeys

Across the previous 12 chapters, we shared various ways teachers can develop global competence dispositions, knowledge, and skills as a means of preparing all students for success within and beyond the classroom. While the 12 elements are portrayed as distinct—and can be focused on as such—they are interrelated. To move toward the sort of global competence for which we advocate, these elements need to work in concert. Not surprisingly, all elements require teachers to embrace a self-reflective stance that emphasizes the connection between the personal and interpersonal, the local and global, a willingness to be open-minded, and a sense of curiosity about oneself, others, and the wider world.

The Journey

Global competence, like great teaching, develops over time. It's important to see its development as an ongoing journey, not a one-time destination. The process of growing and developing across the elements might happen in fits and starts, or it might happen in more formulaic ways. There is no single path to globally competent teaching (Parkhouse, Tichnor-Wagner, Glazier, & Cain, 2015).

For example, an elementary teacher might have the opportunity to participate in a summer-long experience in Belize where she is fully immersed in another culture, living with a local host family and volunteering at a local elementary school. Simultaneously, this teacher may be tweeting about her experience to colleagues back home as she considers ways her experience might provide an impetus for student learning about the world. She is thus working on and across various elements and domains, including understanding global conditions (Element 3), developing an experiential understanding of another culture (Element 5), practicing intercultural communication (Element 6), communicating in two languages (Element 7), and developing international partnerships to support her teaching at home (Element 11). Indeed, this teacher's experience abroad lends itself to working across multiple domains simultaneously.

Alternatively, another teacher may decide to focus entirely on a single element of the domain. Perhaps a new social studies teacher aims to help his students develop multiple and global perspectives during a unit on China. He may spend time exclusively focused on identifying and reading various online resources as he supports his own growing knowledge of current events and global conditions (Element 3). In doing so, he develops his own knowledge and feels better prepared to open these spaces for his students as he integrates this knowledge into his curriculum (Element 10). These investigations may even lead him to discover subsidized opportunities for teachers to travel abroad to China to further cultivate his understanding of the cultures he has researched (Element 5). Suffice it to say, there is no single starting point or way forward in developing global competence. The path will be winding, sometimes circuitous, and unique to the teacher who is venturing on it.

Working with Colleagues and Community Members

Regardless of how a teacher chooses to proceed, we believe that teachers benefit from engaging in this important work with colleagues. In our work with 10 global teacher consultants who engaged in a series of online webinars, observations, interviews, and focus groups, the teacher consultants truly valued the opportunities they had to talk with one another about their teaching practice and the ways they brought the world into their classrooms. One of the teachers shared, for example, how working with other teachers on global competence rejuvenated her and her commitment to instilling global competence among her students. Teaching can be an isolating profession (Britzman, 1986; Hargreaves, 2001). Teachers close their classroom doors and often engage in the practice of teaching alone, yet research on teacher development and retention and on student learning argues that collaboration is an important element to keep teachers and students engaged and growing (Anrig, 2013; Hargreaves & Dawe, 1990; Hindin, Morocco, Mott, & Aguilar, 2007). The National Commission on Teaching and America's Future (2012) has argued that "collaboration is the key to a rewarding career that will attract and retain highly skilled professionals, resulting in higher-impact teaching and deeper student learning. It's time for educators to harness the power of teamwork found in all other successful 21st century professions" (Glazier, Boyd, Hughes, Able, & Mallous, 2017, p. 6).

What does it look like for teachers to collaborate around the elements of globally competent teaching? We have witnessed multiple scenarios. For example, teachers might work together in a book group like the one Melissa initiated (see Chapter 5) where she and a group of teacher colleagues read and discussed young adult literature that reflected the diverse experiences of today's youth. Marlene (Chapter 10) invited fellow teachers from Spanish-speaking countries into her heritage Spanish class. Teachers who form partnerships with classrooms in different parts of the country and world (Chapter 11) not only provide authentic learning experiences for students but also find like-minded colleagues for planning lessons and collaborative projects around global themes.

School administrators can also support opportunities for teachers to share their global learning with colleagues by highlighting their practices during schoolwide or departmentwide professional development. This was the case for Maddy (Chapter 5), who conducted a professional development session with her colleagues about how to successfully incorporate the Global Read Aloud into their classrooms, which resulted in other teachers signing up to have their own classrooms participate. Teachers in the same grade level or department can form professional learning communities (PLCs) that meet regularly around specific elements of global competence to share resources and ideas with one another or coplan lessons, units, and projects. In fact, time for such collaboration is essential for developing interdisciplinary content-aligned investigations of the world.

Collaboration between colleagues is important not only in supporting teacher learning but also in providing support when challenges arise. Teaching for global competence requires teachers to wade into controversies. Issues such as gender equity, global poverty, sex trafficking, climate change, migration, and international conflicts are important issues for teachers to take on as they support student learning about worldwide inequities, global conditions and current events, and global interconnectedness. However, as teachers introduce these challenging topics, they can find themselves at odds with colleagues, administrators, and parents. In moments such as these, it is imperative for teachers to find colleagues—near and far—from whom to seek resources and support.

The Role of School and District Administrators

Global learning falls squarely in the middle of teachers' everyday curriculum. However, teachers need support identifying ways to tie global elements to their everyday practice and finding the time to do so. School administrators play a key supporting role in this. Support can come in a variety of forms. As mentioned previously, school administrators can create the time and space for teachers to regularly collaborate in PLCs or global learning cohorts, make global competence a priority during allocated professional development days, and partner with external organizations that provide instructional support in integrating global learning across the content areas (e.g., Asia Society Global Education Center, International Baccalaureate, Primary Source, World Savvy).

Along with professional learning support, school leaders can also offer financial support in advancing anything from funding abroad experiences for teachers to purchasing classroom materials. Perhaps most important, school leaders can offer dispositional support. Dispositional support can come in the form of schoolwide mission statements that highlight a global focus to regular acknowledgment of the ways teachers are successfully supporting students' global competence growth, vis-à-vis observation feedback, staff newsletters, and schoolwide celebrations (Tichnor-Wagner & Manise, 2019).

Support for advancing global teaching and learning should come not only at the school level but also from the district and state. As found in a case study of two school districts committed to global competence (Tichnor-Wagner, 2016), districts can support globally competent teaching by generating goodwill (e.g., having a superintendent who champions the work, having recognition programs for teachers who excel in global teaching), providing district-level professional learning opportunities, reorganizing office staff so there is a position that directly oversees and supports implementation of global programs and practices, and redirecting extant funds for globally focused instructional programs, materials, and professional development.

State departments of education can support globally competent teaching as well. North Carolina's Global Educator Digital Badge is an example of a successful statewide initiative in support of the growth of global knowledge in K–12 schools. In an effort to ensure "every public school student graduate [is] prepared to be a globally engaged and productive citizen," the North Carolina Department of Public Instruction developed a global educator digital badge program to support teachers' expertise in global education (see www.ncpublicschools.org/docs/globaled/actions/gedb-implement-guide.pdf).

To earn the designation, teachers must complete 100 hours of approved professional development and complete a global education capstone project. This type of opportunity allows teachers to engage deeply in developing their global expertise and to help their students blossom into engaged, responsible global citizens. Similar attention to global education appears in state-level standards for K–12 teachers. For instance, the North Carolina Professional Teaching Standards include the following language (Public Schools of North Carolina, 2013, emphasis added):

> Teachers demonstrate their knowledge of the history of diverse cultures and their role in shaping *global issues*. They actively select materials and develop lessons that counteract stereotypes and incorporate histories and contributions of all cultures. (Standard 2)
>
> Teachers *promote global awareness* and its relevance to the subjects they teach. (Standard 3)

Similar language is also becoming more ubiquitous in national standards for teachers, providing a political impetus for schools to prioritize global teaching and learning. For example, the InTASC (2013) standards of what teachers should know and be able to do include explicit attention to teachers' ability to support student learning of global topics. According to Standard 5: Application of Content: "The teacher understands how to connect concepts and use differing perspectives to engage learners in critical thinking, creativity, and collaborative problem-solving related to authentic and *global issues*" [emphasis added].

As *global* becomes more common across standards for teaching in the United States, it is imperative that school and district leaders support teachers' global competence development. This way, teachers are not alone in deciphering what global teaching should look like. Furthermore, when school, district, and state systems become involved, more and more students will have access to global learning opportunities and therefore greater opportunities to access the curriculum in engaging, meaningful, authentic ways that prepare them for the real world of citizenship and work.

The Role of Schools of Education

Kissock and Richardson (2010) aptly wrote that

> teacher educators are challenged to…begin preparing educators for the globally interdependent world in which they will work and their students will live, by opening the world to students through international experience and integrating a global perspective throughout the curriculum. (p. 89)

The responsibility for supporting teachers in developing global competence does not lie only at the feet of states, districts, and schools. Indeed, schools of education must also play a pivotal role in helping prepare teachers to step into classrooms as confident and competent global educators.

Often, schools of education prepare teachers for present communities, offering little attention to the larger global community (with the exception, perhaps, of the preparation of social studies teachers) (Goodwin, 2010; Kissock & Richardson, 2010). This oversight leaves teachers ill-prepared to engage their students in meaningful global learning. Teacher education programs that intentionally integrate global knowledge, skills, and dispositions into coursework and student experiences provide an important critical step for the development of globally competent—and confident—teachers (e.g., Shaklee & Baily, 2012).

What methods can teacher education programs employ to support preservice teacher learning about the world? First and foremost, programs of education must make explicit their mission to develop teachers as global learners and doers. Second, programs need to establish multiple, coordinated efforts. Although more teacher preparation programs are providing teaching abroad opportunities for undergraduate and masters' students (see Chapter 5), that is just one of many ways to place future and experienced teachers on a global learning pathway. The Association of International Educators (NAFSA) provides a helpful list of opportunities that educator preparation programs may provide for students. This list includes

- Coursework that has integrated global competence into both content and pedagogical development.
- Clinic and field placements in schools that model effective global education.
- Professors and mentors who value global competence and seek out global contexts in all aspects of the teacher preparation curriculum.
- Application of theories of cross-cultural learning, communication, and adjustment across the program.
- Learning about other regions of the world and global current events.
- Reflection on one's own culture and its impact on daily choices and classroom practice.
- Opportunities for experiential learning in other countries and cultures through study abroad, teaching practicums, and/or internships. (Moss, Manise, & Soppelsa, 2012, p. 4)

These efforts take time to implement. As schools of education seek to better prepare their students to be globally competent educators, we look forward to additional examples of what this looks like in practice.

In the meantime, individual teacher educators can make a difference in their teacher preparation courses, even when these do not include an explicit focus on global awareness. They can infuse global competence into their course descriptions and objectives, materials, and instructional activities, as well as through designing cross-cultural learning experiences for students (Parkhouse, Glazier, Tichnor-Wagner, & Cain, 2015). Jocelyn, a teacher educator at the University of North Carolina at Chapel Hill, decided to redesign one of her courses to focus more on global competence. The topic of the course, part of a master's program for experienced teachers, was culturally responsive teaching. Jocelyn added readings and instructional activities that allowed students to compare education and culturally responsive teaching across local and global contexts. Students also rated themselves along the GCLC at the beginning and end of the semester, which allowed Jocelyn to evaluate the extent to which students believed they had progressed in their global competence development and allowed students to reflect further on the significance of global learning. Students did advance in some areas, and, as important, many expressed a greater interest in global connections.

We live in an interconnected world, but our classrooms are often not as interconnected with the outside world as they could be. Students might conduct internet searches that expose them to information from around the world, but mere exposure is unlikely to develop an appreciation for diverse cultures and empathy for people around the world they've never met. Global competence attributes must become explicit learning objectives, woven throughout the P12 curriculum across grades and subject areas. Consequently, teachers of all grades and subject areas need to become committed to instilling global competence in students—and receive the necessary training to pursue it. As we expect our students to be prepared to engage with world partners, so too must we support our teachers in developing this knowledge (Shaklee & Baily, 2012; Zhao, 2010). Otherwise, teachers will be hard-pressed to help their students be ready to meet and transform the world.

Appendix

The Globally Competent Learning Continuum Self-Reflection Tool

Step 1: Carefully read the twelve elements of globally competent teaching and the five corresponding levels (nascent, beginning, progressing, proficient, and advanced) on the Globally Competent Learning Continuum.

Step 2: Rate yourself nascent, beginning, progressing, proficient, or advanced for each element. Explain why you chose that level, and provide evidence from your professional and/or personal experiences.

Step 3:

Which element(s) do you feel are your greatest strengths?

Which element(s) do you feel you have the greatest room for growth?

Element	Level	Evidence
1. Empathy and valuing multiple perspectives		
2. Commitment to promoting equity worldwide		
3. Understanding of global conditions and current events		
4. Understanding of the ways the world is interconnected		
5. Experiential understanding of diverse cultures		
6. Understanding of intercultural communication		
7. Communicating in multiple languages		
8. Creating a classroom environment that values diversity and global engagement		
9. Integrating learning experiences that promote content-aligned explorations of the world		
10. Facilitating intercultural conversations		
11. Developing local, national, or international partnerships		
12. Developing and using appropriate methods of inquiry to assess students' global competence development		

References

Agirdag, O. (2009). All languages welcomed here. In M. Scherer (Ed.), *Supporting the Whole Child*. Alexandria: VA: ASCD: Retrieved from www.ascd.org/publications/books/110058e4/chapters/All-Languages-Welcomed-Here.aspx

Alexander, M. (2012). *The new Jim Crow: Mass incarceration in the age of colorblindness*. New York: New Press.

Alfaro, C., & Quezada, R. L. (2010). International teacher professional development: Teacher reflections of authentic teaching and learning experiences. *Teaching Education, 21*(1), 47–59.

Alim, H. S., & Paris, D. (2017). What is culturally sustaining pedagogy? In D. Paris & H. S. Alim (Eds.), *Culturally Sustaining Pedagogies* (pp. 1–21). New York: Teachers College Press.

American Academy of Arts & Sciences. (2017). *America's languages: Investing in language education for the 21st century*. Cambridge, MA: American Academy of Arts & Sciences. Retrieved from www.amacad.org/publication/americas-languages-investing-language-education-21st-century

American Council on the Teaching of Foreign Languages (ACTFL). (2015). *World readiness standards for learning languages*. Retrieved from www.actfl.org/publications/all/world-readiness-standards-learning-languages

American Council on the Teaching of Foreign Languages (ACTFL). (2018). *What does research show about the benefits of language learning?* Retrieved from www.actfl.org/advocacy/what-the-research-shows

American Councils. (2017). *The National K–16 Foreign Language Enrollment Survey Report*. Retrieved from www.americancouncils.org/sites/default/files/FLE-report.pdf

American Educational Research Association, American Psychological Association, and National Council on Measurement in Education, Joint Committee on Standards for Educational & Psychological Testing. (2014). *Standards for educational and psychological testing*. Washington, DC: American Educational Research Association.

Amit, M., & Abu Quoder, F. (2017). Weaving culture and mathematics in the classroom: The case of Bedouin ethnomathematics. In M. Rosa et al. (Eds.), *Ethnomathematics and its diverse approaches for Mathematics Education* (pp. 23–50). New York: Springer International.

Anderson, S. R. (2010). *How many languages are there in the world?* Washington, DC: Linguistic Society of America. Retrieved from www.linguisticsociety.org/content/how-many-languages-are-there-world

Andonova, E., & Taylor, H. A. (2012). Nodding in dis/agreement: A tale of two cultures. *Cognitive Processing, 13*(1), 79–82.

Andreotti, V. (2006). Soft versus critical global citizenship education. *Policy and Practice: A Development Education Review, 3,* 40–51.

Andreotti, V., & Pashby, K. (2013). Digital democracy and global citizenship education: Mutually compatible or mutually complicit? *The Educational Forum, 77*(4), 422–437.

Anrig, G. (2013). *Beyond the education wars: Evidence that collaboration builds effective schools.* New York: Century Foundation Press.

Armstrong, N. F. (2008). Teacher education in a global society: Facilitating global literacy for preservice candidates through international field experiences. *Teacher Education and Practice, 21*(4), 490–506.

Asia Society. (2009). *Going global: Preparing our students for an interconnected world.* Retrieved from http://asiasociety.org/files/Going%20Global%20Educator%20Guide.pdf

Asia Society. (2013). Global Leadership Performance Outcomes. New York: Asia Society Center for Global Education. Retrieved from https://asiasociety.org/education/leadership-global-competence

Asia Society & Longview Foundation. (2016). *Preparing a globally competent workforce through high-quality career and technical education.* Retrieved from http://asiasociety.org/sites/default/files/preparing-a-globally-competent-workforce-june-2016.pdf

Associated Press. (2016, September 15). Where do Trump and Clinton stand on Syrian refugees coming into the United States. *Haaretz.* Retrieved from www.haaretz.com/world-news/where-do-trump-and-clinton-stand-on-syrian-refugees-coming-into-the-united-states-1.5435724.

Avery, P. G., Levy, S. A., & Simmons, A. M. (2013). Deliberating controversial public issues as part of civic education. *Social Studies, 104*(3), 105–114.

Bailey, A. L., & Kelly, K. R. (2013). Home language survey practices in the initial identification of English learners in the United States. *Educational Policy, 27*(5), 770–804.

Baldwin, J. (1979, July 29). If Black English isn't a language, then tell me, what is? *The New York Times.* Retrieved from www.nytimes.com/books/98/03/29/specials/baldwin-english.html

Ball, D. L., & Forzani, F. M. (2011). Building a common core for learning to teach: And connecting professional learning to practice. *American Educator, 35*(2), 17.

Banks, J. A. (2008). Diversity, group identity, and citizenship education in a global age. *Educational Researcher, 37*(3), 129–139.

Banks, J. A. (2014). Diversity, group identity, and citizenship education in a global age. *Journal of Education, 194*(3), 1–12.

Barton, K., & McCully, A. (2007). Teaching controversial issues where controversial issues really matter. *Teaching History, 127*, 13–19.

Bigelow, B., & Peterson, B. (2002). *Rethinking globalization: Teaching for justice in an unjust world.* Milwaukee, WI: Rethinking Schools Press. Retrieved from http://rethinkingschools.aidcvt.com/publication/rg/RGIntro.shtml.

Bishop, R. S. (1990). Mirrors, windows, and sliding doors. *Perspectives: Choosing and using books for the classroom, 6*(3), ix–xi.

Bridgeland, J. M., Dilulio, J. J., & Morison, K. B. (2006). *The silent epidemic: Perspectives of high school dropouts.* Washington, DC: Civic Enterprises.

Britzman, D. P. (1986). Cultural myths in the making of a teacher: Biography and social structure in teacher education. *Harvard Educational Review, 56*(4), 442–456.

Brody, C. M., & Davidson, N., (1998). Introduction: Professional development and cooperative learning. In C. M. Brody & N. Davidson (Eds.), *Professional development for cooperative learning: Issues and approaches.* Albany: State University of New York Press.

Brookhart, S. M. (2013). *How to create and use rubrics for formative assessment and grading.* Alexandria, VA: ASCD.

Bucholtz, M., Casillas, D. I., & Lee, J. S. (2017). Language and culture as sustenance. In D. Paris & H. S. Alim (Eds.), *Culturally sustaining pedagogies: Teaching and learning for justice in a changing world.* New York: Teachers College Press.

Buck Institute for Education. (2015). *Gold standard PBL: Essential project design elements.* Retrieved from www.bie.org/object/document/gold_standard_pbl_essential_project_design_elements

Byford, J., Lennon, S., & Russell, W. B. (2009). Teaching controversial issues in the social studies: A research study of high school teachers. *Clearing House, 82*(4), 165–170.

Cantor, P., Osher, D., Berg, J., Steyer, L., & Rose, T. (2018). Malleability, plasticity, and individuality: How children learn and develop in context. *Applied Developmental Science*, 1–31.

Center for Applied Linguistics. (2016). *Heritage FAQs.* Retrieved from www.cal.org/heritage/research/faqs.html

Chappuis, J., & Stiggins, R. J. (2017). *An introduction to student-involved assessment FOR learning* (7th ed.). London: Pearson.

CNN Staff. (2017, December 16). From coding to literacy: These youth are changing the game. CNN. Retrieved from www.cnn.com/2017/12/13/us/cnn-heroes-2017-young-wonders/index.html

Collier, V. P., & Thomas, W. P. (2004). The astounding effectiveness of dual language education for all. *NABE Journal of Research and Practice, 2*(1), 1–20.

Columbus World Affairs Council. (2017). *The Global Report 2016–2017*. Retrieved from https://columbusworldaffairs.org

Colvin, R. L., & Edwards, V. (2018). *Teaching for global competence in a rapidly changing world*. Paris: OECD Publishing.

Cummins, J. (1979). Linguistic interdependence and the educational development of bilingual children. *Review of Educational Research, 49*(2), 222–251.

Cushner, K. (2012). Intercultural competence for teaching and learning. In B. D. Shaklee & S. Baily (Eds.). *Internationalizing teacher education in the United States* (pp. 41–58). Lanham, MD: Roman & Littlefield.

D'Ambrosio, U. (2001). What is ethnomathematics, and how can it help children in schools? *Teaching Children Mathematics, 7*(6), 308.

Dantas, M. L. (2007). Building teacher competency to work with diverse learners in the context of international education. *Teacher Education Quarterly, 34*(1), 75–94.

Deardorff, D. K. (2006). Identification and assessment of intercultural competence as a student outcome of internationalization. *Journal of Studies in International Education, 10*(3), 241–266.

Deardorff, D. K. (2018, January 31). How to assess global competence [blog post]. *Education Week Global Learning Blog*. Retrieved from http://blogs.edweek.org/edweek/global_learning/2018/01/how_to_assess_global_competence.html

Engel, L. (2018). K–12 study abroad linked with improved learning outcomes [blog post]. *Education Week*. Retrieved from http://blogs.edweek.org/edweek/global_learning/2018/03/k-12_study_abroad_linked_with_improved_learning_outcomes.html?cmp=soc-edit-tw&print=1

Ernst-Slavit, G., & Mason, M. (n.d.). *Making your first ELL home visit: A guide for classroom teachers*. Retrieved from www.colorincolorado.org/article/making-your-first-ell-home-visit-guide-classroom-teachers

Eslami, Z. R. (2005). Global education: Instructional strategies used and challenges faced by in-service teachers. *Teacher Education and Practice, 18*(4), 400–415.

Fillmore, L. W. (2000). Loss of family languages: Should educators be concerned? *Theory into Practice: Children and Languages at School, 39*(4), 203–211.

Freire, P. (1970). *Pedagogy of the oppressed*. New York: Continuum.

Friedman, T. (2007). *The world is flat*. New York: Picador.

Gallavan, N. P. (2008). Examining teacher candidates' views on teaching world citizenship. *Social Studies, 99*(6), 249–254.

García, O. (2009). *Bilingual education in the 21st century: A global perspective*. West Sussex: Wiley-Blackwell.

García, O., & Wei, L. (2014). *Translanguaging: Language, bilingualism and education*. London: Palgrave Macmillan.

Gaudelli, W., & Hewitt, R. (2010). The aesthetic potential of global issues curriculum. *The Journal of Aesthetic Education, 44*(2), 83–99.

Gay, G. (2000). *Culturally responsive teaching: Theory, research, and practice*. New York: Teachers College Press.

Gee, J. (1989). Literacy, discourse, and linguistics: Introduction. *Journal of Education, 171*(1), 5–17.

Gerber. E. (2018). *The best books on globalization recommended by Larry Summers.* Retrieved from https://fivebooks.com/best-books/larry-summers-globalization

Gibson, M. A. (1988). *Accommodation without assimilation: Sikh immigrants in an American high school.* Ithaca, NY: Cornell University Press.

Gibson, M. A. (1998). Promoting academic success among immigrant students: Is acculturation the issue? *Educational Policy, 12*(6), 615–633.

Glazier, J., Boyd, A., Hughes, K., Able, H., & Mallous, R. (2017). The elusive search for teacher collaboration. *The New Educator, 13*(1), 3–21.

Goetz, P. J. (2003). The effects of bilingualism on theory of mind development. *Bilingualism: Language and Cognition, 6*(1), 1–15.

Goodwin, A. L. (2010). Globalization and the preparation of quality teachers: Rethinking knowledge domains for teaching. *Teaching Education, 21*(1), 19–32.

Gorski, P. C. (2016). Poverty and the ideological imperative: A call to unhook from deficit and grit ideology and to strive for structural ideology in teacher education. *Journal of Education for Teaching, 42*(4), 378–386.

Gudykunst, W. B. (2003). *Cross-cultural and intercultural communication.* Thousand Oaks, CA: Sage.

Haidt, J. (2012). *The righteous mind: Why good people are divided by politics and religion.* New York: Pantheon.

Hall, E. T. (1976). *Beyond culture.* New York: Doubleday.

Hammer, M. R., Bennett, M. J., & Wiseman, R. (2003). Measuring intercultural sensitivity: The intercultural development inventory. *International Journal of Intercultural Relations, 27*(4), 421–443.

Hanvey, R. G. (1982). An attainable global perspective. *Theory into Practice, 21*(3), 162–167.

Hargreaves, A. (2001). The emotional geographies of teachers' relations with colleagues. *International Journal of Educational Research, 35*, 503–527.

Hargreaves, A., & Dawe, R. (1990). Paths of professional development: Contrived collegiality, collaborative culture, and the case of peer coaching. *Teaching & Teacher Education, 6*, 227–241.

Hasso Plattner, Institute of Design at Stanford. (n.d.). *Guide for creating a design challenge.* Retrieved from https://dschool-old.stanford.edu/sandbox/groups/k12/wiki/37c88/attachments/d6fae/Scoping%20Suite.pdf

Hayakawa, H. (2003). *"The meaningless laugh": Laughter in Japanese communication* (Unpublished doctoral dissertation). University of Sydney, Australia. Retrieved from https://ses.library.usyd.edu.au/bitstream/2123/656/2/adt-NU20050104.14424602whole.pdf

Heejung, A. (Ed.). (2016). *Handbook of research on efficacy and implementation of study abroad programs for P–12 teachers.* Hershey, PA: IGI Global.

Heineke, A. J., Davin, K. J., & Bedford, A. (2018). The seal of biliteracy: Considering equity and access for English learners. *Education Policy Analysis Archives, 26*(99), 1–12.

Hess, D. (2011). Discussions that drive democracy. *Educational Leadership, 69*(1), 69–73.

Hinchey, P. H. (2004). *Becoming a critical educator: Defining a classroom identity, designing a critical pedagogy* (Vol. 224). New York: Peter Lang.

Hindin, A., Morocco, C., Mott, E., & Aguilar, C. (2007). More than just a group: Teacher collaboration and learning in the workplace. *Teachers and Teaching: Theory and Practice, 13*, 349–376.

Hofstede, G. (2011). Dimensionalizing cultures: The Hofstede Model in context. *Online Readings in Psychology and Culture, 2*(1).

Howard, T. C. (2003). Culturally relevant pedagogy: Ingredients for critical teacher reflection. *Theory into Practice, 42*, 195–202.

iEARN. (2014). *iEARN teacher's guide to online collaboration and global projects*. Retrieved from https://iearn.org/assets/resources/32498_iEARN-Teachers-Guide.pdf

InTASC. (2013). *Model Core Teaching Standards and Learning Progressions for Teachers 1.0.* Washington, DC: Council of Chief State School Officers. https://ccsso.org/sites/default/files/2017-12/2013_INTASC_Learning_Progressions_for_Teachers.pdf

IREX. (2018). *World Smarts STEM Challenge*. Retrieved from www.irex.org/project/world-smarts-stem-challenge

Jack, R. E., Garrod, O. G., Yu, H., Caldara, R., & Schyns, P. G. (2012). Facial expressions of emotion are not culturally universal. *Proceedings of the National Academy of Sciences of the USA, 109*(19), 7241–7244.

Journell, W. (2016). Teacher political disclosure as parrhesia. *Teachers College Record, 118*(5), 1–36.

Kammerman, S. (2006). *Spanish for educators* [audiobook]. Ventnor, NJ: KAMMS Consulting.

Kirkwood, T. F. (2001a). Our global age requires global education: Clarifying definitional ambiguities. *Social Studies, 92*(1), 10–15.

Kirkwood, T. F. (2001b). Preparing teachers to teach from a global perspective. *Delta Kappa Gamma Bulletin, 67*(2), 5–12.

Kirshner, J., Tzib, E., Tzib, Z., & Fry, S. (2016). From pen pals to global citizens. *Educational Leadership, 74*(4), 73–74.

Kissock, C., & Richardson, P. (2010). Calling for action within the teaching profession: It is time to internationalize teacher education. *Teaching Education, 21*(1), 89–101.

Kotthoff, H., & Spencer-Oatey, H. (Eds.). (2008). *Handbook of intercultural communication* (Vol. 7). Berlin: Walter de Gruyter.

Koutonin, M. R. (2015). Why are white people expats when the rest of us are immigrants? *The Guardian*. Retrieved from www.theguardian.com/global-development-professionals-network/2015/mar/13/white-people-expats-immigrants-migration

Kunda, Z. (1990). The case for motivated reasoning. *Psychological Bulletin, 108*(3), 480–498.

Laal, M., & Ghodsi, S. M. (2012). Benefits of collaborative learning. *Procedia-Social and Behavioral Sciences, 31*, 486–490.

Ladson-Billings, G. (1995). Toward a theory of culturally relevant pedagogy. *American Educational Research Journal, 32*, 465–491.

Ladson-Billings, G. (2011). "Yes, but how do we do it?": Practicing culturally relevant pedagogy. In J. G. Landsman & C. W. Lewis (Eds.), *White teachers/diverse classrooms: Creating inclusive schools, building on students' diversity and providing true educational equity* (2nd ed., pp. 33–46). Sterling, VA: Stylus.

Larmer, J., Mergendoller, J., & Boss, S. (2015). *Setting the standard for project-based learning: A proven approach to rigorous classroom instruction.* Alexandria, VA: ASCD.

Levine, P. (2007). *The future of democracy: Developing the next generation of American citizens.* Lebanon, NH: University Press of New England.

Lindsay, J. (2016). *The global educator.* Eugene, OR: International Society for Technology in Education.

Lippi-Green, R. (1997). *English with an accent: Language, ideology, and discrimination in the United States.* New York: Routledge.

Mansilla, V. B. (2016). How to be a global thinker. *Educational Leadership, 74*(4), 10–16.

Mansilla, V. B., & Jackson, A. (2011). *Educating for global competence: Preparing our youth to engage the world.* New York: Asia Society.

Marks, H. M. (2000). Student engagement in instructional activity: Patterns in the elementary, middle, and high school years. *American Educational Research Journal, 37*(1), 153–184.

Martin, F., & Griffiths, H. (2014). Relating to the "other": Transformative, intercultural learning in post-colonial contexts. *Compare: A Journal of Comparative and International Education, 44*(6), 938–959.

Martin-Kniep, G. O. (2000). *Becoming a better teacher: Eight innovations that work.* Alexandria, VA: ASCD.

Marx, H., & Moss, D. M. (2011). Please mind the culture gap: Intercultural development during a teacher education study abroad program. *Journal of Teacher Education, 62*(1), 35–47.

Matsumoto, D., Hee You, S. H., & LeRoux, J. A. (2007). Emotion and intercultural adjustment. *Handbook of Intercultural Communication*, 77–97.

McGraw, G. (2018, March 22). For millions of Americans, lack of access to water isn't just a drought problem. *Los Angeles Times.* Retrieved from www.latimes.com/opinion/op-ed/la-oe-mcgraw-water-poverty-data-20180322-story.html

McGury, S., Shallenberg, S., & Tolliver, D. E. (2008). It's new but is it learning? Assessment rubrics for intercultural learning programs. *Assessment Update, 20*, 6–9.

McLaughlin, M. W. (1990). The Rand change agent study revisited: Macro perspectives and micro realities. *Educational Researcher, 19*(9), 11–16.

Merrit, A. (2013, June 19). Why learn a foreign language? Benefits of bilingualism. *The Telegraph.* Retrieved from www.telegraph.co.uk/education/educationopinion/10126883/Why-learn-a-foreign-language-Benefits-of-bilingualism.html

Merryfield, M. M. (1998). Pedagogy for global perspectives in education: Studies of teachers' thinking and practice. *Theory and Research in Social Education, 26*(3), 342–379.

Merryfield, M. M. (2000). Why aren't teachers being prepared to teach for diversity, equity, and global interconnectedness? A study of lived experiences in the making of multicultural and global educators. *Teaching and Teacher Education, 16*(4), 429–443.

Merryfield, M. M. (2002). The difference a global educator can make. *Educational Leadership, 60*(2), 18–21.

Miller, A. (2017). Project-based learning for global readiness [blog post]. *ASCD InService*. Retrieved from http://inservice.ascd.org/project-based-learning-for-global-readiness

Moll, L., Amanti, C., Neff, D., & Gonzalez, N. (2001). Funds of knowledge for teaching: Using a qualitative approach to connect homes and classrooms. *Theory into Practice, 31*(2), 132–141.

Morgan, W., & Streb, M. (2001). Building citizenship: How student voice in service-learning develops civic values. *Social Science Quarterly, 82*(1), 154–169.

Moss, D., Manise, J., & Soppelsa, B. (2012). *Preparing globally competent teachers: Background paper for CAEP commissioners*. Washington, DC: NAFSA.

National Center for Education Statistics (NCES). (2016). *Status and trends in the education of racial and ethnic groups 2016* (NCES 2016-007). Washington, DC: U.S. Department of Education. Retrieved from https://nces.ed.gov/pubs2016/2016007.pdf

National Council for the Accreditation of Teacher Education (NCATE). (2008). *Professional standards for the accreditation of teacher preparation institutions*. Washington, DC: Author. Retrieved from www.ncate.org/~/media/Files/caep/accreditation-resources/ncate-standards-2008.pdf?la=en

National Council for the Social Studies (NCSS). (2016). Academic freedom and the social studies educator: A position statement of National Council for the Social Studies. *National Council for the Social Studies, 80*(3), 186.

National Governors Association Center for Best Practices and Council of Chief State School Officers. (2008). Common Core State Standards Initiative. Retrieved from www.corestandards.org/about-the-standards/development-process

National Research Council. (2014). *The growth of incarceration in the United States: Exploring causes and consequences*. Committee on causes and consequences of high rates of incarceration. Washington, DC: National Academies Press.

Neason, A. (2016, June 8). How Hawaiian came back from the dead. *Slate*. www.slate.com/articles/life/tomorrows_test/2016/06/how_the_ka_papahana_kaiapuni_immersion_schools_saved_the_hawaiian_language.html

Negri-Pool, L. L. (2017). Welcoming Kalenna: Making our students feel at home. In E. Barbian, G. Cornell Gonzales, & P. Mejia (Eds.), *Rethinking Bilingual Education*. Milwaukee, WI: Rethinking Schools.

Noddings, N. (1984). *Caring*. Berkeley, CA: University of California Press.

Noddings, N. (2005). Global citizenship: Promises and problems. In N. Noddings (Ed.), *Educating citizens for global awareness* (pp. 1–21). New York: Teachers College Press.

O'Connor, K., & Zeichner, K. (2011). Preparing US teachers for critical global education. *Globalisation, Societies and Education, 9*(3-4), 521–536.

Organisation for Economic Co-operation and Development (OECD). (2018a). *Preparing our youth for an inclusive and sustainable world: The OECD PISA global competence framework.* Paris: OECD Publishing. Retrieved from www.oecd.org/pisa/Handbook-PISA-2018-Global-Competence.pdf

Organisation for Economic Co-operation and Development (OECD). (2018b). *Inequality.* Paris: OECD Publishing. Retrieved from www.oecd.org/social/inequality.htm

Oxley, L., & Morris, P. (2013). Global citizenship: A typology for distinguishing its multiple conceptions. *British Journal of Educational Studies, 61*(3), 301–325.

Palmer, P. J. (1998). *The courage to teach: Exploring the inner landscape of a teacher's life.* San Francisco: Jossey-Bass.

Panitz, T. (1999a). *The case for student centered instruction via collaborative learning paradigms.* Retrieved from https://files.eric.ed.gov/fulltext/ED448444.pdf

Panitz, T. (1999b). *Collaborative versus cooperative learning: A comparison of the two concepts which will help us understand the underlying nature of interactive learning.* Retrieved from https://files.eric.ed.gov/fulltext/ED448443.pdf

Paris, D. (2012). Culturally sustaining pedagogy: A needed change in stance, terminology, and practice. *Educational Researcher, 41*(3), 93–97.

Parker, W. C. (2008). "International education": What's in a name? *Phi Delta Kappan, 90*(3), 196–202.

Parkhouse, H., Glazier, J., Tichnor-Wagner, A., & Cain, J. M. (2015). From local to global: Making the leap in teacher education. *International Journal of Global Education, 4*(2), 10–29.

Parkhouse, H., Tichnor-Wagner, A., Glazier, J., & Cain, J. M. (2015). "You don't have to travel the world": Accumulating experiences on the path toward globally competent teaching. *Teaching Education,* 1–19.

Parkhouse, H., Turner, A. M., Konle, S., & Rong, X. L. (2016). Self-authoring the meaning of student teaching in China: Impacts on first-year teaching practices. *Frontiers: The Interdisciplinary Journal of Study Abroad, 18*, 78–98.

Payne, K., Niemi, L., & Doris, J. M. (2018, March 27). How to think about "implicit bias." *Scientific American.* Retrieved from www.scientificamerican.com/article/how-to-think-about-implicit-bias

Peacock, J. L. (2007). *Grounded globalism: How the U.S. South embraces the world.* Athens: University of Georgia Press.

Perez-Sotelo, L., & Hogan, E. (2008). *The essential Spanish phrase book for teachers.* New York: Scholastic.

Pike, G. & Selby, D. (2000). *In the global classroom.* Toronto: Pippin.

Pike, G., & Selby, D. (2001). *In the global classroom.* Toronto: Pippin.

Pilonieta, P., Medina, A., & Hathaway, J. (2017) The impact of a study abroad experience on preservice teachers: Dispositions and plans for teaching English language learners. *The Teacher Educator, 52*(1), 22–38.

Pinxten, R. (1994). Ethnomathematics and its practice. *For the Learning of Mathematics, 14*(2), 23–25.

Pitler, H. (2017). Twitter and your professional learning network [blog post]. *ASCD Inservice.* Retrieved from http://inservice.ascd.org/twitter-and-your-professional-learning-network

Public Schools of North Carolina. (2013). *North Carolina Professional Teaching Standards.* Retrieved from www.ncpublicschools.org/docs/effectiveness-model/ncees/standards/prof-teach-standards.pdf

Ray, B. (2012, December 7). How to use Twitter to grow your PLN [blog post]. *Edutopia.* Retrieved from www.edutopia.org/blog/twitter-expanding-pln

Reeves, D. (2011). From differentiated instruction to differentiated assessment. *ASCD Express, 6*(20).

Reimers, F. (2009). Educating for global competency. In J. E. Cohen & M. B. Malin (Eds.), *International Perspectives on the Goals of Universal Basic and Secondary Education* (pp. 183–202). New York: Routledge.

Ribble, M. (2011). *Digital citizenship in schools: Nine elements all students should know* (3rd ed.). Eugene, OR: International Society for Technology in Education.

Rickford, J. (n.d.). What is Ebonics (African American English)? *Linguistic Society of America.* Retrieved from www.linguisticsociety.org/content/what-ebonics-african-american-english

Roberts, A. (2007). Global dimensions of schooling: Implications for internationalizing teacher education. *Teacher Education Quarterly, 34*(1), 9–26.

Robertson, R. (1995). Glocalization: Time-space and homogeneity-heterogeneity. *Global Modernities, 2,* 25–44.

Samovar, L. A., & Porter, R. L. (2002). *Intercultural communication: A reader* (10th ed.). Belmont, CA: Wadsworth/Thomson Learning.

Sanders, T., & Stewart, V. (2004). International education: From community innovation to national policy. *Phi Delta Kappan, 86*(3), 200–205.

Sandoval, C., & Latorre, G. (2008). Chicana/o artivism: Judy Baca's digital work with youth of color. *Learning Race and Ethnicity: Youth and Digital Media,* 81–108.

Selby, D., & Pike, G. (2000). Civil global education: Relevant learning for the twenty-first century. *Convergence, 33*(1), 138–149.

Selby, D., & Pike, G. (2001). *In the global classroom.* Toronto: Pippin.

Shaklee, B. D., & Baily, S. (Eds.). (2012). *Internationalizing teacher education in the United States.* Lanham, MD: Rowman & Littlefield.

Shulman, L. S. (1986). Those who understand: Knowledge growth in teaching. *Educational Researcher, 15*(2), 4–14.

Simons, G. F., & Fennig, C. D. (2018). *Ethnologue: Languages of the world* (21st ed.). Dallas, TX: SIL International.

Singmaster, H., Norman, G., & Manise, J. (2018, June 26). Why states, districts, and schools should implement global certificate programs [blog post]. *Education Week.*

Retrieved from http://blogs.edweek.org/edweek/global_learning/2018/06/why_states_districts_and_schools_should_implement_global_certificate_programs.html

Spencer, M. B., Noll, E., Stoltzfus, J., & Harpalani, V. (2010). Identity and school adjustment: Revisiting the "acting White" assumption. *Educational Psychologist, 36*(1), 21–30.

Spencer, S. J., Steele, C. M., & Quinn, D. M. (1999). Stereotype threat and women's math performance. *Journal of Experimental Social Psychology, 35*(1), 4–28.

Spires, H. A., Himes, M., & Wang, L. (2016). Cross-cultural inquiry in science. *Educational Leadership, 74*(4), 72–74.

Steele, C. M., & Aronson, J. (1995). Stereotype threat and the intellectual test performance of African Americans. *Journal of Personality and Social Psychology, 69*(5), 797.

Steele, D. M., & Cohn-Vargas, B. (2013). *Identity safe classrooms: Places to belong and learn*. Thousand Oaks, CA: Corwin.

Steele, J. L., Slater, R. O., Zamarro, G., Miller, T., Li, J., Burkhauser, S., & Bacon, M. (2017). Effects of dual-language immersion programs on student achievement: Evidence from lottery data. *American Educational Research Journal, 54*(1 suppl.), 282S–306S.

Stewart, V. (2010). A classroom as wide as the world. In H. H. Jacobs (Ed.), *Curriculum 21: Essential education for a changing world*. Alexandria, VA: ASCD.

Stewart, V. (2012). *A world-class education: Learning from international models of excellence and innovation*. Alexandria, VA: ASCD.

Strickland, T., & DePalma, K. (2016). *The barefoot book of children*. Cambridge, MA: Barefoot Books.

Taie, S., & Goldring, R. (2018). *Characteristics of public elementary and secondary school teachers in the United States: Results from the 2015–16 National Teacher and Principal Survey*. U.S. Department of Education. Washington, DC: National Center for Education Statistics. Retrieved from https://nces.ed.gov/pubs2017/2017072rev.pdf

Tate, K. J. (2011). Integrating humane education into teacher education: Meeting our social and civic responsibilities. *Teacher Education and Practice, 24*(3), 301–315.

Tavangar, H. S., & Mladic-Morales, B. (2014). *The global education toolkit for elementary learners*. Thousand Oaks, CA: Corwin.

TESOL. (2017). *Principles of language learning and the role of the teacher*. Retrieved from www.tesol.org/docs/default-source/books/14077_sam.pdf?sfvrsn=2

Thorpe, H. (2018). *The newcomers: Finding refuge, friendship, and hope in America*. New York: Scribner.

Tichnor-Wagner, A. (2016). *Global education politics and policy: Discourses, coalitions, and co-construction amongst globally committed national, state, and district actors* (Unpublished doctoral dissertation). University of North Carolina at Chapel Hill.

Tichnor-Wagner, A. (2017). Inspiring glocal citizens. *Educational Leadership, 75*(3), 69–73.

Tichnor-Wagner, A., & Allen, D. (2016). Accountable for care: Cultivating caring school communities in urban high schools. *Leadership and Policy in Schools, 15*(4), 406–447.

Tichnor-Wagner, A., & Manise, J. (2019). *Globally competent educational leadership: A framework for leading schools in a diverse, interconnected world.* Alexandria, VA: ASCD. Retrieved from http://files.ascd.org/pdfs/publications/general/ascd-globally-competent-educational-leadership-report-2019.pdf

Tichnor-Wagner, A., Parkhouse, H., Glazier, J., & Cain, J. M. (2016). Expanding approaches to teaching for diversity and social justice in K–12 education: Fostering global citizenship across the content areas. *Education Policy Analysis Archives, 24*(59), 1–35.

Tomlinson, C.A., & Moon, T. R. (2013). *Assessment and student success in the differentiated classroom.* Alexandria, VA: ASCD.

Tony Blair Faith Foundation. (2015). *The essentials of dialogue.* London: Author.

Tye, K. A. (Ed.). (1990). *Global education: School-based strategies.* Orange, CA: Interdependence Press.

UNESCO. (2015). *Global citizenship education: Topics and learning objectives.* Paris: United Nations Educational, Scientific, and Cultural Organization. Retrieved from http://unesdoc.unesco.org/images/0023/002329/232993e.pdf

United Nations. (2015). *Transforming our world: The 2030 agenda for sustainable development.* Retrieved from https://sustainabledevelopment.un.org/post2015/transformingourworld

United Nations. (2016). Progress towards the sustainable development goals: Report of the Secretary General. Retrieved from https:/sustainabledevelopment.un.org/sdg4

U.S. Department of Education. (2017). U.S. Department of Education [website]. Retrieved from www.ed.gov

Valenzuela, A. (1999). *Subtractive schooling.* Albany: State University of New York Press.

Van Reken, R. E., & Rushmore, S. (2009). Thinking globally when teaching locally. *Kappa Delta Pi Record, 45*(2), 60–68.

Virtual Exchange Coalition. (2018). What is virtual exchange? [website]. Retrieved from http://virtualexchangecoalition.org

Vygotsky, L. (1978). Interaction between learning and development. *Readings on the Development of Children, 23*(3), 34–41.

Watson, L. (1985). 'Decade for Women.' Speech given at United Nations Conference, Nairobi, Kenya, July 15–26.

Wiggins, G. (2012). Seven keys to effective feedback. *Educational Leadership, 70*(1), 10–16.

Willard-Holt, C. (2001). The impact of short-term international experience for pre-service teachers. *Teaching and Teacher Education, 17*, 505–517.

Wilson, B. G. (1996). *Constructivist learning environments: Case studies in instructional design.* Englewood Cliffs, NJ: Educational Technology.

World Savvy. (2018). *Global competence matrix.* Retrieved from www.worldsavvy.org/global-competence

Zhao, Y. (2010). Preparing globally competent teachers: A new imperative for teacher education. *Journal of Teacher Education, 61*(5), 422–431.

Zhou, M., & Li, X. Y. (2003). Ethnic language schools and the development of supplementary education in the immigrant Chinese community in the United States. *New Directions for Youth Development, 2003*(100), 57–73.

Index

The letter *f* following a page locator denotes a figure.

About the Authors

Ariel Tichnor-Wagner, Hillary Parkhouse, Jocelyn Glazier, and J. Montana Cain are the codevelopers of the Globally Competent Learning Continuum (GCLC), an online self-reflection tool for professional growth around globally competent teaching. They have presented on the GCLC at numerous national and international conferences and local workshops and have coauthored multiple articles on globally competent teaching, including 'You don't have to travel the world': Accumulating Experiences on the Path Toward Globally Competent Teaching" in *Teaching Education;* "Expanding Approaches to Teaching for Diversity and Justice in K–12 Education: Fostering Global Citizenship Across the Content Areas" in *Education Policy Analysis Archives;* and "From Local to Global: Making the Leap in Teacher Education" in the *International Journal of Global Education.* Each of their individual bios are below, highlighting the unique perspectives that each brings to inspiring educators to teach with and through the world.

 **Ariel Tichnor-Wagner** is a senior fellow of global competence at ASCD. In her role, she advocates for, develops, and implements innovative frameworks, tools, and professional learning experiences that support educators in fostering the knowledge, skills, and attitudes students need to succeed in

a diverse, interconnected world. Tichnor-Wagner began her career as an elementary school teacher in a high-poverty school district in Phoenix, Arizona, where she taught primarily English language learners. She has also led student trips and volunteered in educational programs in Nicaragua, Guatemala, Costa Rica, Peru, and Israel. She graduated summa cum laude with a BA in history from the University of Pennsylvania. She received a master's degree in Elementary Education from Arizona State University, and a doctoral degree in Education Policy, Leadership, and School Improvement from the University of North Carolina at Chapel Hill. As an educator and researcher, she is committed to identifying and leveraging policies and practices that improve academic and social-emotional outcomes of culturally and linguistically diverse students and that foster global citizenship. Her writing on global competence and school improvement has appeared in a variety of outlets, including *Education Week, Educational Administration Quarterly, Leadership and Policy in Schools, Journal of Educational Change, Teaching Education, Education Policy Analysis Archives,* and *Educational Policy.*

 **Hillary Parkhouse** is an assistant professor of teaching and learning at Virginia Commonwealth University School of Education. She began her career as an English and history teacher in Santo Domingo, Dominican Republic. She then taught high school social studies and English as a second language in the Washington Heights neighborhood of New York City. Her research focuses on issues of diversity and equity in education, particularly how teachers create inclusive environments and curricula and how students develop the critical citizenship skills necessary for creating a more just future. Dr. Parkhouse has published "Pedagogies of Naming, Questioning, and Demystification: A Study of Two Critical U.S. History Classrooms" in *Theory and Research in Social Education;* "Teaching Culturally Relevant Pedagogy and Transformational Resistance Using the Film *Precious Knowledge*" in *The New Educator;* and "'Calling Out' in Class: Degrees of Candor in Addressing Social Injustices in Racially Homogenous and Heterogeneous U.S. History Classrooms" in *The Journal of*

Social Studies Research. She also coedited the book *Possibilities in Practice: Social Justice Teaching in the Disciplines*, published by Peter Lang.

Jocelyn Anne Glazier is an associate professor of education at the University of North Carolina at Chapel Hill. Her research and teaching focus is on supporting teacher development of innovative and empowering pedagogies to support all students, particularly those most marginalized in schools. Her qualitative work raises important questions about the potential of transformative, experiential teaching practices at all levels of education and across multiple contexts—local, national, and international. An important element of this work focuses on teacher learning about diversity, inequity, and social justice, both locally and abroad. Her research has appeared in *The Harvard Educational Review, Teachers College Record, The New Educator*, the *Journal of Experiential Education*, and *Teaching Education*. Recently, Glazier served as a 2017–2018 mentor in the Global Teacher Education Fellowship program and was a 2018 Transformative Teacher Educator fellow. With book coauthors, Glazier has researched, presented about, and published on the preparation of K–12 teachers for global competence. Prior to her work in higher education, she was a high school English teacher.

J. Montana Cain currently serves as the senior evaluator with the Children's Trust of South Carolina, where she leads evaluation activities and works to build evaluation capacity, both externally and internally. She holds a PhD from the University of North Carolina at Chapel Hill in Educational Psychology, Measurement, and Evaluation. Dr. Cain pairs her interest in education and evaluation with her commitment to equity. In addition to teaching Spanish at the secondary level, she has taught courses related to multicultural education and social justice for preservice teachers and school counselors. With the goal of bridging the gap between equity-centered practices and measurement, she developed the Multicultural Teacher Capacity Scale.

Related ASCD Resources: Global Competence

At the time of publication, the following resources were available (ASCD stock numbers in parentheses). For up-to-date information about ASCD resources, go to www.ascd.org. You can search the complete archives of *Educational Leadership* at www.ascd.org/el.

Print Products

All Teaching is Social and Emotional: Helping Students Develop Essential Skills for the Classroom and Beyond by Nancy Frey, Douglas Fisher, and Dominique Smith (#119033)

Building Equity: Policies and Practices to Empower All Learners by Dominique Smith, Nancy E. Frey, Ian Pumpian, and Douglas E. Fisher (#117031)

Catching Up or Leading the Way: American Education in the Age of Globalization by Yong Zhao (#109076)

How to Teach Now: Five Keys to Personalized Learning in the Global Classroom by William Powelll and Ochan Kusuma-Powell (#111011)

Keeping it Real and Relevant: Building Authentic Relationships in Your Diverse Classroom by Ignacio Lopez (#117049)

Using Understanding by Design in the Culturally and Linguistically Diverse Classroom by Amy J. Heineke and Jay McTighe (#118084)

ASCD myTeachSource®

Download resources from a professional learning platform with hundreds of research-based best practices and tools for your classroom at http://myteachsource.ascd.org/.

For more information, send an e-mail to member@ascd.org; call 1-800-933-2723 or 703-578-9600; send a fax to 703-575-5400; or write to Information Services, ASCD, 1703 N. Beauregard St., Alexandria, VA 22311-1714 USA.